# McCall's
## Book of
## Entertaining

# McCall's
# Book of
# Entertaining

### EDITED BY
# Jean Read

Recipes Edited by
**Mary Eckley,**
Food Editor of McCall's

The McCall Publishing Company

Random House  New York

Copyright © 1979 by The McCall Publishing Company
All rights reserved under International and Pan-American Copyright
Conventions.
Published in the United States by Random House, Inc., New York, and
simultaneously in Canada by Random House of Canada Limited, Toronto.

Library of Congress Cataloging in Publication Data
Main entry under title:
McCall's book of entertaining.
Includes index.
1.   Entertaining.   2.   Cookery.   I.   Read, Jean B.
II.   Eckley, Mary.
TX731.M23      642'.41      78–21813
ISBN 0–394–50073–3

Manufactured in the United States of America
3   5   7   9   8   6   4   2
First Edition

# Preface

In this book you will find information on all kinds of parties. Naturally, not all of them will be for you. Like most experienced party-givers, eventually you'll settle on the form of entertainment that suits you best, that works for your space and the way you live.

How you entertain will also have something to do with the way people live in your community, but mostly it will depend on the kind of person you are and what you enjoy. If you're a busy, gregarious person with a large group of acquaintances, you may prefer the ease and conviviality of a large cocktail buffet. If small groups are what you like best, then an intimate dinner for six or eight may be the way you choose to entertain most of the time. If you live in the country or the suburbs with a sizeable family and have fallen in love with your barbecue, that could very well be your standby whenever you give a party.

However you choose to entertain, there are two things to remember: keep things simple, and no matter who your guests are, don't try to impress them. When Franklin and Eleanor Roosevelt entertained the king and queen of England at the White House during World War II, they widened the eyes of the whole country by serving hot dogs. You don't necessarily have to serve hot dogs, but there's a message there about being oneself. Too many trimmings, too much fancy food, will only make you an anxious host or hostess who has lost sight of the real purpose of a party—to give pleasure to others and to yourself. By staying within your own capacities and resources, it's possible to avoid the moment of panic that besets the overextended party-giver—the one who, looking around at the cigarette burns in the rug, the crush at the bar, the dwindling ice supply and the fancy but fast-melting fish mousse that has taken a day and a half to make, asks herself "Who are all these people and what are they doing here in my house?"

In this book, you will find out how to plan and carry out most forms of entertainment—and how to deal with some of the problems that go with them. Wherever food is served, you will find menus and recipes for each occasion at the back of the book. Today there are no rules, only guidelines, for giving parties, so relax and enjoy yours.

Although the book is addressed to both the host and hostess and naturally refers to guests of both sexes, to bypass the clumsy repetition of "his and her" we have settled on the female pronoun for the party-giver and the male pronoun for the guest.

# Contents

# McCall's
## Book of
## Entertaining

# 1

# Party Preliminaries

## Making a Master Plan

You've decided to give a party. The date is set, but even before you decide on the guest list and send out the invitations, stop right now and allow yourself the luxury of daydreaming about how you'd like that party to be. Let's say it's a cocktail buffet for twenty people.

In your daydream, the guests arrive a little after seven. The living room is filled with flowers. The table looks beautiful and inviting with an array of artfully arranged dishes and your best glassware and china, set off by candlelight. Dressed in your nicest caftan, you're looking calm and rested as you greet your guests. By seven-thirty or so they have finished their cocktails; the party moves to the buffet table and then breaks up into small groups for dinner according to the seating play you've arranged beforehand. Coffee and dessert are served, the dishes magically whisked away, and then everybody settles back to talk until it's time to go home.

*Getting Down to Business:* This is the way you see the party in your daydream. But to make it come true it's time to stop dreaming and get down to specifics. Get a pad and pencil and begin to ask yourself some questions, jotting down the answers as you go along. For instance, who will be there to open the door for the guests? And where will they put their coats? At a smaller party you would simply clear out the hall closet, but with twenty people coming you'll have to think of something else. You could use a bedroom—or rent a coatrack from one of the firms that specialize in party equipment. If you entertain this many people frequently, it may be more economical to buy a rack. If you live in an apartment, you'll probably have to get permission from the landlord to put it in the outside hall. And don't forget to think of where guests can go to freshen up. Can you get the children out of the bathroom in time to tidy it? These may seem like small details compared to the bigger considerations of what you're going to give your guests to eat and how much liquor you'll need to order, but they too can contribute to a smoothly run party.

In your daydream the glassware and china add to the effect of the buffet table. The question is, do you have enough of both? If the answer is no, consider the alternatives. If a large party is what you enjoy and are likely to be giving again, you may want to invest in more china and some stainless-steel flatware. You may choose to borrow or rent glasses, or to buy a stack of plastic throwaways. They're inexpensive, simply designed and widely used these days. Make a note of what you decide.

*Check Your Space:* Get up and take a walk around the ground floor of your house, or your one-bedroom apartment. Take a look at your space. Where are you going to put the bar? It should be off to one side, away from the entrance to the living room and well out of the main party space. An unused corner of the living room, a study (use the desk for the bar), or even a hallway are possible places for the bar—the main thing is to put it where it won't create a traffic jam. Or, consider having two bars. If you have a porch or deck, and the weather is right, think of having one bar indoors, the other out. Or one in the living room, the other in a basement playroom. If you're pressed for space, you might even put the second bar in the bedroom. Wherever you put it, don't forget to tell your guests that it's there.

While you're inspecting your floor plan, check to be sure that twenty people can move about freely. You may find that you have to push some furniture back against the walls and perhaps transfer some pieces, like the big wing chair by the living-room fireplace, to another room. Make a note of these changes. And while you're at it, now—before you send out the invitations—is the time to consider whether you ought not to shorten your guest list.

Once you've located the bar, decide where you'll put the buffet. The dining room is the logical spot; if you don't have one, you'll have to improvise. The big flat-topped desk in the alcove off the living room could double nicely as a table. After your guests have served themselves, where will they settle down to eat? Is there enough seating and enough surfaces (coffee tables, occasional tables, even a piano bench) for guests to put down their plates and drinks? If not, check on the number of chairs that can be brought in from other rooms, or borrowed from a neighbor, and decide now whether you ought to invest in some folding chairs and small, inexpensive stackable or folding tables.

*Creating a Menu:* The buffet in your daydream is covered with an array of tempting dishes. So jot down a tentative menu. Remember that you should be able to eat buffet foods with a fork alone. Hot dishes should be chosen so that they can be prepared ahead and kept warm over an alcohol burner or on a hot tray.

And what about cost? The sweetbreads in wine sauce, or that shrimp-and-crabmeat dish that have earned you so many compliments at small dinners may be too expensive for a large group. Curried chicken or moussaka might be a more practical choice.

As you plan your menu, think a bit about what your guests would enjoy. If most of the people you know are on diets, you'll want to include some low-calorie dishes. And if you know that some are vegetarians, include at least one substantial meatless dish.

*Drinks:* How much liquor and wine will you need for twenty people? (See Chapter 17.) Who is going to mix the drinks and who will serve them? Even though you may have decided to get along without a professional bartender, you'll need to think of who is going to do the job. Or you could do what many people do these days and have somebody in your family or a friend make a drink for each arrival and then tell that guest to help himself on the next one. However, you will still need to appoint someone to keep an eye on the bar and be responsible for restocking ice, glasses or other dwindling supplies. Finally, ask yourself whether you can manage alone, or whether you should hire someone to help you in the kitchen. (See Chapter 2.)

There will be other questions, of course, for other kinds of entertaining. For example, for a small dinner party your questions will focus more on food. But once you've answered the preliminary questions in your own mind—and jotted down the answers on your pad—you're ready to start some serious planning. Begin by turning to the chapter in this book that talks about the type of party you've decided to give.

## Party Timetable

*Invitations:* At least four weeks before a big party (two to three weeks before a dinner party), plan your guest list and mail out (or begin telephoning) the invitations. If you're doing the inviting by telephone and it's not too big a party, three weeks ahead will do—but don't leave it much later.

Formal invitations are rarely used anymore in private life except for big important occasions such as weddings, and sometimes not even then. If you want to use them, the stationery or department store will have various samples to choose from.

When you're planning for so many guests that written invitations are necessary, keep your stationery simple. For almost any party you can use a fold-over card, either plain or with your name printed on the front. Or, you might choose a printed card with envelopes to match, and space on the card to fill in the necessary information. In considering the possibilities, don't overlook postcards. Old ones are nice if you can find them, and there are some very handsome new cards around, especially in museum shops.

What you write on the invitation is up to you—there's no set form except that it should explain the kind of party you're having, give the date, the time, the address and the fact that you expect a reply. If you want your guests to come in formal dress, add that, too. When the party is a large one, many people these days save time for themselves and their guests by simply writing "Regrets only," followed by the telephone number, instead of the more formal RSVP. That way, only those people who can't make it will need to call.

For a relatively small party it's easiest to telephone the invitations. It also means immediate acceptance or regrets, which can simplify your life considerably. On the telephone you can also explain the party in a way that you can't on written invitations. If it's a dinner party, most guests like to know two things: who will be there, and what to wear. In a telephone conversation you can say, "It's just a small dinner for my sister who's visiting; Tom and Lucy, whom you know, and some of my office friends are coming." Then you might add, "I'm wearing a long skirt, but do what you feel like." Or, "Since we're going on to the museum opening, it's black tie." Or, "We're doing a barbecue, so don't dress up. I'm wearing blue jeans."

*Party Helpers:* If you're hiring professional help, you'll want to make the arrangements at least four weeks ahead. Party helpers often need as much, if not more, advance notice as the guests. Some caterers need as much as six weeks' advance notice. Even your trusty teenager, the one who helps out at every party you give, may not be available if you wait too long. If you live in the country, the same goes for the young person whom you may need to direct the parking.

*Party Equipment:* If you've decided to rent extra china, glassware or flatware, order it now for delivery the day before the party. If you've decided to buy it, don't postpone your shopping until the week of the party. Do it at once and get the job out of the way. If your hall closet or bedroom space is too small to hold the number of coats you expect, get coatracks now, too.

The timing for something like a buffet dinner for twenty might continue like this:

*Three Weeks Ahead:* Draw up your menu in final form, with a separate list of the ingredients you will need for each dish. If there are any special foods to be ordered in advance—a fresh turkey or smoked ham, fresh crabmeat, veal kidneys, or a fancy frozen dessert—get on the telephone. If you're planning something like a curried dish, don't wait until the last minute to discover that your local grocer has run out of chutney, or that raisins have suddenly disappeared from the shelves of all the neighborhood supermarkets. Check these supplies now and go elsewhere if necessary.

*One Week Ahead:* The week before the party make your final preparations. Do what has to be done one day at a time—it's that much easier. For instance, early in the week prepare anything on your menu that lends itself well to freezing, such as pie crusts, pastries, some soups and hors d'oeuvres, and put them in the freezer. The next day get the real chores out of the way, like washing a seldom-used dinner service and party glasses, and polishing whatever silver you're planning to use. In the middle of the week, order the wine and liquor and arrange for it to be delivered on the day of the party. (See Chapter 17.) You can start making ice cubes and store them in plastic bags in the freezer or, if you haven't the room, order ice in advance.

*Two Days before the Party:* Shop for, or order, all the foods that will keep. (Fish or shellfish should be bought the day of the party or a day ahead at the most.) Prepare as much as you can in advance, before putting the food away in the refrigerator: salad greens can be washed, dried and placed in the crisper along with garnishes such as parsley and watercress. Meats can be trimmed and stored in the refrigerator, or placed in a marinade, ready to be cooked the day of the party.

*The Day before the Party:* Do all the serious cooking that can possibly be done. If you're having shrimp, cook and shell them and leave them, covered in the refrigerator. Some main dishes can be partially cooked ahead: beef stroganoff, for example. A blanquette de veau or a goulash are even improved with a day of rest. All you have to do on the evening of the party is add the finishing touches and heat up the dish.

If your menu includes sauces and condiments, check now to be sure you have them. If, for example, you're serving a sauce made with currant or mint jelly, and you think you have the jelly somewhere, make sure. If you're wrong there's still time to get it. It also helps if you put these things in one place where you can reach them easily when you need them. Prepare the lemon peel for drinks and after-dinner coffee, wrap it in plastic and stick it in the refrigerator. It's a small chore, but one less to be done on the day of the party.

Set up the bar ready for the liquor to be delivered the next day, and put out the glasses. If you care about the table or chest where you're going to put the bar, cover it first with an old clean bed pad, newspapers or a plastic tablecloth before you put on the top cloth.

The day before the party you'll also probably want to buy (or pick) flowers or leaves to "dress up" your house or apartment. Arrange them now while you have a quiet moment and put them away in a cool place. Decide, too, on what your table decoration is going to be and include whatever's necessary in your shopping or picking.

If you're planning to move some furniture to make more space for guests, this is a good time to call in a friend or someone in the family to help you. Tomorrow, you'll be glad you did it today. And before you go to bed don't forget to take out whatever frozen party foods need defrosting overnight.

At the end of the day, sit down and pick out some records to play at the party. Background music is always pleasant to have when you're entertaining, especially at a cocktail party where it can be a big help to those first few arrivals who have to stand around talking in a room cleared for twenty-five. But don't forget to turn the record player off when the party really hits its stride; it only adds to the din and no-body will be able to hear it anyway.

*A Kitchen Schedule:* This is also a good time to make out a time-table for yourself and whoever is going to be helping you. You've invited guests to come at 7:30 and you're planning to serve dinner at 8:15. The menu is: shrimp marinated in dill dressing, to be served with cocktails, a veal dish (which you've just put out for defrosting), buttered noodles, a tossed green salad with split buttered rolls and individual raspberry cream tarts for dessert, with coffee or tea for those who prefer it. The work schedule in the kitchen might go something like this:

| | |
|---|---|
| 6:30 | Put out butter to soften for rolls |
| | Arrange salad greens, return to refrigerator |
| 6:45 | Arrange shrimp on serving platter; return to refrigerator |
| 7:00 | Heat oven |
| | Get out ice and supply bar |
| 7:15 | Uncork wine, put on service table |
| 7:20 | Put defrosted veal dish to heat in oven |
| | Split and butter rolls for heating |
| 7:35 | Heat water for noodles |
| 7:45 | Bring shrimp platter to living room |
| 7:50 | Start noodles |
| | Put butter on stove to melt for noodles |
| | Put dinner plates in warmer |

8:00    Dress salad, put on buffet table
        Start coffee; begin water for tea
8:05    Drain noodles, add butter and place in covered serving dish
8:10    Put rolls in oven
        Put veal dish and noodles on hot plates on buffet table
        Light candles
8:15    Remove rolls from oven
        Announce dinner
        Put rolls on table
8:20    Clear away glasses from living room
8:30    Remove dessert from refrigerator
        Fill cream pitcher for coffee
9:15    Clear buffet table
        Put out dessert, coffee and tea
9:30    Remove main course plates
10:00   Remove dessert plates and coffee cups
        Replenish ice at bar

*Party Day:* On the day of the party, set the buffet table, including any devices you'll be using to keep the serving dishes warm. If you're planning to have guests sit down in small groups to eat, it's a good idea to set up these tables with tablecloths now, if they don't interfere with your cocktail space. Otherwise you'll have to do it under much more pressured conditions while your guests are at the buffet table. However, if this is the only plan practical for you, put all the tables together out of the way in one spot, where you or a helper can get at them easily. If you're using small individual folding tables, stack them in a corner now, ready to bring out for dinner.

Stock the bar, including the things like cocktail onions, olives, etc. that you'll need for garnishing drinks. Set up the coffee service. Put the flowers where you want them, tidy the house and take care of last-minute details such as filling nut dishes, putting out extra ashtrays and coasters; and don't forget the guest towels in the bathroom.

Of course, if you work, many of these preliminary jobs will have to be fitted into the hours you spend out of the office. The chances are you won't feel quite as unharried as the party-giver who has been home all week; but having planned ahead so well, you'll at least have time to bathe and change your clothes before your guests arrive.

# 2

# Help

Let's face it, professional help at a party is always expensive and unless you live in a big city, it's not that easy to get. With the exception of the very well-to-do, most party-givers get by these days with a minimum of assistance and the helpers they do use they have usually trained themselves. How do they manage? By creating their own style of entertaining based on convenience rather than the "correct" way of doing things. What it takes is a lot of careful preliminary planning, the ability to give clear directions to the person who may be there to help, plus clockwork timing about how the party is to proceed, not to mention a certain sleight of hand in arranging for guests to take care of themselves whenever possible.

*What Kind?:* The first step in giving any kind of party is to decide what jobs you can do yourself and which to delegate, either by asking friends or family members to do them, or getting outside help. You're probably not going to ask a friend to stay and help clean up after a party, but you would feel free to ask her to greet people at the door or help you put the dinner on the buffet table. And you would certainly ask any of these duties of a teenage son or daughter—that is, if you've begun your indoctrination early enough.

Let's say you work and have to entertain on a weekday. In this situation you're likely to be most interested in having someone to clean up. What you could do is either set the date of the party for the night before a weekly cleaner comes in; or if you don't have such a person, hire someone to come in to do that. If you're having a sit-down dinner, you might get someone to come in to help serve and stay on to leave you with an orderly kitchen in the morning. It all depends on what your situation is and your inclinations are as to the kind of help you want. If you have a tiny dining area, you probably won't want to cramp things further by having yet another body to do the serving. If you hate to cook, you might be happy to settle for someone to come in and prepare the meal, then serve it yourself, family style, and do the cleaning up yourself.

If you do have someone who regularly comes in to help with the cleaning, and she's indicated an interest in cooking, consider that idea. But before you commit yourself, have a trial run. First discuss what your helper likes to prepare. If she has a specialty that might be good for your party, ask her to fix the dish for you or your family first, rather than suggesting something she's not familiar with. If it doesn't work out, explain kindly, but make other arrangements. If it does, plan to have her do the same dish for your party.

For a large cocktail buffet, if you can afford the expense, you might want someone to tend bar and another person to help in the kitchen, collect plates and glasses after the meal and do the washing up.

One way to find such helpers in a small town is to ask the proprietor of a good local restaurant if he knows of someone who does freelance jobs. Supermarkets and tobacconist shops often have bulletin boards where people advertise such services.

*Student Help:* Many students work regularly as party helpers. Check the vocational office of a nearby college or your local high school. Some communities have a Youth Employment Service where you can get help at a modest hourly rate. Or consider a teenager in your neighborhood who would like to earn extra money. You'll have to take more trouble explaining their duties than you would to the more experienced helper, but a fourteen-year-old doesn't go off to college until he or she is eighteen, and in the meantime, with any luck, you've found a cherished standby to cover your parties for the next four years. Also, think of a pair of teenage helpers. Young people like to work together and can make a very good team.

*Instructing Your Helper:* Whomever you get to help you, don't assume that he or she will automatically know what to do—or even what to wear. If your helper is a young girl who comes for a preliminary interview in blue jeans, you might ask her to wear something else on the night of the party, especially if she will be helping out at the dinner or buffet table. If you're getting someone in to cook, discuss the entire menu with her beforehand, including such details as which of you is going to do the shopping, what time your guests will arrive, when to serve the hot canapés, if you're having them, and finally, what time you want to have the meal ready.

Think of yourself as a stage director and know ahead of time exactly how you want your play to proceed. You don't actually have to stage a dress rehearsal, but talk to your helpers before the party and spell out in detail what their duties are. If one of them is to set the table for a sit-down dinner, show him or her where the dinner service and the linen you are going to use is kept, where the flatware and serving dishes are, and the wineglasses you plan to use. Draw a plan showing how you want the table set and pin it on the kitchen bulletin board. Now write a timetable, similar to the one in the previous chapter, of what is to be done when and pin it there, too. The best rule with untrained help is not to assume *anything*—spell it all out. Before you know it you may have an invaluable helper whom you wouldn't exchange for the fanciest butler or maid in town.

*A Little Help from Your Friends:* When and how to accept help from your friends is a question that comes up in the life of anyone who gives a party. (As does the more thorny problem of how to refuse it.) As a general rule, most of us would prefer not to have guests helping out in the kitchen when we entertain. With too many bodies in it, the kitchen can become a disaster area where everything gets out of hand. But there is no reason why a guest, who is also a good friend, should not help you at a large cocktail party by passing the hors d'oeuvres (and at the same time make a few introductions if she knows the guests.) A friend might serve the dessert at a sit-down dinner or help with the coffee afterward. Or, if you are giving a formal tea party, you could ask someone to pour in the old-fashioned way, or to help older guests. Another friend might go to meet out-of-town guests at the airport and bring them to the party.

*How to Say No:* If you do want to turn down offers of help, try to do it nicely, but firmly. It helps if you can think of something this person *can* do and so you might say "Thanks, no, but if you'd just check on the ice supply at the bar . . ." Or, "No, thanks, not just now, but it would be great if later you'd help take out the empty glasses before we go in to dinner." Remember that offers of help often come from people who feel uncomfortable at a party, so don't turn them off completely.

Weekend guests are different: you're likely to treat them more casually, especially if they also happen to be good friends. Before a weekend party, you may even relax your rule of no guests in the kitchen and ask one of them to prepare the salad greens, or help cut up a platter of *crudités*. If you happen to have a friend staying whom you know makes great salad dressing, you'd certainly ask him to do that. Over a long weekend, some gourmet guests with a passion for cooking have even been known to produce an entire meal.

The best way is to stay loose and don't be too rigid about not accepting help. Kitchens are a natural environment for intimacy. If you've invited a friend to a party whom you haven't seen for a long time, what better place to catch up while the two of you arrange the canapés or assemble the salad? And no matter how much you pride yourself on your self-sufficiency you can never tell what may come of letting an interesting guest stay on after the party and help clean up.

# 3

# Entertaining
# Alone

Who says that entertaining is for couples only? A lot of single people seem to think so, and unfortunately they miss a lot as a result.

Their excuses are many. Young people with full-time jobs often get into the habit of eating out; they tell themselves they'll begin to entertain at home when they marry, or have more room or more time. The widowed, divorced or separated say that their party-giving days are over because friends have drifted away or their present quarters are too small. If they can't give the parties they used to give, why give them at all?

For all sorts of reasons. The purpose of entertaining is to enjoy yourself and your guests. You can do this just as well in a one-room apartment as in a twenty-room house—except that the ground rules are different. As for the excuse that you've lost touch, what better way to renew old friendships or start making new ones than to give a party?

One thing to remember about entertaining at home is that you don't have to invite a lot of people to make it a party. Some of the best parties can happen when there are only one or two guests involved. If an old acquaintance calls to say he or she is going to be in town; if your son's college roommate—who is your friend, too—turns up with his girlfriend; if you have a colleague at work whom you'd like to know better, what could be more natural than to invite these people for dinner? It will be a lot cheaper than going out to a restaurant and a lot cozier to spend the evening at home. Even if you decide you're not up to serving more than spaghetti with a green salad and cheese, the chances are that any of these friends will appreciate it a lot more than being taken out to dinner.

*Making the Most of Your Space:* Let's say you're a single person either starting or beginning to entertain again in a small apartment.

First look at the amount of room you have. If the floor space is limited, you can simplify your party-giving, as well as your daily living, by having furniture that serves more than one purpose. If you don't already have one, consider an expandable dining table, either the drop-leaf kind or the more contemporary type that folds up like an accordian, or has leaves that can be stored under the top. Other pieces of furniture that can do double duty are a storage cabinet that doubles as a sideboard, or a low chest that can serve as a coffee table or a bar. You might also think of a modular wall system, with room for a record player and space for records underneath, or a desk unit that you can also use as a bar. Stools that stack have more than one purpose: use them as small tables as well as for seating. When you don't need them, stick them away in a corner.

Unfortunately, guests aren't stackable, so learn to use every inch of space you have. A small apartment foyer can serve as a dining area, and if you have a separate bedroom, never mind that you sleep there, use it, too. If your bed has a conventional head- and footboard, get rid of them. The bed itself, set against a wall with bolsters and throw pillows, can double as a couch. Clear off a dresser and use it for a bar; or rearrange the furniture and set up your buffet table in the bedroom. In other words, don't be rigid about your use of space: according to what you need at a party, a bedroom can be a barroom, a dining room or just a place to put the coats.

A separate dining room is a big asset when it comes to giving a party; it makes the perfect setting for a seated dinner or a buffet. However, in newer houses and apartments it seems to have vanished along with the pantry. If what you have is a dining area that opens off the kitchen, you might consider a folding screen to separate the two areas at a formal dinner party. Or you could do just the reverse, and emphasize the connection by setting out the meal on the kitchen counter and letting your guests help themselves. This method of serving presupposes, of course, that you've planned a menu with no last-minute procedures and unwashed pots to detract from your party landscape.

*Party Equipment:* If you've gone back to living alone, and perhaps moved from a house to an apartment, you may already have more china and glassware than you can find places for. Before you decide to get rid of some of it, consider other uses certain items might be put to: for instance, those hot-chocolate cups inherited from your grandmother could be used for *pots de crème;* the old-fashioned washbowl, picked up at auction and kept in the guest room before you moved from a house to an apartment, could make a great punch bowl, or you might use it to serve salad at your next buffet supper. Even if you have to keep it under the bed, you'll certainly want to hang on to something like the odd huge platter you only use once a year—and then wonder how you'd do without it. On the other hand, you might think twice before holding on to the dozen seafood-cocktail glasses you got as a wedding present—maybe let those go.

*Starting from Scratch:* If you're at the stage in life when you're starting from scratch, all you really need are as many plates and soup bowls as your expandable table will take at its full capacity, the flatware to go with them and some decent looking glasses, preferably simple and stackable. Of course, if you're planning a buffet supper for a large crowd rather than a seated dinner, you'll need more tableware, and again, the stackable type is more practical for storage between parties. Table mats and some heavy-duty mats to take hot dishes when you're serving family style at the table will take care of the linen department, although you may want one tablecloth to make an occasional change from the mats. If your quarters are small, choose a plain one: patterns have a way of seeming to absorb space. Add some after-dinner coffee cups and dessert plates and you're in business.

This doesn't mean, of course, that you won't want the fun of finding a few accessories, but before you buy them think about how often you will actually use them, and if you have storage problems, where you will put them between parties. The chances are you'll be hard put to find space to store that enormous Mexican casserole you saw, designed to hold food for twenty. You might be better off with two smaller ones, one of which can be used at parties for six or eight.

*Kitchen Strategy:* If your kitchen is like most apartment kitchens or those in most small houses, it's as short on work space as it is on storage space. One way of creating an additional work surface is to have a carpenter make you a simple table that, when not in use, folds down against a wall or even the back of a kitchen door. You may want to splurge on a Formica top; it will be more expensive, but it's a lot easier to keep clean than a wooden surface.

A tea cart is a useful thing to have and can always double as something else between parties. At a dinner party, use it to take the dishes from the table out to the kitchen and to bring in the dessert and coffee. At a large gathering it can serve as a bar. Between parties, use it to hold your plants (put them in the bathtub when you're entertaining), or to show off a nice-looking tea set or some pottery.

In preparing for a party, lack of space on the stove can be a problem—unless of course you're lucky enough to have a restaurant stove. A two-tiered rattan steamer, set over a wok filled with simmering water (both available in oriental stores) can save space—and vitamins. Use it to cook vegetables and do away with an array of saucepans cluttering up your stove top. At the same time, you might be steaming a fish on the bottom tier. Off the stove, a steamer is nice to look at, its separate tiers hooked on a wall, or the whole thing set on a chest or on the floor by a chair or sofa.

*Staying Ahead of the Game:* A way of overcoming the problems of entertaining alone is to work ahead of your party. If you're having a sit-down dinner, plan a menu where you can do most of the meal ahead of time. Then all you have to do is boil up a batch of rice, potatoes or noodles to go with your main course, toss your prepared salad greens and heat the bread after your guests arrive. Also, think of foods that can be cooked in one pot or served together on one platter: a subtly flavored beef stew, seasoned with thyme, cinnamon and lemon peel, cooked with pears and sweet potatoes; or cioppino, a mixture of seafoods stewed in a red-wine-and-tomato sauce; or beautifully roasted Cornish hens kept warm in the oven, then placed on a bed of rice, and surrounded by a border of vegetables. For dessert, serve fruit and cheese.

*Alternatives to Home Cooking:* The easiest, if perhaps not the most imaginative way of dealing with the problem of preparing food for a party, is to bring it in from the outside. However, this doesn't mean you have to hire a professional caterer, or that the results have to be routine and uninteresting. Take the time to explore your neighborhood. Talk to the butcher and the man who runs the fish market, or drop in on the proprietor of your local restaurant. One of them may know of a good home cook who does a few special dishes—chicken Kiev or turkey Tetrazzini, for instance—that can be ordered ahead. Investigate the bakeries; many of them carry excellent appetizers, such as cheese-and-spinach tarts, and homemade desserts.

But don't, for Heaven's sake, go to the place that all your friends go to to get that same old quiche Lorraine; think of something else. Consider asking your fish man to poach you some salmon. You'd be surprised how many fish markets have this service, which a lot of customers don't know about and don't think to ask for. Or go out of your way to find a Japanese fish store; ask them to cut sashimi for a really adventurous first course.

In your search, don't overlook the delicatessen. Many of them can do a lot better than the usual office-party fare. Go when the place isn't crowded and have a chat with the person who runs it. Sample the chopped chicken livers and the herring salad, try a little of the Brie and the Tilsit—have an informal cheese-tasting right there at the counter. If the proprietor is of Middle Eastern origin, he'll probably have both hummus and tabbouleh, as well as fine, flaky baklava for your next cocktail buffet.

If the place where you live is short on delicatessens but strong on fund-raising food sales, it's worth checking these out. It could be that you'll find the perfect carrot cake or baked lasagna and be able to make a deal with the maker to do the same thing for your party.

In relying on the neighborhood for your menu, don't leave everything until the last minute and end up having to take whatever you can get. Over a period of time, try out various facilities either for yourself alone or at dinner with a friend or two. Gradually, by a process of elimination, you'll be able to work up a list of really good take-out places that can supply you with an excellent party menu.

*Yes, but . . . :* Having dealt successfully with problems of space, party equipment and food, many single women are still put off by the idea of entertaining without a man, and many single men by having guests without a woman's help. Certainly any party is easier when there are two people involved, whatever their sex. A team of two, whether it's husband and wife, roommates or friends, can share the work beforehand and at the party divide the roles of host and hostess. The single person not only has the job of making all the preparations, but has to play both roles. Even the career woman who prides herself on her cool and efficient performance at the office can suddenly begin to worry about who is going to do the "man's job" at her party, who is going to carve or serve the wine. Single men can be concerned about the food preparation and table-setting, and about who is going to sit where. Divorced or widowed men particularly, being used to entertaining with a wife, find it hard to think of entertaining without one.

One answer to the problem of giving a party by yourself is to ask a guest to help you. This person could be a friend of either sex. Who says that carving is necessarily a man's job? Or, if you are a single hostess, that a woman friend can't take the host's place at the head of the table, or pour the wine?

The single women whose guests are mostly couples does have a special problem: she could be misunderstood in asking a married man for help. So before you ask your best friend's husband to serve as host, be sure that it's clear what you're asking—a friendly gesture that will help your party run smoothly. When the guests are mostly single, pick out the shyest person at the party and ask him or her to assume the role of helper. Bartending, pouring wine or carving meat will give that person something to do—and that's always helpful to the shy.

The single man is more likely to want to act as his own bartender, but he, too, can fall back on his guests. His best friend's wife is not likely to be enchanted by being asked to pass the hors d'oeuvres, but again, the most retiring person at the party might welcome the request.

In entertaining alone, remember that the point of your party is to bring people together, not to put on an elaborate production, or even to give the kind of party you may once have given. Remember, it's *you* who's entertaining—not your mother or your ex-husband or wife; you can make the occasion anything you want. Work ahead, keep things simple, accept a little help from your friends and your parties may well be the ones that people enjoy most.

# 4

# Party Politics

People are the most important ingredients in any successful party. The right mix can make almost any party go; the wrong one can sometimes mean disaster.

At a big party, the mix more or less takes care of itself; everyone is bound to find someone to talk to. With a smaller group, who you invite with whom can be crucial.

You can, of course, play safe when you entertain by routinely inviting a group of old friends—people who already know and like each other. But eventually this grows as dull as if you were to serve the same menu every time you gave a dinner party. So make a point of including some new faces: the young accountant in your office, for instance. He might enjoy the new art teacher at school your children have talked about so much. If it doesn't work as an exercise in match-making, don't worry, they're bound to find others to talk to and their presence is likely to make your party of old friends more lively.

In drawing up your guest list, try to include people with different lines of work and different interests. If the party is made up mostly of people in the same profession—doctors, teachers, lawyers—or people in the same business (worse yet, the same office) the conversation is apt to degenerate into shop talk, leaving those guests who aren't members of the "in" group feeling out of it and not providing much refreshment to those "in the shop."

*Mixing Generations:* The same idea holds for mixing people of different ages as for mixing those of different professions. The "generation gap" is an outmoded idea and certainly has no validity when it comes to planning a guest list. The dinner party where guests linger longest at the table is likely to be one where young and old are exchanging views. And if you have a group of mixed ages at a sit-down dinner, don't put the younger ones together at one end of the table. Try putting your twenty-year-old niece next to the oldest guest there;

you may be surprised and proud to see a whole new facet in your young relative.

*Mismatched Guests:* As for mixing temperaments at the table, we all know about not putting two "talkers" or two "nontalkers" together. But what to do when you've unwittingly put two guests with strongly opposing views together, and their conversation begins to escalate beyond the bounds of friendly argument? If the meal has reached that stage, you can diffuse the situation by inviting everyone to come into the living room for coffee. If not, you can deliberately interrupt the conversation with a change of subject, or even more directly, say quietly "I wish you'd continue this conversation another time." The two combatants will usually subside. If this should happen at a cocktail party, the easiest thing is to move into the angry twosome by introducing a third guest. Or you could split them up by taking one away with the excuse that you've been wanting him to meet so-and-so, or that you need his help at the bar.

*The Visible Hostess:* Don't rely on your guests to keep a party going. The responsibility is yours to see that they meet each other, that people circulate and no one gets stuck permanently in a corner. At a large cocktail party of more than twenty people, you can't be expected to introduce every guest to every other guest, but as soon as a new arrival gets his drink, see that he meets one or two people before you leave him on his own. And try to keep your eyes open during the evening for people who may need rescuing—a guest trapped behind the coffee table with a longwinded conservationist, or a noncommunicating twosome who look as if they would welcome a third person.

At a big party, even if you've asked a friend or helper to be at the door to show people where to put their coats, don't wander too far from that door yourself. You may be the only person some of your guests know at this particular gathering. Be visible, so that the shy guest can find you quickly and get your help in getting launched.

On the other hand, don't be a strongarm hostess and try so hard to see newcomers meet everyone that they don't have a chance to continue a conversation with anyone. A few introductions will do at the start. And if a particular group is off and running, don't interrupt. Find a single guest or twosome to whom to introduce the newcomer.

*Introductions:* As you introduce people, give them some common ground to go on. "Mary, I want you to meet Paul Jones" can lead to an awkward silence after you've left them. Simply by adding, " 'Mary's the director of our new day-care center,' or 'Paul's just back from a trip to Greece' " you give them something to start talking about. And a note to guests: if you find yourself in a room full of strangers and are at a loss for something to say beyond the rather clumsy "And what do you do?" a useful, all-purpose question is "And how do you know our hosts, Jennie and Bob?" This will always bring forth some sort of answer, such as "I went to school with Jennie" or "I work with Bob," and the conversation is on its way.

*The Problem Guest:* The guest who drinks too much and becomes either amorous or belligerent or just plain obnoxious is a painful problem to any party-giver. Telling that person that he or she has had too much to drink and ought to go home rarely works. In fact, it usually makes things worse. Your best bet is a discreet word to the spouse—if there is one present. If not, recruit a good friend of the same sex as the guest to walk him around the block—and hopefully, into a taxi. What you want most is to get that person out of your house where he can no longer be an embarrassment. However, don't apologize to your other guests; what's happened is strictly between you and the culprit.

A good way to forestall such mishaps at a dinner party, especially if you know that one of your guests is a heavy drinker, is to cut the cocktail hour short. This is also helpful to guests who don't drink. Half an hour to forty-five minutes is time enough for everyone to have one cocktail, or, at most, two. After that, serve dinner.

Other problem guests are the ones who don't go home. As every experienced hostess knows, at almost every party there is always a little band of hangers-on who are reluctant to call it a day. One way of handling this is to see that the bar is closed; you may have to quietly begin putting the bottles away yourself. Or, if it's a cocktail party, you might suggest going on to your local Chinese restaurant or pizza parlor as a means of getting lingerers out of the house. Or, after a dinner, you might just begin cleaning up.

Another method, which always gets results, is to say you have to walk the dog. Get your coat, call the dog, put on his leash and proceed firmly to the front door, where any guest with the slightest sensitivity will follow you. Of course, if you don't have a dog you'll have to think of something else. As a last resort you can simply be honest and break up the group around the piano or the poker game that's brewing by saying "Sorry, I'm really tired and I've got to say the party's over. Let's do this again soon."

# 5

# The
# Well-Dressed Table

How a table is set helps to create the mood of a party. If you've inherited a fine china service with the silver and crystal to go with it, by all means use it. The very fact that you have these beautiful things is reason enough to give a formal dinner party.

On the other hand, if all you possess is a starter set of pottery and stainless steel, don't think you have to put off giving parties until you acquire something grander. Instead, capitalize on what you have, plan a mood of informality and build your table setting around the pottery, with earthenware serving dishes, a rough-textured tablecloth or placemats, colorful napkins and bread baskets.

*Mix-and-Match:* If, like many people, your dinner service has pieces missing, don't worry. Some of the best-dressed tables are often mix-and-match. And the matching can be minimal. Cups should match their saucers, but dinner plates and salad or dessert plates can vary. Learn to create a dramatic setting by alternating dinner plates—one patterned one and one plain. If, for instance, your dinner service is in a blue-patterned earthenware, and all you've got left are salad plates and two or three soup plates, forget the soup plates and invest in eight to ten attractive white ironstone or deep-blue glass bowls and serve them on the salad plates. Add wine or water glasses in deep-blue pressed glass, use blue placemats and bright red napkins, and you have a simple table setting that's a pleasure to the eye. The mix-and-match principle works just as well with any kind of dinner service: pottery or stoneware, or really elegant bone china or porcelain. The only rule is that the colors should blend, and pieces should be similar in feeling and their degree of formality.

*Flatware:* Let's admit that silver looks best on a formal candlelit dinner table, especially if you're using an elegant tablecloth. But there's no law about this, and nowadays there's such a broad range of plain and fancy stainless steel to choose from that there's really no argument for using silver—and a lot to be said against it when it comes to polishing all those forks, spoons and knives.

*Glassware:* At a formal dinner, if you're serving wine it's better to stick to clear glass in traditional shapes (see Chapter 17.) For an informal dinner where you may be serving more modest table wines almost anything goes except perhaps the jelly glass—unless it's really pretty: colorful glassware from Mexico, some unmatched antique goblets that you may be collecting, or short, straight-sided glasses that double for cocktails.

*Linens:* Table linen can be anything from a lace or damask tablecloth to finely embroidered place mats or crossed table runners, or for a more informal feeling, the same type of thing in heavy linen, fiber or even laminated plastic. It all depends on the effect you want. For an attractive, not too expensive and easily laundered tablecloth, have a look at some of the no-iron designer sheets in department stores—or consider a batik or India print bedspread. The twin size fits nicely on a table for six, with plenty of overhang. For a longer table, seating eight to ten, use two twin spreads and overlap them. If you have a wide rather than a narrow table, try the double spread or sheet.

Use either plain cotton napkins or ones with a pattern that harmonizes with your tablecloth. For an informal dinner, slip napkins into raffia holders, or the Victorian silver napkin rings you've been collecting.

If you're putting guests at card tables at a buffet supper try to use matching tablecloths. You'll find they help to pull the scene together.

*Decorating the Table:* In planning the table decoration for a seated dinner, remember that a large arrangement of flowers is probably the most effective way of cutting off communication between diners on opposite sides of the table. If you're using flowers, plan on a low arrangement. A bowl of fruit (to double later as dessert with cheese), or an arrangement of vegetables: shiny eggplant, violet-tinged young turnips and artichokes set out on a long narrow silver or wooden tray or simply on a bed of green leaves, also make attractive centerpieces. Or try breaking up the centerpiece into three or four smaller ones, depending on the length of your table. Or put a tiny vase with a flower or two at each place. A great-looking table could also be almost bare except for tall white candles in simple stone or glass cubes, and a few choice shells from last summer's vacation strewn over the surface.

Use your ingenuity and try to work from materials that you have on hand: for example, if you have an unusual collection of stones, china birds or animals, a grouping of them can be very attractive. Another idea might be to use small footed dishes set at intervals, each holding three or four perfect lemons. If you're using pottery and planning a Mexican or Spanish menu, you might want to put small pots of cacti from the dime store at each place. If you lack ideas, don't be afraid to steal. Look at the display settings in department stores, even in museums, and clip and save ideas that appeal to you in magazines.

In decorating a buffet table, think small; remember you have a limited surface for all the utensils, napkins and serving dishes that are going to go on it and you don't want your decoration to take up too much space.

*Lighting:* Lighting has a lot to do with the general ambience of a party, and being able to adjust it with a touch of the hand can make a big difference. By now, we all know about rheostats ("dimmers"), which for a few dollars can be attached to a light switch. If you don't have one, get one.

Candles are a great accessory when it comes to setting a table, especially now that you can get them in all shapes, sizes and colors. Of course, you may want to stick to the conventional taper, especially if you have some nice-looking candle-holders to go with them. Or you might try the dramatic effect of a single candelabra on your buffet table. However, if you're using these tall and substantial pieces at a sit-down dinner, be sure to place them so your guests can still see and talk easily across the table. Experiment with different types of candles. A line of short, square or globe-shaped candles arranged the length of the table give a low, intimate light. Tall tapers give distance and a strong sense of formality that diminishes appropriately as they burn down and the wine has been passed a few times.

For an informal dinner party try kerosene lamps. You can find them in any hardware store; they aren't expensive and in the long run kerosene costs much less than candles. Remember to store the kerosene in a safe place; keep the lamp wicks trimmed and wash the chimneys when they need it.

# 6

# Cocktail Parties
# and
# Cocktail Buffets

*The Cocktail Party:* Most people, even the people who give them, have a high degree of ambivalence about cocktail parties. The general complaint is that they are too crowded, poorly ventilated and noisy, and that the chance for any real conversation is small, Also, that it's not much fun to drop in for a brief moment of partying and then have to go home and cook dinner.

Those in favor of cocktail parties like the sense of gaiety that a large gathering conveys. They see it as an opportunity to meet new people who later—going on to dinner, perhaps—become good friends. The cocktail party is also not a bad place to have a conversation with an old friend in a private oasis cut off from the surrounding din. And because it is a freewheeling affair where introductions aren't really necessary, it's a time when you can enjoy talking to a variety of people and not have to stick with any one group.

It could be that the cocktail party survives because it is still the easiest way to entertain a large number of people without having to prepare a tremendous amount of food. It is a convenient way to entertain business and professional friends, to celebrate something like the completion of a community project or a political campaign to raise funds for a candidate, or to honor a visiting celebrity or public figure. Although it's less intimate and personal than a small party, it can be a convenient way to welcome new neighbors and introduce them to the community.

Since the cocktail party is a stand-up affair, you can fit a sizeable number of people into a fairly limited space without worrying about where they are going to sit. Some guests may come at the appointed hour and stay until the end, but many more will drop in, stay for a drink or two and leave. Usually, the hostess can count on a high turnover and invite a few more people than there's actually room for on the theory that they won't all be there at one time. However, be cautious: look carefully at your available space and limit the invitations accordingly; a hot and overcrowded room will only make everybody uncomfortable and bring out the worst features of this kind of entertaining.

*Clocking the Guests:* The cocktail party usually lasts from two to three hours, beginning after work, if it's on a weekday. Weekend parties are likely to begin a bit later. Make it clear on your invitations when you expect your guests to arrive and leave: 5:30 to 7:30 (or 8); 6 to 8 (or 8:30); depending on what suits you best, or what the custom is in your community. This serves as fair warning to guests that the bar will close at the last hour given on the invitation, when you expect them to go home. (See Chapter 4 for what to do about guests who linger.)

*Setting Up the Bar:* You will need a full bar—that is, the makings of the drinks that your friends like best (see Chapter 17.) At a party for twenty-five, count on fifty drinks an hour during the first two hours and forty drinks an hour thereafter. The idea is that everybody has two drinks at the beginning of a party and after that they taper off proportionally. However, don't forget that with the emphasis on health sweeping the country nowadays, many people do more running than drinking, and when they do drink they often prefer a mild beverage to hard liquor. Depending on the number of guests and their drinking habits, you will need at least a gallon of red and another gallon of chilled white wine, as well as nonalcoholic drinks. And if you value your furniture, remember to supply coasters or cocktail napkins for each guest.

If you're having more than twenty-five people, it's a good idea to set up two bars in different rooms to avoid the sardine effect that can beset even the best-planned large party. This way, you can disperse your guests between rooms without having to resort to such wiles as "Do come look at the view from the sun porch." Even so, guests have a terrible habit of clinging together and you will have to either fight like a tiger or use all your talents of persuasion to spread them out.

*Food:* Cocktail-party food can be anything from nuts, raw vegetables, dips and chips set out where they are easily accessible, to elaborate hot and cold canapés arranged on a buffet table, or passed around on a tray. But it should always be food that can be eaten out of hand, or from a small plate while standing up. The rule is, if it needs a knife, don't serve it.

On the whole, finger foods are easier to manage—but easier doesn't have to mean unimaginative. Miniature quiche, tiny puff pastries filled with shrimp mousse, toast rounds with chopped chicken livers mixed with a little mayonaise and sherry, hot fishsticks with a tartar sauce dip, cold cooked asparagus spears wrapped in a slice of white bread thinly spread with mayonaise, rounds of cucumber with cream cheese, topped with a little lumpfish caviar and a sprinkling of lemon juice are delicious and all can be eaten with the fingers.

*The Cocktail Buffet:* This, too, is a drop-in, drop-out affair and like the cocktail party, all your guests are unlikely to be present at the same time. However, since the food served is more elaborate and the hours longer you'll have to think where they can sit and where they can put their plates. Since few households can produce the necessary seating for twenty-five to thirty people, don't hesitate to use footstools, ottomans and pillows on the floor. Or you can borrow some occasional chairs from your neighbor and buy some small folding tables you may have use for anyhow.

*Drinks:* Again, you'll need a full bar (see Chapter 17) and enough additional wine for two glasses per guest if you're going to be serving it with the meal. For twenty guests you should plan on three to four drinks per person, not including the wine drunk during dinner.

*Food:* The food at a cocktail buffet is a bit different from what you'd serve at a cocktail party: it's substantial enough for guests to make a dinner of it if they wish. Though the "no-knife rule" no longer applies, it is still better to keep the food easy to handle, since many guests will be eating with plates perched on their laps. A cold ham or turkey, sliced cold cuts, potato and rice salads, various cheeses and breads are all good foods to have for a cocktail buffet, as they can stay on the table for several hours without drying out. But it's also nice to have one hot dish, kept warm on a hot tray. This could be something like a shrimp Creole, Swedish meatballs or Italian sausage rolls, or a big baking dish of noodles with cream cheese and sour cream.

The buffet can be set up just before your guests arrive, or brought out a little later in the evening when you decide that everyone is getting hungry. Dessert isn't really required, but it's a good idea to have plenty of coffee on hand, especially if some of the guests are facing a long drive home.

*Help:* For either a big cocktail party or a cocktail buffet you really need help. You can't, for instance, greet twenty-five to thirty guests at the door and still keep an eye on the canapés under the broiler. Try to arrange things so that your wife or your husband, an older child, or even a good friend who knows most of the guests, is there to greet people at the door and make a few introductions. It's a friendly gesture and one that makes things easy for the shy person who would otherwise have to enter a crowded room alone. At a cocktail buffet, you're going to need help in taking away the cocktail things before people begin to eat, refilling dishes on the buffet table and clearing away when your guests have finished dinner. As to who these helpers might be and where you can find them, see Chapter 2.

*Alternatives:* Instead of giving a large cocktail party, why not consider a series of small informal cocktail parties for as few as ten to twelve people whom you invite by phone? If you know what they like to drink, you don't have to have a full bar, just the makings of the drinks these people prefer. You don't even have to have help. This kind of entertainment works particularly well for the person whose quarters are small. And the chances are that guests enjoy it more than a big bash. In the same way, you could make it a cocktail buffet; the food can be the same, you just think in terms of fewer people. Or, you might want to do something more interesting that you can't do for a crowd, such as a fondue kept bubbling over a spirit lamp, with plenty of fondue forks and a big pile of chunky French bread. Again, with careful preparations and a simple menu, you can get away without help.

# 7

# The Buffet Dinner

This kind of entertainment differs from a cocktail buffet in that what you serve is definitely dinner. There's no dropping in and out; guests are invited to come for cocktails and dinner at a specified hour. Just as at a seated dinner, there's a short period for drinks and hors d'oeuvres beforehand and then everyone is invited to come to the buffet table. After serving themselves, guests sit down wherever you've arranged for them to eat.

*Seating:* At a buffet dinner there should be seating and table space for everybody. At an elaborate party, you may want to set up a cluster of bridge tables, covered with tablecloths and set for four. In this case, you will probably want to use place cards to avoid the confusion of guests having to decide on their own where to sit. These can be anything from a simple white card to offset the beautiful script you learned at that calligraphy course, to an old-fashioned greeting or postcard, illustrations cut from an old book, or works of art you've commissioned from one of your children.

*The Buffet Table:* If you have a dining table, you'll probably want to use that for your buffet. If the surrounding space allows, open the table up to its fullest extent. If not, think of moving it to another area where you can. The important thing is to have plenty of room for guests to maneuver easily as they serve themselves.

If you don't want to mar the table, treat it as you would your bar and cover it with one or two plastic tablecloths, without a pattern to show through the "company" one you're going to put on top. Of course, it's possible to leave the table bare if you're not worried about the surface, and if that's the effect you like. Place mats or runners won't work at a buffet because they tend to slide about as people serve themselves.

*Substitute Tables:* If your dining table isn't large enough to serve as a buffet, you might use a sideboard if you have one; or if you do enough entertaining of this sort, consider buying a long folding plywood table that can be stored in a hall closet or some other out-of-the-way place.

*Setting the Table:* There are no formal traditions for setting a buffet table, no special place for the napkins, tableware or glasses, but there are some practical guidelines for how to go about it. One is to place things in sequence, according to the order in which the guests will serve themselves. For instance, napkins and cutlery first, the latter either wrapped in a napkin or laid out in neat rows, if no knives are required. Then the stacked dinner plates. Next, the main dish in its casserole or on a platter set on a hot plate or other warming device. Serving utensils go beside it. If a condiment or sauce is to be served with it, put that next, then the side dishes, also kept warm, with their serving utensils. The salad, if you're having one, comes next and finally the hot buttered bread.

Another guideline is not to crowd things. Be sure there's enough space between dishes so that guests can put their plates down while they help themselves. You could set out the dessert plates and coffee cups at the far end of the table to be used later in the meal, but only if there's room. If not, put them out on a side table or bring them in later. If you're serving wine, it's a good idea to put it and the wine glasses in a separate spot where guests can serve themselves after they've been through the buffet line. This way, you're more likely to avoid spills. Or, of course, you could serve the wine after the guests have settled themselves to eat.

One way to speed up the buffet line is to set each side of the table with identical dishes and split the line in two. Another problem that often comes up is the tendency for the men to hang back politely and wait for the women to go through the line first. Do everything you can, short of shepherding your guests like a nursery school teacher, to discourage this. If you're not assigning seats, the result is a little band of women who have already served themselves, not knowing quite where to sit, or worse still, all seated together by the time the men have gone through the line.

*Variations on the Buffet:* A variation on the buffet on a plate that you might want to consider is the buffet on a tray, served cafeteria style. A stack of lightweight trays is placed on a separate table near the buffet. Guests help themselves to plates, napkins and flatware and put them on the tray before coming to the buffet table. This method of self-service makes it possible to manage not only a dinner plate, but a small salad plate and sometimes—if the tray is large enough—a dessert plate, too. While the tray is not really a substitute for a table surface when the guest settles down to eat, it does make it simpler when it comes to clearing things away.

Another practical idea, particularly for an informal gathering, is the lapkin. This is an oversized napkin, with a pocket to hold flatware. Lapkins are rolled, tied and set in rows next to the stacked plates. When the guests sit down to eat, they have ready-made place mats.

*Food:* The food served at a buffet dinner can be fairly elaborate, but unless you are providing small individual tables where guests can put down their plates while they eat, there should be nothing that needs to be cut with a knife. Casseroles, cold salads, and platters of thinly sliced meats are the mainstays of any buffet. But you don't have to stick with cold cuts and potato salad. Try serving a moussaka with wilted cucumbers in dill with sour cream dressing, thin slices of buttered pumpernickel and Middle Eastern pastries for dessert. Or a bubbling baked manicotti with a cool endive salad and Italian bread, followed by a Danish fruit pudding. Shrimp pilaf makes a good party dish, with cold cooked young string beans and almonds marinated in French dressing, buttered finger rolls and perhaps a mousse for dessert.

*Service:* At a sizeable buffet dinner, the point when you need help most is getting the meal on the buffet table. If there is some food that needs to be cut, or that may be difficult for self-service, you or someone else will have to be at the table to do that, too. Afterward, you'll want help in clearing away the dishes, whisking off the tablecloths and putting away the tables, especially if your guests are going to be spending the evening in the room where they've eaten. Here, you can call on your kitchen helper (if you have one), family members or a couple of good friends to help you out.

# 8

# The Seated Dinner

The formal dinner isn't what it once was, with as many as eighteen to twenty guests, a five-course menu and a bevy of waitresses in black uniforms and white aprons serving from opposite ends of the table. But the seated dinner is still the most satisfying way of enjoying good conversation with a group of congenial friends.

Today, the menu has been pared down to three, or at the most, four courses and the uniformed waitress has disappeared. What you're likely to be serving is an appetizer (perhaps a big platter of antipasto or cold marinated shrimp with a dip, eaten with drinks in the living room), or soup, a main course, salad and dessert.

Since few people can afford or even want the kind of help that another generation used to have, most of us learn to handle a formal dinner party on our own. What it takes is meticulous planning, a sensible menu, careful preparation and a certain ingenuity in cutting corners. For example, if you're entertaining alone, without help, you'll probably decide to skip those canapés with drinks that require your last-minute attention in the kitchen. Nor will you have time to clear each place at the table between courses in the same way as a professional maid. What you'll probably do is stack the plates on a cart and push it out to the kitchen. But just so you'll know the "correct" way of doing things at a formal seated dinner, we'll run through the table setting and the service. At the same time, we'll also point out the short cuts that any host or hostess in his or her right mind, without help or with very little help, will take today.

*Choosing a Menu:* What you serve will depend to a certain extent on the number of people you are having. If you've having as many as ten people, you may decide to skip the soup course, serve the appetizer in the living room during cocktails and start with the main course at the table. For this number of guests baby lamb might not be all that practical, whereas a filet of beef or chicken pieces would work well. Artichokes are delicious, but they require extra plates and side dishes for melted butter, so you might decide to serve them another time to a smaller group. The same goes for asparagus. Broccoli is always a good choice with beef; dress it up with a hollandaise sauce that goes very well in combination with red meat. Rich desserts will never go entirely out of fashion, but you'll be doing most of your guests a favor by sticking to something fairly simple and noncaloric.

For a summer dinner you might serve a cold veal dish with fresh dilled string beans and little new potatoes, with a chilled lemon soufflé for dessert. If you want to have a first course, try an iced zucchini soup and substitute a simpler dessert: fresh peaches and blueberries with cream and perhaps a plain spongecake. For a cold winter night, think of a roast tenderloin of pork or old-fashioned fried chicken with creamed onions and peas, a crisp green salad and maybe an apple tart for dessert.

The real message here is not to overextend yourself by creating (or worse still, trying to create) a lot of rich, complicated dishes, with the result that when everyone sits down to dinner you are anxious and exhausted and nothing about the meal comes off really well. Better to stick to a few simple, well-prepared dishes that everyone enjoys. For example, when one well-known cooking expert gave a dinner for some of her most eminent colleagues, her choice of menu was: ripe melon balls, broiled liver with lemon wedges and new potatoes, Boston lettuce with French dressing and a cake for dessert. Everything was beautifully fresh, and perfectly timed and presented. It was a memorable meal.

Another good rule to follow in planning your menu is not to try something new: stick with familiar recipes where you can be sure of the results. And unless you're a very practiced cook, avoid dishes that require a lot of last-minute preparation—soufflés, for instance, or something like a Baked Alaska which require your prolonged absence from the table or, worse still, your uneasy presence there as you listen for the timer in the kitchen.

*Dinner Party Tips:* In planning your menu, try to avoid repeating a dinner you may have served two months ago to some of the same guests. It's not a bad idea to keep a notebook listing what you've served when to whom in order to avoid such duplications.

If there are to be elderly people at your dinner party, it's considerate not to include highly spiced dishes or foods, such as corn on the cob, which are difficult to eat.

One problem you can't avoid are food allergies, for unless you know your guests well you can't be expected to know which ones they may have. But if you're serving praline ice cream and one of the guests turns out to be allergic to nuts, don't fuss, just offer him a piece of fruit instead.

The smoking problem is more easily handled. If you'd prefer not to have guests smoke during dinner, simply leave the ashtrays off the table.

*Midweek Dinners:* Having guests in for dinner in the middle of the week is not so formidable an undertaking as some working people think. All you have to do is give up any ideas about an elaborate menu, or of doing everything yourself from scratch. Instead, concentrate on preparing one main dish (you might choose one that can be made the day before the party), or think of having a steak, not broiled, but baked in the oven. Buy the first course from one of your trusty sources, such as a spinach-and-crabmeat roll from a local gourmet specialty store. For dessert, all you need is fruit and store-bought cookies. If you want to be a bit fancier, buy a good brand of ice cream and serve it with a drizzling of liqueur. But whatever menu you plan, remember that the food is always less important than the spirit of the party and the guests' enjoyment.

# Setting the Table and Serving

*The Place Setting:* The traditional place setting is arranged as follows: forks to the left, beginning at the outside edge according to the order in which they're to be used. The only exception is the small fish fork used for a first course, such as oysters, shrimp cocktail, etc., which goes on the outside to the right of the place setting. Knives go on the right and are always placed directly beside the plate, the blade turned toward it. Spoons are placed to the right of the knife, beginning at the outside edge in order of use.

If the place setting gets to look too elaborate, or to take up too much room beside the plate, try putting the dessert fork and/or spoon horizontally, at the top of the plate as the English do.

Water- and wineglasses go above the knives and spoons, at the upper right-hand corner of each place. As part of the move toward simplification, butter plates aren't used very much anymore. The rule used to be to use them only at an informal dinner and to place them above the forks in the upper left hand corner. Napkins are placed to the left of the forks or, depending on what you're serving as a first course, in the center of the service plate. If you're having something like a shrimp cocktail, already set at each place when guests come in to dine, of course you'll put the napkins to the side.

Service plates, like butter plates, are one more thing to wash and handle and aren't used as much as in the past. They have their uses, though, in addition to giving guests something to look at beside a bare tablecloth or place mat. For instance, they can form the base for the appetizer (if you prefer to serve that at the table rather than with cocktails), and then for the soup, after which they are removed unless the meat course is to be carved and served in the dining room. In this case, the service plate traditionally is left at each place until you (or your helper) is ready to replace it with a hot plate with a serving of meat. If this seems inconvenient, take it off whenever you please. The old rule for serving is: take away from the right of the guest and place or pass on this left. This seems to work nicely, but again, it doesn't make too much difference whether you follow the rule or not. For example, if a place at the table is easier to reach from the left, serve and clear from that side. No one is marking your performance; it's your dinner, your table, do what's convenient for you.

One problem that always comes up at a seated dinner (even at one where the hostess has help), is the guests who have already been served whose food grows cold as they wait politely for their hostess to begin. As yours are served, encourage them not to wait for you. The old way used to be for guests to watch the hostess and begin when she did. Now the custom is to do as the French have always done and begin when served, so the food doesn't get cold. On the other hand, it can feel pretty lonely if, by the time you're seated yourself, the first-served guests are finished. If you see that service is taking too long, by all means get one of the guests to help speed things up. And certainly, if it's a cold supper, everybody can wait until the host and/or hostess are seated.

If you are the one who is doing the serving, remove the first course while someone else carves. Have the plates warmed—in the oven, in an electric warmer, or in the dishwasher. Side dishes can be passed around family style. However, a much better way is to do the carving ahead of time in the kitchen and arrange the platter of meat with the side dishes on the sideboard. While you're clearing the dishes from the first course, your guests can then go to the sideboard or a table where you've set up the buffet and serve themselves. This way of doing things has become more and more popular even for a very formal seated dinner. One can see why—it's a lot simpler and also helps to ensure a warmer meal.

Salad is served on side plates with the meal. It doesn't matter whether they 're placed on the left or the right of the diner as long as it's clear which plate belongs to whom. Few guests enjoy plunging a fork into someone else's salad. Or you can serve the salad as a separate course, especially if you're planning to have cheese with it. Just pass the salad bowl from hand to hand. It helps to have a small table or cart beside you on which to put it once it's passed.

If you're getting someone to serve dinner, you may want to have the dessert plates, on which a spoon and fork was placed, set in front of each guest before the dessert is passed. Without help, it's simpler to serve it yourself, or ask a friend to do it, and have the necessary utensils already set at each place.

If you're serving fruit either as dessert or after dessert, give each guest a plate with a fruit knife and fork, and either pass the fruit bowl yourself or have it passed informally from guest to guest.

*Serving Wine:* Wine is poured from the right as the shortest and least hazardous route to the glass. It may be poured by a helper, by the single hostess, by the host or surrogate host. Or you can simply place a bottle at either end of the table and ask guests to help themselves. If the wine is chilled, the custom is to wrap the bottle in a napkin to absorb any drips and spare your tablecloth. And if you're going all out with a separate wine with the soup and dessert, glasses used during the earlier part of the meal are usually removed before the new wine is served.

A good way to keep the table neat is to remove salts and peppers, sauces and relishes and brush away the crumbs with a folded napkin and a plate before you serve dessert. This is another nonrule. Do it if you like, forget it if it seems to be too much trouble.

*Serving Coffee:* Whether you serve coffee at the table or in the living room depends on you—and perhaps on how well your seating arrangements are working out. This might be the moment for everyone to change partners. However, if your guests are obviously having a good time, don't break things up by moving them to the living room. Just bring the coffee to the table. The formal way to serve is: empty demitasse cups and saucers, with demitasse spoons on the saucers, placed to the right of the diner. Coffee is customarily poured from the right, and sugar and cream passed on a small tray from the left. All this, of course, do only if you have a helper and only if you feel comfortable with that degree of formality. The easy way is to serve from your place at the table and pass the coffee, with the cream and sugar, family style, among your guests. If you should decide to serve coffee in the living room, it's a nice, if old-fashioned, gesture of friendship to ask a guest if she would do the honors. It also gives you time to replace the ashtrays or put perishables away in the refrigerator.

*Putting It All Together:* If you're entertaining with someone else, but without outside help, it's a good idea for the two of you to get into a huddle before the party and decide the following. Who is going to greet the guests, and who is going to tend bar, or will you decide to cut another corner and let guests help themselves? Which of you is going to provide the final touches to the dinner (many men these days do the cooking), and get the first course on the table? But, most important, figure out who is going to clear the table between courses. This way, you can avoid the jumping-jack effect that happens when these decisions haven't been made beforehand. Agree ahead of time on how you're going to serve the wine. Will you have your guests help themselves, or will one of you do the pouring? And, while you're at it, decide which of you is going to slip off to the living room before the gathering at the table breaks up to take out the used glasses, plates and dirty ashtrays left from cocktails.

*Seating Arrangements:* Who sits next to whom at a seated dinner is usually up to the party-giver except when there is a guest of honor. In this case, if the guest is a man the custom is for him to sit on the right of the hostess; if it's a woman, she sits at the right of the host. If they have spouses present, they sit at the right of the host or hostess, depending on their sex. If you are a woman entertaining alone and your guest of honor is also a woman, there is no reason why you should not put her on your right. Husbands and wives are generally not seated together, men and women are usually alternated. Guests are seated around the table according to your judgment of who would enjoy whom, or who might be helpful in drawing out a particularly quiet guest. A dinner table is not like an orchestra where you put all the basses together and settle an ensemble of woodwinds in another spot. You want to avoid putting people next to each other who, together, are likely to get lost.

Today, it's no longer necessary to balance out the sexes at any kind of party, including a seated dinner. You may choose to invite more women than men, or vice versa. All the old rules about such matters of gender have happily passed on. But it is still a good idea to have place cards, or a little seating plan you can consult as the guests are seated. Even the most confident hostess or host can sometimes get confused when it comes to assigning seats verbally.

# 9

# Breakfast, Brunch and Lunch

## Breakfast and Brunch

You don't have to ride to the hounds to entertain at breakfast, nor do you have to live in the country. However, some of the best daytime parties take place after skating or bicycling in the park, cross-country skiing, bird watching in early spring, or a hot volleyball or softball game. Still, even if you're allergic to exercise, there's nothing to say you can't invite a few friends in for Bloody Marys and brunch on a Saturday or Sunday. And with or without the athletic preliminaries, breakfast or brunch is a good way of entertaining weekend guests.

*Food:* Here, again, the idea is to keep things simple. One main dish, plenty of coffee and tea and fruit juice, and some hot breads or sweet rolls are all you need. It's better not to attempt omelets, eggs Benedict or pancakes for a group of more than six—unless you enjoy being a short order cook. However, blini or a stack of crêpes (made ahead and kept warm), together with a variety of fillings for the crêpes from which guests can make their own choice, work well. Steak Tartare is also delicious and easy to do. Corned-beef hash, fried so that it has a nice crust and surrounded with soft scrambled eggs, is a good candidate for a wintry morning. If you're not having that many people, you might consider a cheese or beef fondue for a sit-down breakfast, brunch, or even lunch. Either set the pots at intervals down the table, to be shared by two or three guests across the board, or set up card tables to seat four with one fondue pot to each table.

*Service:* What you do about service at a brunch or breakfast depends on how many people you've invited, and what you're having as a main dish. As a rule, these are very informal occasions where it's nice to be casual about how things are done as long as everybody gets plenty to eat and has a good time. Coming in from the softball field or the skating rink, your guests won't be too particular even if they have to sit on the floor.

Provided you have enough hot plates, most menus lend themselves to buffet service, or semi-buffet service. However, if you are having something like a fondue, it's essential for everybody to have a place at the table. And for a smaller group at breakfast it's warm and cozy if everyone can sit together, even if it's at the kitchen table. Have the coffee on a warming tray at one end of the table, a pot of tea at the other, and a Lazy Susan in the middle with jams, jellies, butter, syrup, sugar and cream so people can help themselves.

If you're having a really large group, you could transpose all this to a buffet table. Here, you might do best with a twenty-four-cup electric coffee maker that you can plug in and leave to turn itself off and stay hot. Surround it with the necessary number of coffee cups and saucers with spoons, as well as sugar and cream; this way, you can tell your guests to help themselves and don't have to think of it again. Also, invest in a large teapot, and keep plenty of hot water going in the kitchen for refills.

Have the glasses for fruit juice set up on a table and pitchers of chilled orange, grapefruit and tomato juice ready to be taken from the refrigerator.

*Drinks:* Since fewer and fewer people want to drink in the middle of the day, you can restrict your alcoholic drinks to something mild like Campari or vermouth with soda, or orange juice spiked with an inexpensive champagne. For a cold day, you might even want to consider serving a mulled wine, or other hot mildly alcoholic drink.

# Lunch

The "ladies' luncheon" still survives in some communities, especially among groups of women who don't work in an office and who enjoy bridge or some other activity together in the afternoon. They might, for example, get together once a month to discuss a book they have read, or listen to a paper one of them has written, or simply to enjoy each other's company. Lunchtime is also a good time to get together a group of men and women to plan a community project. But at this kind of a working session, you'll want to see that things keep moving, so make the prelunch drink a short one; that way, you can get down to the business at hand and people can get back to work.

*Food:* Whatever the purpose, business or pleasure, choose a menu that's simple and calorie-conscious. Almost no one these days likes to eat heavily in the middle of the day. Soup, salad, a light dessert and coffee or tea are all most people want. In hot weather, you might serve gazpacho or vichyssoise, followed by chicken or shrimp salad, or avocados filled with crabmeat, served with hot buttered rolls, and a fruit cup flavored with kirsch or cassis for dessert. On a chilly day, you could serve something simple like a homemade lentil soup and a big chef's salad, accompanied by French bread, with a simple apple dessert and full-sized cups of coffee to follow.

*Drinks:* If you know the drinking habits of your guests, plan accordingly. If you don't, have on hand the makings of a Bloody Mary, and an aperitif or two, such as sherry or Dubonnet. And if you're serving wine at lunch, you can always open a bottle to be sampled beforehand by those who prefer it.

*Service:* If you've planned a seated lunch, you'll want to have the table set before your guests arrive, the cold soup, if you're having it, already ladled out into cups or bowls on a tray in the refrigerator, the salad platter arranged and put in a cool place, the rolls buttered waiting to be heated, and the fruit cups on plates ready to be served. When the time comes to eat, all you have to do is pop the rolls in the oven for a moment or two, set out the soup with its small plate or saucer, on serving plates that will later hold the salad, and ask your guests to come to the table. If you're serving a hot soup, a good way of ensuring that it is not lukewarm by the time everyone is seated is to serve it yourself from a big tureen. Have your guests do the passing, family style, but once two or three people have been served, ask them to begin. Otherwise, you've defeated your purpose.

Alternatively, you can still have a seated lunch, but set out everything, including the soup tureen, on a buffet table and let your guests serve themselves. While they are helping themselves to the second course, you can quietly remove the soup course.

For any group, whether it's an eight-member bridge club or thirty people involved in an environmental campaign, there's nothing wrong with having a strictly buffet lunch with the same kind of simple menu. You will, though, need places for everybody to sit down when they eat, and enough table surfaces to hold their plates, just as you would at a buffet dinner.

Remember that though most guests will want coffee, many people prefer tea, and that both types often like to drink their favorite brew right through lunch. So have plenty of both ready by the time you serve the second course.

If your heart is into something fancier than the two luncheons described above, you can, of course, make your party as elegant as you like. Let's say you're having a sit-down luncheon for eight in honor of your daughter's mother-in-law-to-be, who has come for a prenuptial visit. This is a time when you may want to use your prettiest things and make the table look as attractive as you can, with a beautiful tablecloth or handworked place mats and placecards for the guests.

On this occasion, you might think of serving a delicate home-made chicken broth with a good lacing of white wine and thin slices of lemon with parsley. (If it's a hot day, serve it jellied.) And instead of chef's salad consider creamed sweetbreads in patty shells and a watercress salad with a slightly tart French dressing. For dessert, you'll want something simple after all that cream sauce. You could still have the fruit cup, but consider serving it in stemmed glasses with a helping of sherbet. Or, if the season is right, think of halved straw-berries with lemon sherbet.

For wine, you might investigate a crackling (not sparkling) rosé. It's a nice light wine for drinking in the middle of the day, but effervescent enough to put your party on its toes.

# 10

# Tea and Coffee Parties

## The Tea Party

The tea party is another casualty of social custom that occurred during World War II, when so many women went to work. But for those who are nondrinkers, or who have a strong feeling of nostalgia for the past in their recollection of childhood tea parties—and perhaps a silver tea service inherited from a grandmother—it's still an excellent way of entertaining friends during the week after work, or of providing refreshment for a late afternoon committee meeting. It's also a pleasant Sunday afternoon alternative to having people in for drinks.

We're going to tell you here the old-fashioned way of doing things but, by all means, improvise as you like. Use ceramic pots and a selection of herb teas; a samovar, if you're lucky enough to have one; lighter or heartier food, as suits you and your friends. Children, for example, love tea parties, and simple cinnamon toast, cut in triangles, will seem very special to them.

*Invitations:* For a small informal tea of ten to twelve people you will probably want to telephone your invitations. For a larger group written ones are easier.

*Service:* At a tea party, which usually begins at four or five, it's traditional—and easy—to do the serving yourself or to ask a good friend to help. Your tea tray could include: a teapot; an attractive-looking kettle for hot water, set over a spirit lamp to keep hot; a bowl of lump sugar with tongs if you have them, or other sugar if you don't; a creamer filled with milk; and a small dish of thinly sliced lemon with a fork to serve it. Nearby are cups, saucers and spoons, as well as tea napkins and small plates for cookies, sandwiches, cakes or whatever other food is being served.

If you don't have a formal tea service with its own hot-water kettle, use a vacuum jug (with a pouring lip and handle) attractive enough to come to the table. Keep a kettle of water boiling in the kitchen ready for brewing a second or third pot of tea and to replenish the kettle on the teatray.

As you pour, ask each guest how he takes his tea and serve it to him accordingly. The custom is for guests to come to the table to be served and then help themselves to food. However, if there are older guests present it's courteous to ask a friend to invite them to sit down, ask them how they like their tea and then bring it to them.

At a large tea party you aren't expected to have seats for everyone, but you will want to see that there are places for them to set down empty teacups and plates.

*Brewing Tea:* For best results, rinse out the pot with boiling water, then add the tea, either loose or in tea bags. Bring the water to a full boil once more and fill the teapot. Tea should steep from three to five minutes before serving.

If in making tea you're using loose tea leaves and your teapot lacks a built-in strainer, you will need one: china, silver or even bamboo will do nicely.

*Types of Tea:* The tea we all know is Orange Pekoe, but for a party why not try one of the fancier varieties? You'll find them in gourmet shops and even in some supermarkets.

Teas fall into three categories, depending on how the leaves are processed. Black teas are fully fermented and produce a strong, rich brew. Green teas are not fermented at all, simply dried; the flavor is mild and pleasant but doesn't have the hearty flavor we associate with tea. The oolongs are a compromise between the fermented and non-fermented. The leaves are semiprocessed and give a brew that's light in color, but with a definite tea taste.

Earl Grey, English Breakfast and Keemun are popular black teas. Their robust flavor goes well with sweet things. Lapsang souchong is also a black tea, but with a pronounced smoky or tarlike flavor. Some people dislike it; others are addicts. It tastes best with simple, non-competitive fare: cucumber sandwiches, a slice of loaf cake, or a simple sugar cookie.

Formosa oolong is a mild and delicate tea that also goes best with foods that are not too sweet. The same is true of jasmine tea—an oolong that's subtly flavored with white jasmine blossoms.

Green tea—the best-known kind is Gunpowder—is an acquired taste, and since it has a lot in common with herbal teas you might try it first on friends who go in for health foods.

For herbal tea-lovers, also try camomile, one of the refreshing mint teas, or rosehip—it's full of vitamin C.

*Food:* All sorts of light foods may be served with tea. Tiny sand-wiches (use thin-sliced white and wholewheat bread) cut in quarters, and with the crusts trimmed have been the traditional fare. Keep the fillings simple: cream cheese, liver pâté, or thin slices of wilted cucum-ber with a dash of salt and just a touch of mayonnaise or plain butter. You can make the sandwiches ahead of time and keep them moist on their serving platter, covered with plastic wrap and a dampened tea towel.

Homemade cookies, bite-size jam tarts, small filled puff pastries or cake are other good choices. However, when it comes to cake, slices of plain loaf cake or any kind of fruit or nut cakes that can be eaten without a fork are best. Between juggling teacup, saucer and plate, guests usually have all they can handle without the additional prob-lem of dealing with a rich and gooey concoction.

# Coffee Parties

These are held at any hour of the day or evening. The morning kaffee-klatsch with coffee and Danish pastry or doughnuts is still an institu-tion in some communities. And at an afternoon tea party you might very well serve coffee as well as tea, with another pourer at the coffee tray at the other end of the table. In this case, you would serve the same food with both.

A good time to invite guests specifically for coffee is after dinner in the evening, especially at times when you'd like to see friends but don't feel like coping with a full-scale dinner party. You can either serve dessert and coffee, or skip the dessert and serve the coffee in true Viennese fashion "mit schlagobers,"—with sweetened whipped cream. And if you're going in that direction, don't forget Irish coffee. All you need is good strong coffee, Irish whiskey and a bowl of whipped cream. You don't even have to have cups and saucers—ordi-nary mugs will do. For each serving heat together one jigger of whiskey and one to two teaspoons of sugar. Put in a mug, fill to within a half inch of the top with coffee, then add the whipped cream.

*Types of Coffee:* To make things more interesting, you might want to investigate some more exotic coffees than the ones ready-ground in your supermarket. They aren't as difficult to find as they once were, but like all coffee they are expensive. Look for a delicatessen or spe-ciality store that carries a wide range of whole beans. Think about buying a hand or electric coffee grinder—a blender or food processor won't do a fine enough job. Or ask the store to grind the coffee for you.

The chief thing that affects the flavor of coffee is how long it's been roasted. There are three main roasts. The mildest in flavor (and the shortest in roasting time) is the American roast (medium brown and somewhat darker than the typical canned coffees.) Next in line is the French or Viennese roast (slightly darker and more tangy), which is recommended for the demitasse or for *café au lait*. The strongest in flavor is the Italian roast, which has a definite bittersweet tang and is usually used for espresso.

Different kinds of coffee get their names from the degree to which the bean has been roasted, the place where it was grown, or the dealer's name for a special blend of beans. Blended coffees, like Mocha and Java, are a mixture of two or more straight coffees from a single country, region or crop. Many experienced coffee-lovers like to mix different types of coffee and invent their own blends.

Whatever the flavor of the bean, the *strength* of a cup of coffee has to do with the proportion of coffee to water. The more coffee you use per cup, the stronger the brew.

*What to Use When:* For an afternoon or morning coffee party, you will probably want to use a milder-flavored coffee, such as Mocha Java. For an evening party, especially after a rich dessert, the Italian roast with its rich, bittersweet flavor, tastes best. Serve it double-strength with a thin slice of lemon peel, and in demitasse cups, as a little goes a long way. Also, don't forget to have some decaffeinated coffee on hand for those who never touch the real stuff after noon.

*Turkish Coffee:* Sometimes, for a change of pace, try serving Turkish coffee. Use a blend of beans from Kenya and Brazil, very finely ground. For each cup put one tablespoon of coffee together with a heaping teaspoon of sugar (more, if you like it sweeter) and a small coffee cup of fresh cold water in a saucepan and heat until the coffee begins to rise. Remove from the heat for a moment and let the coffee subside. Repeat the process a second and third time. Serve it, thick, sweet and hot from the beautiful brass or copper *tanaka* you may have brought back from your travels, or bought in an import shop. Or serve it from a small ceramic or enamel pitcher. And just to persist with your theme, have baklava or other Turkish pastries for dessert.

*Cappuccino:* You don't have to have an Italian espresso machine to make cappuccino. For each three-quarter cup of strong Italian roast coffee add a quarter cup of hot milk that has been given a froth with the help of a blender. Serve with a grating of nutmeg or a dash of cinnamon.

*To Make Good Coffee:* Among the hundreds of stories about Abraham Lincoln is the one about the time when he was served a particularly pallid brew. The President is quoted as saying, "If this is coffee, please bring me some tea. But if this is tea, please bring me some coffee."

With this story in mind, begin with a scrupulously clean glass, not metal, coffee maker. (If you're having a large party you may have to settle for a metal one to get the capacity you want.) Using the drip method, with a filter, measure out two level tablespoons for each six to eight ounces of fresh cold water, depending on how strong you like it. Make only as much as you need at one time, and in reheating, never let the coffee boil. The best coffee is made from freshly ground beans which can be stored in the freezing compartment of your refrigerator.

# 11

# The Wine
# and
# Cheese Party

Since fewer and fewer people are drinking hard liquor anymore, why not invite a few friends in for a late afternoon or after-dinner glass of wine? It is an uncomplicated and pleasant way to entertain, easier than the party where you're serving spirits. It's also something you can do pretty much on the spur of the moment and with very little preparation.

If you don't know a great deal about wine, you might try a wine-tasting. This is a good way to learn—through trial and error. In this chapter we'll give you a few guidelines about what wines go best with certain kinds of cheeses. If you want to learn more about wines see Chapter 17, and also have a talk with your wine dealer; he will be able to tell you a lot more about types, vintage years and prices.

*What Goes with What:* Wines and cheeses vary in flavor from mild and light to hearty and robust. Generally speaking, the lighter wines go with the lighter cheeses and the heartier wines with stronger cheeses. The only cheeses we don't recommend are Limburger and Liederkranz, which are a bit strong for the average taste. They demand beer, onions—and like-minded friends.

In choosing your cheeses, think of the wines that are going to accompany them. For instance, a blue-veined cheese such as Stilton, Danish blue or Roquefort needs a robust wine like a Burgundy or a port; a soft cheese with a crust (Brie, Coulommiers or Camembert) tastes best with a red wine such as Beaujolais or Médoc; a soft mild cream cheese, (Boursin, Monsieur Fromage or Crema Danica) takes a medium dry wine like a Moselle, a New York State Riesling, Pouilly or rosé; pungent semi-soft cheeses, (Münster or Port Salut) take a full-

bodied dry white wine, such as a white Burgundy, a California Chablis
or dry champagne; Cheddar is good with red wine, sherry or port. If
you're serving an Italian Soave, try it with a mild Fontina or Bel
Paese; with Chianti, try a Gorgonzola.

With the cheese serve bread or crackers that are bland and unob-
trusive: French bread, thin-sliced black bread, English water biscuits
or mild unsalted crackers are best.

Whatever you do, try to make your choice of wines an interesting
one, not necessarily limited to one price. You might decide to stay
with American regional wines; or a mixture of the lesser-known European wines, such as the ones from Yugoslavia, Rumania and Hungary;
or if you know of a particularly good Chilean Riesling have another
Riesling from Germany or the Alsace area and compare the two.

*How Much to Buy:* You'll want to buy five or six different types
of cheeses and as many wines. The general rule in buying wine is
to allow a total allotment of a half bottle per person. A bottle each of
six different wines should be enough for a party of twelve. But to play
it safe, especially if you know your guests are real wine-lovers, you
could add an extra half bottle of each wine for anyone coming back
for seconds. A pound of each cheese should be ample—if there is any
left over you can always wrap it in foil and store it in the refrigerator.
For those cheeses that come individually wrapped, like Boursin, you
may want two packages.

While you're doing your shopping, include some fruit—apples,
pears and grapes—to arrange in the center of your serving table for
guests to eat between wines. You might also put together a platter of
crunchy *crudités,* such as celery, cucumber and carrot sticks; unsalted
almonds or walnut halves also make a nice accompaniment to cheese
and wine.

*Service:* At a party like this one, the service is strictly each person
for himself. Simply place each cheese on a small tray, board or plate
of its own and set it out on the table, with a knife or cheese server
to go with it. Nearby, place the wine that goes best with it, or make a
list of what wine goes with what cheese and post it near the serving
table. If you want to be really educational you could label the cheese.
But encourage experimentation, too. Who knows what interesting
combinations your guests may come up with?

Serve the cheeses and the red wines at room temperature; white or
rosé wines, either sparkling or still, are served chilled. A plastic pail,
or an old-fashioned galvanized washtub makes a good wine-cooler
for several bottles. Or use a tall ice bucket or large glass vase for
chilling bottles individually. If you don't have a very large selection
of glasses, plastic wineglasses, or four-ounce plastic old-fashioned
glasses work well at a tasting as each guest will need a fresh glass for

each wine. You'll also need fruit knives and plates for the fruit—and plenty of paper napkins.

A wine and cheese party is the kind of small informal gathering where you can manage nicely without help. With the exception of sparkling wines (save these for the finale), open the bottles before your guests arrive; then, as you greet them all you have to say is "Won't you take some wine from the table and come and join us?" Soon everyone is comparing notes on what they're drinking, and eventually they sit down to talk. Because each guest gets his own drink and food, he can use this as an excuse to circulate. Given the right mixture of people and some interesting wines, this kind of gathering makes a nice change from the cocktail party and more or less takes care of itself.

# 12

# Barbecues
# and
# Picnics

## Barbecues

The barbecue, which is basically a buffet supper cooked and served outdoors, has come a long way from the simple hamburger or grilled steak cookout, although these are still fun to do. New grills come in about every shape and size; some are portable and many are mounted on wheels. In choosing yours, think first about how often you are likely to use it and whether the investment is worthwhile. Maybe you'll be just as well off with a simpler, inexpensive model. Also consider what the average number of guests you'll be serving is likely to be. This will help you decide on the type and size grill you'll need.

*Types of Equipment:* If you prefer entertaining small groups of people, and want something you can also take along on picnics, you can get by with the simplest, most basic form of charcoal grill—the portable type made of lightweight metal which stands six to eight inches from the ground and will hold the equivalent of six large hamburgers or one good-sized steak. Of course, your choice of menus will be limited with this grill.

Larger grills are usually mounted on wheels and can be adjusted to three positions above the level of the coals—a useful device when you want to vary the temperature of your cooking. Some have metal hoods and electrical attachments, such as a revolving spit for roasting chicken, a pork, beef or lamb roast, or even a good-sized turkey. For baking, all you have to do is drop the hood. Try to get one of the larger grills that has additional work space on either side of the grill.

Other types of grills are the trough-shaped firebox with folding legs, and the vertical grill which, with its drop sides, looks something like an old-fashioned toaster. With the latter type you can avoid flare-up of fat because the meat cooks in front of the fire rather than on top of it. The experts say, however, that with this type you miss the full flavor of the charcoal smoke.

Another type of charcoal grill is the Japanese hibachi, available in single, double or triple sizes. It's very attractive looking, easy to use set on a table, and would be a good choice for a small apartment balcony. The smallest size will hold the equivalent of four large hamburgers or six to eight kabobs; three large hibachi, used together, should be enough for a party of twelve, although you may have to stand there overtime working on second helpings. The hibachi can also be used for surface cooking, with a skillet or wok set over the fire.

The ultimate in fancy equipment for the truly dedicated barbecue giver is the gas or electric-fired charcoal stove, which uses a kind of permanent briquet, and is almost the equivalent of bringing your kitchen stove outside.

*Additional Equipment:* In addition to your barbecue, you will need:

long-handled fork
pair of tongs (for turning meat)
spatula
large, long-handled cooking spoon
skewers
potholders and mitts
work gloves or asbestos gloves for handling coals
sharp kitchen knife
basting brush
platter or plank for carving and serving
salt shaker with large holes for coarse salt
pepper grinder
meat thermometer (for roasts)
sprinkler bottle (for dousing flare-ups)
hinged broiler with fine grids (for broiling tidbits)
basket grill with long handle (for broiling whole fish)
a good working-height table
a large apron

*Charcoal:* The best type of charcoal is the briquet, a pressed oval about the size of an egg. It burns longer and more evenly than unprocessed charcoal and is a lot less messy to use. You can find it in supermarkets and hardware stores.

*Starting the Fire:* In starting your fire never use anything but a commercial fuel starter (in liquid or jelly form), or kerosene or odorless paint thinner. Gasoline is highly combustible and should *never* be used nor even kept anywhere near your barbecue area. Also, after you've used your fire starter, be cautious and put it away before you put a match to the charcoal.

As a general rule, twelve to eighteen briquets will do you for eight to six hamburgers or hot dogs. Large amounts of chicken or pork require a second lot of at least sixteen briquets, and an extra-thick steak takes a replenishment of from eighteen to twenty. Follow the directions that come with your barbecue for more precise amounts. If you do a lot of this kind of entertaining, buy the large-size bag of charcoal and save.

*Timing:* The intensity of the fire is vital to the success of what you are cooking. For instance, the juiciest, tenderest steak will be ruined if the fire isn't hot enough to seal the juices, just as a chicken broiled over a too-hot fire will burn on the outside and remain half raw on the inside. So, if you're planning to serve your chicken at 7:30 you'll have to start your fire about 5:30, adding additional briquets when the first lot dies down. The cooking time for small chickens is about thirty minutes; larger ones take closer to fifty minutes. The cooking time for steak or lamb is relatively short: fourteen to twenty minutes for a 1½-pound steak; but it takes a bit longer to get the fire to the correct heat. Whatever you're cooking, it's important to plan ahead accordingly.

*Preparation and Serving:* Before your guests arrive, set up the buffet table with plates, cutlery, napkins and glasses. Put out what side dishes you can while you're at it. Set up the bar, if you're having one, and if you're serving at picnic tables, set them up, too, with colorful matching tablecloths and perhaps some bandanas from the dime store to use as napkins.

If you're cooking with charcoal, get the fire going in plenty of time. All meats, except steak, should be at room temperature (70°) before cooking. If the main dish is something that cooks quickly, have it on a table near the grill. If it's something that takes a long time to cook, get it started before your guests arrive, unless you're prepared for a very long drink period. If what you're serving lends itself to individual cooking, such as shish kebab, think of having guests cook their own. Or ask one or two people to do the first batch and let another pair take on the second, and so on until every guest has had a turn. This way, if the guest list is right, you can always do a little quiet matchmaking, or at the least your guests will have the fun of participating in the cooking.

Once the main dish is ready, guests can either come to the barbecue to be served and then move to the buffet table for side dishes, or the barbecued dish can be taken to the table for guests to serve themselves. Dessert and coffee can either be brought to the buffet table, once you've cleared it after the main course, or to a side table where, again, guests can serve themselves. At a barbecue you don't have to be too particular about clearing everything away between courses; just remove the less attractive bits and pieces.

# Picnics

A picnic can be anything from an elegant chicken in aspic packed in a portable refrigerator and served with a chilled bottle of Chablis on a cloth-covered picnic table, to a couple of peanut-butter-and-jelly sandwiches stuck into an old bread wrapper. We're assuming that the picnic you might be planning is somewhere between the two, and that you'll be cooking some of the food at the picnic site. Nevertheless, there's still quite a lot of preparation and gathering together of equipment to be done ahead.

*Ahead of Time:* Write down your picnic menu and make a list of the ingredients such as mustard, mayonnaise, ketchup, pickles, and relishes, that you want to take to the site. Now make another list of the picnic equipment you'll need. Too many al fresco affairs have been ruined by the absence of a corkscrew, a can-opener, or a salt shaker for the hard-boiled eggs. And don't forget matches, a fire-starter, kindling and charcoal (if that's what you're using)—not to mention a grill—so that you can get things going the minute you get there.

Check to be sure that you have enough insulated bags, buckets, or a portable icebox to keep your cold foods and soft drinks chilled. If you're bringing wine and beer you'll need insulated carriers for them, too. Have a look at your thermos. Is it big enough to hold enough coffee for the number of people who are coming? If not, borrow or buy another, or ask one of your guests to bring coffee, too. And if you feel comfortable about it, you could simplify things by asking someone else to bring the salad makings, some crisp vegetable sticks, or a selection of fruit for dessert. If you have a friend who makes great brownies, ask him or her to bring along a batch. A picnic is for participants, not a spectator sport, and few people will mind being asked to make a contribution to the menu, or to help out at the picnic.

If you're planning on a large crowd, with children, consider feeding the youngsters first with a do-it-yourself method—something like hamburgers or hotdogs-on-a-stick—while the grownups are having a drink. And don't forget the marshmallows to roast over the fire for dessert.

*Choosing Your Menu:* In planning the menu for a picnic, it helps to consider ahead of time where you will be eating. If you're going to a beach, you won't want to bring along a whole roast chicken and carve it there with all that sand about, even if you have a table. Instead think of frying chicken pieces beforehand. Wrap them individually in foil, and let each person eat directly from the wrapping. On the other hand, if you're picnicking in some grassy spot, you don't have to worry too much, once it's there, how the food is going to stand up to its surroundings. However, you will want to consider how well it will travel. A lemon meringue pie, for instance, is not too happy on its way to a picnic.

*A Fish Fry:* If you live near a good fishing hole or trout stream, you might consider having a fish fry. All you need is a good catch of fresh fish, a sharp knife to clean them, several skillets, corn meal or flour in which to bread the catch, and plenty of butter, lard or oil in which to fry them. (You'd better be pretty confident about the catch, though, or you're in for starvation. Bring along some hot dogs, just in case.) With something to drink, a big bowl of coleslaw and wedges of homemade apple pie, your menu is complete.

*A Clambake:* A clambake is a little more complicated and it takes time, especially if you have a clamming license and are planning to dig your own. A good idea is to plan this party around an afternoon at the beach so there's plenty of time to prepare the cooking site. Who knows, by the time you get around to eating, there may even be a moon.

First, separate your guests into groups and send each one off to collect firewood, dry rocks and bushels of seaweed. Keep behind a couple of helpers, and while the others are gone take turns digging a hole in the sand, about four feet long, three feet wide and one-and-a-half feet deep. For this, you'll need to bring along a heavy shovel. Now line the hole with the rocks and set a big fire blazing with the wood your friends have collected. When the fire has died down (this will take anywhere from two to three hours) cover the coals with seaweed. Between them, the hot rocks, coals and damp seaweed will create the steam that does the cooking. Top the seaweed with a stretch of chicken wire (brought with you to the picnic), add clams (cleaned with a stiff brush if you've dug your own), more seaweed, then a layer of live one to one-and-a-half-pound lobsters you've picked up at a local fish market on your way to the beach. Set them on their backs so the juices don't run out. Now, add more seaweed, partially shucked corn on the cob (also bought on the way to the picnic), and potatoes wrapped in foil and brought from home. Top with more seaweed, cover with a tarpaulin and weight it with stones at the edges. Leave everything to steam from thirty minutes to one hour. Check first, before you open up the whole thing, to be sure the potatoes are done. Serve with plenty of butter, bread, wine or beer, soft drinks for the young—and piles of paper napkins.

Since this is the kind of operation that presupposes an uncertain dinner hour, it's a good idea to include some snacks for hungry swimmers, clammers and seaweed gatherers. You might want to bring along a simple grill and do some cocktail sausages or small tidbits of marinated beef to serve in toasted finger rolls.

*In Case of Rain:* The danger of planning a barbecue or any kind of picnic is, of course, the problem of the weather. If a rainy day should happen to you, most menus can be transposed indoors. Your chicken or pork roast may not have the same smoky flavor cooked in the kitchen oven, but if you have a covered porch you might prepare it there on a grill and then serve it indoors, buffet style. If you've planned something like a clam bake, all you have to do is steam the clams and corn on your stove top and boil the lobsters. Traditionally, the clams and corn are eaten first, so you'll have plenty of room to cook the lobsters after these are done. If you're planning a fish fry, you'll have to switch to something else, unless you want to *buy* fish for a crowd.

# 13

# Weekend Entertaining

Entertaining guests for the weekend could be a reason for consulting almost every chapter in this book, from the cocktail party to the barbecue. However, no guests need or even want a perpetual round of entertainment from Friday to Sunday; after all, they are coming to see you, not a hostess already exhausted by preparations for their visit. Depending on your circumstances, the demands of a job or your family life, decide how much you can do in the way of having other people in and still enjoy your guests. Whatever you plan, keep the party small and the preparations simple.

*Before a Guest Comes:* Take a moment to check out the room where your guest or guests are going to sleep. Is there a good reading light? A place to put suitcases other than on the floor? A small chest or a couple of luggage racks (which have other possibilities—to hold a tray for after-dinner coffee or a collection of plants) is a good idea. Is there a bureau with at least one empty drawer for whatever your guests may want to unpack and put away? They won't be staying for a week, but still a little space for them to stow their belongings is a considerate gesture. Take a look at the closet and find other places to store your old riding jacket, seldom-used evening dresses, the bits and pieces you've been meaning to give away to the thrift shop. Throw out those old wire hangers from the cleaners (you'll soon be getting more) and either substitute some good ones from your own closet or buy new ones. And don't forget a couple of large hangers for men's jackets and a skirt/trouser hanger or two. Also, be sure there's an extra blanket and something to read.

If you're fortunate enough to have a second bathroom, check on tissues, bath powder, hand lotion and toothpaste. A new cake of soap at the basin and in the tub or shower helps make a bathroom look fresh and attractive, even if this is the one you usually use for hanging up your drip-drys and storing wet mops. Take a look at the bathroom glass; either put it through the dishwasher or substitute a new plastic one.

If your guests are going to share your bathroom, give it an eagle eye for tidiness. Check over the items listed above, and put away as many of your personal things as you can. If there isn't enough space for their towels, put them on a portable towel rack in the room where they're going to be.

*Entertaining Your Guests:* If your guests arrive on a Friday, that's a good time for a family dinner when you can quietly catch up on their activities. On Saturday, you might want to ask a small group of friends to come in after dinner for wine and cheese or coffee and dessert. Or you might plan a small dinner party with a few friends whom you know your guests will enjoy. Whatever you decide for Saturday, you'll want to start the day with a substantial, leisurely breakfast. Since lunch is likely to be an informal, pick-up affair, this is the time to go all out with a platter of eggs Benedict, pancakes and sausage, French toast or even big bowls of Irish oatmeal and cream if it's a cold day.

After breakfast, you might take your friends to a museum or an art gallery, or suggest a walk through some interesting sections of town. Never mind if the place where you live isn't strong on sight-seeing attractions; every town has something to interest outsiders: a block of old Victorian buildings or the embattled railroad station you and your friends are trying to save, a lovely park or a new housing project. The real point of the expedition is the companionship and the exercise. Later, you can bring your guests home to help with the preparations for dinner or other plans for the evening and a rest before the party begins.

*The Out-of-Town Weekend:* If you live in the suburbs or have a weekend place in the country, your entertaining could revolve around the same kinds of entertainment that you would give in town; or if the season is right, you might plan a barbecue or a picnic for Saturday evening (see Chapter 12). Sunday brunch or a late luncheon party are also good ways of entertaining weekend guests before they start back home. (See Chapter 9.)

For a suburban or country weekend, you might think of getting up a badminton or croquet tournament, or a game of volleyball. For less strenuous entertainment you might drive everybody to a nearby fair, if there is one. It all depends on your inclinations—and what your guests enjoy.

*Shopping for Food:* If your entertaining is being done at a weekend place, it will take some advance planning to be sure you have what you need. For example, it helps to know ahead of time what foods will be available in the country and what you'll have to order ahead or bring with you. Interesting greens for salads, out-of-season fruits and some vegetables like endive and artichokes are sometimes hard to find in country supermarkets, as are some delicatessen items and many wines. So be prepared: make a list of what you'll be serving and bring the hard-to-get items with you. Last-minute shopping can be done in the country on Saturday morning. In fact, a pleasant way of spending the morning with your guests is to combine a shopping trip with a tour of the local points of interest or a particularly nice stretch of countryside. You might include a couple of antique shops if that's what interests your guests, or stroll through an old graveyard before stopping to shop.

If you live in the suburbs and work, you're still likely to have last-minute shopping. On Saturday, you might drop by with your guests to see the craft show in the local high school on your way to the supermarket. Or spend a few minutes watching a Little League baseball game.

In planning the weekend, remember that most house guests enjoy helping. Let them. If their talents don't extend to the kitchen, or you'd prefer not to have them there, give them other chores to do like splitting some kindling for the barbecue, helping you fix the screen door, or hoe a row of beans in the garden.

*Briefing Your Guests:* Make a point of telling your house guests beforehand what kinds of clothes they will need: boots if it's muddy and you're thinking of a hike on Saturday, tennis things if there's a court near you and you know tennis is what they enjoy, extra sweaters if the temperature in your eighteenth-century farmhouse is unpredictable. Let them know too, if you're planning to dress up on Saturday evening.

If you're having a party, take a few minutes before it begins to tell your weekenders something about the people who will be coming, what they do or what their special interests are. This way, your guests will have something to go on when they meet your friends.

Weekend entertaining can be a pleasure for everyone as long as the hostess and/or host is relaxed and allows guests to feel the same. Make sure that the amount of entertainment you plan is balanced out by an equal amount of free time for all. Remember, it's your weekend too, and don't go back to the office on Monday feeling as if you'd been through Armageddon. The best weekends with guests are those where no one is worrying too much about social arrangements and schedules or rushing off to see the sights. Two or three days together can be a wonderful opportunity to talk quietly and intimately with friends. And if you don't know your guests too well, what better way to get to know them than to share small chores or sports, or being together out of doors?

# 14

# Parties for the Young

Entertaining children takes as much, if not more, planning as giving a party for grown-ups. Without a certain amount of organized activity, older children tend to get out of hand. This can lead to a lot of running around, playing "sardines" in the linen closet, or bowling in the living room with whatever's at hand. Younger ones are likely to become bored, whiny and quarrelsome. So plan ahead and see that the hours between four and six or three and five are filled with amusing things for them to do. If you live in the country or the suburbs, you can relax a little, especially if the weather is nice, and turn them outdoors for a short period. But in an apartment some form of planned activity for the young is essential for every minute of the time they are there.

*Very Young Guests:* If your guests are very young (from four to six years), think of limiting the party time to two hours. Whatever you do, begin it early and let the parents know exactly when you'd like them to pick their children up. Otherwise, you may find yourself with exhausted youngsters, including your own, hanging around up to your dinner time.

If your child is old enough to write his own invitations, by all means have him do it; otherwise, write them yourself or get on the telephone.

*A Birthday Party:* If the party is to celebrate a birthday, a good way of doing things is present-opening first, games or entertainment second, with food served immediately afterward. Pin-the-Tail-On-the-Donkey, Musical Chairs, or a simpler version of the game where the children simply dance around to the music and then sit down on the floor when its stops, are still favorites. If you have the time and energy, you might set up a "cobweb" of different colored strings leading to a small prize for each child. However, this takes a certain amount of supervision for a young child to follow so don't try it unless you have someone to help you. Drop-The-Handkerchief, London Bridge and Farmer-in-the-Dell are good games if you have the space for a circle of children in your living room.

As an alternative to games, you might get that friend of your oldest son who's such a great magician to perform, or someone else who plays the guitar and is good at getting kids to sing together. In any case, an hour of games or entertainment is enough; then shepherd everyone to the table.

*Decorating the Table:* A pretty table is as much appreciated by little children as by the older guest. What goes on it doesn't have to be expensive and certainly this isn't a time to bring out your best china. A brightly colored paper tablecloth, paper napkins, and plates are fine. With small children mugs are better than paper cups; they aren't as likly to tip over. However, don't count on this—have a couple of sponges on hand for spills. A bunch of balloons tied to your dining table light fixture makes a festive decoration, and if it survives long enough, it's fun for each child to take one home.

*Favors:* There's a broad range of party favors available in department and stationery stores, as well as those devoted entirely to party novelties. It all depends on what you want to spend. With a little imagination, you can do as well in the dime store. Tiny baskets make nice favors, filled with candies. Or make party cups out of paper napkins. Clam shells are for free (if you live near a beach, or have recently had clams for dinner) and make interesting and attractive containers for gumdrops and other tidbits. What you want to do about party crackers depends on how you feel about them. They seem to be the reason why many grown men and women have never recovered from their terror of birthday parties.

*Service and Food:* Self-service is *not* for the very young; on the other hand, given their favors and a few paper whistles they aren't too particular if the service is slow. So serve whatever you've planned on individual plates from the kitchen or a sideboard. Or better still, stick to finger food and have it ready on the plates when the youngsters come to the table. Depending on the time you have to prepare it, this could be tiny meatballs with catsup, or small hamburgers, shaped in rectangles to fit a toasted frankfurter roll cut in half. Don't worry if the food isn't that warm. Stuffed eggs or egg sandwiches cut in quarters, with carrot sticks and perhaps some dates filled with creamed cheese are also finger foods that children like.

You will, of course, want to provide the obligatory birthday cake, but there's nothing that says it has to be ordered from a fancy bakery as long as it has icing and candles. And since half the food at a party for little children winds up in the Disposall or the garbage can, think simple (and decoratively), with small servings to each guest.

By the time the cake is served your eye will be wandering to the clock. This is the moment to get out the sherry decanter. It may look like a nice hospitable gesture to the parents who come to pick up their children; only you will know who it's really for.

*Older Children:* For older children, a party is often built around an event such as an ice-hockey game, a Little League match, an amateur musical at school, a popular film or the circus. Your job is to feed them either before or afterward.

For this age group (nine to fourteen) parties are often a disaster. Children can be rambunctious, overexcited and generally difficult to manage in a large group. Don't invite too many guests and keep things simple. Don't bother too much about decorations. The pre-teenager is more interested in filling his stomach than satisfying his aesthetic sense, so why waste your energies? Concentrate instead on the food.

*Food:* Think of serving chili with plenty of toasted tortillas, or a big dish of spaghetti and crusty Italian bread, or bread sticks—they make great poison darts. And then there's always pizza—the standby of the "now" generation. If you want to appeal to the adventurous do-it-yourself strain in your guests, you might consider a beef fondue. You'll need one fondue pot for each three to four guests, some long-handled forks, two or three sauces for dipping, and a lot of tolerance for messiness. Consider a tablecloth made up of the Help Wanted pages in your local newspaper. It makes a consistent, not unattractive pattern and the kids certainly won't care. After a hearty dessert, such as pie or ice cream, you can either speed them on their way, or pile them into the car and get them wherever it is they're going.

*Teenagers:* Teenagers fourteen years and over are quite capable of planning and carrying out their own parties—with a little help in the culinary department. Once you've performed your duties as a cook your presence is very likely to be vetoed, but the chances are you will want to be there behind the scenes, a friendly but firm presence. Monitor the noise level if you live in an apartment and the neighbors are likely to complain; intervene if the party seems to be taking a turn you or the parents of other youngsters might not approve. You may also want to remind your son or daughter when the time has come for guests to go. If you don't want to intrude, make some arrangement with your child beforehand—for instance, that the party's over when the kitchen timer goes off.

*Food:* The menu could be the same as for younger children. Hamburgers and French fries and homemade "grinders" are also popular, along with huge bowls of potato chips and gallons of cola. This is one time when you forget your pious pronouncements about empty calories and poor complexions and lay it all on. Some teenagers, however, can surprise you with the sophistication of their palates, so be sure to consult your son or daughter about the menu and keep your cool if the request is for something like shrimp, sushi, or sukyaki. Just hope you can afford it.

*Entertainment:* A record player is a vital piece of teenage party equipment (if you have a teenager you undoubtedly have one), and with it space for dancing. So put any treasures out of the way and let your guests do what's necessary about pushing back the furniture and rolling up the rugs. It's also a good idea to leave out a few games like backgammon, Parcheesi and Chinese checkers, and a pack or two of playing cards.

*Young and Old:* In mixing anyone up to fourteen with grown-ups, a good thing to remember if you're not a parent is that many kids of that age do not share the exotic taste in food of their elders. Be sure to have one smple dish on your menu when your mixture of generations is extreme. Another useful thing to know is that youngsters rarely find waiting easy, especially waiting to eat. Either feed the young while the grown-ups are drinking, or at least be sure that they have plenty of snacks to sustain them before the meal is served.

# 15

# Home Weddings

A home wedding can be anything from a small gathering of close friends who bring lovingly made dishes for the reception after the ceremony, to the most elaborate affair, with a cluster of attendants, a lavishly catered reception, an outdoor marquee and an orchestra. It all depends on what the couple and you (the family) want to make it, and what you think you can afford. It could be that your daughter and her husband-to-be would rather take the money and run—across country, to Mexico or to Europe. Before you start planning, get together with the bride and groom and find out what they really want. Too often both principals and parents are pushed into a costly affair simply because they find it hard to give up the conventional picture of an elaborate wedding with engraved invitations sent out to two hundred people, ushers in hired morning coats and bridesmaids in picturesque but expensive dresses they never wear again. Of course, if this is what your young people want, you'll do all you can to provide it, with perhaps some realistic adjustments to suit your facilities and pocketbook.

On the other hand, *you* may be the one who has always dreamed of your dauther in your wedding gown, getting married under an ancestral portrait in the living room, or the rose arbor in the garden—only to find that she and her fiancé have other ideas in mind. Maybe what they want is to be married at sunrise, barefoot and dressed in East Indian costume, to the strains of a sitar. Whatever it is, remember it's their wedding and go cheerfully along with them. For the purposes of this chapter we're assuming that they won't be barefoot and that they've decided to have both the ceremony and reception at home.

*Invitations:* Invitations to a wedding are usually sent out four weeks before the event. They may be engraved or printed and follow the conventional form that any stationer can show you. If it's a small wedding you may prefer to send personal notes. Nowdays, it is not unusual for the bride and groom to issue the invitations themselves.

*The Ceremony:* One of the first things you will want to do is have the couple choose the spot, indoors or out, where they would like to have the ceremony take place. This could be in front of a fireplace or bay window banked with greens, plants or flowers; or if it's to be an outdoor wedding, in some attractive spot in your yard or garden. However, here you'll have to have an alternative plan in case of rain.

For a Catholic or High Church Episcopal ceremony, you will want a small rug or two pillows for the couple to kneel on. For a Jewish ceremony, a beautiful piece of embroidery or small handworked tablecloth makes a nice *chuppah* or canopy, and it's all the nicer if it's something that has been handed down in the family. A canopy of flowers or that rose bower are also traditional *chuppahs*. You will also need a small table, such as a card table, covered with a cloth.

If there is to be a bridal procession of some kind, you may want to have music, although it isn't absolutely necessary. This could be anything from a small three-piece orchestra to a friend at a portable organ, or even a record player. The choice of music is, of course, up to the bride and groom. A certain amount of rehearsing is necessary so that the principals have some idea of how they're going to proceed— where they're going to appear from (the groom, let's say, from a sunporch off the living room, the bride and her father from the front hall), and how they are going to stand at the altar. Here, the clergyman or rabbi who is going to officiate, can help you. Don't forget that this isn't a professional performance, and mix-ups are easily dismissed with a smile. However, it's nicer, and helps to focus attention on the seriousness of the ceremony itself, if these procedures are planned in advance and carried out smoothly.

Parents can be startled and sometimes upset by some of the alternative marriage ceremonies many young people choose nowadays. If yours decide to include readings from *The Prophet* or Omar Khayyám or to recite other love poetry to each other—even if they decide to forget tradition entirely and write their own service—don't let it upset you. The chances are that whatever off beat form they choose for exchanging vows, their sincerity and feeling for each other will shine through the irregularities, enveloping everyone at the wedding and dispersing your concern.

*Who Goes Where?:* These days, families come in such a variety of patterns that there's no telling who will be playing what roles at a wedding except, of course, for the bride and groom. If the father of the bride is absent or deceased, she may want a brother or an uncle or a good friend of the family to give her away. Or she may decide to dispense with this tradition entirely and simply take her place at the altar with the groom. If either of their parents are divorced and remarried a family council is probably in order to decide what step-parents, if any, will appear in the receiving line, or whether they should come to the wedding at all. It all depends on what seems most natural and comfortable to the chief participants. Whatever is decided, it should be done before the wedding day.

After the ceremony the custom is for the bride and groom, their parents and any attendants to form a receiving line. This is a nice convention that gives each guests a chance to offer congratulations to the couple and exchange a few words with the parents.

*The Reception:* Depending on the time of the ceremony, a home wedding reception usually takes the form of a buffet luncheon or supper. At a four o'clock wedding, a selection of canapés and small thinly cut sandwiches would be enough—along with the traditional wedding cake.

Champagne is another tradition at weddings, and is usually served as soon as the guests have passed through the receiving line, but it doesn't necessarily have to be imported. Some New York and California brands can hold their own with French champagne. As a general rule, twelve to fifteen bottles will serve twenty-five people, and you will need plenty of ice tubs to keep it chilled. If you'd prefer not to serve champagne, why not choose a less expensive white wine, either domestic or imported, or serve a white wine punch.

A toast to the couple is another nice tradition at weddings, pro-posed by either the bride's father, another close relative, or the best man. Afterward, guests can be asked to come to the buffet table. Or the toast can be proposed later, at the moment when the bride and groom are the focus of the assembled guests as they prepare to cut the wedding cake.

Traditionally, nobody makes the move to go home until the bride and groom have left the reception. Again, these traditions are passing, but this is another sweet one that you may want to hold on to.

If you're serving a buffet lunch or supper at the reception, you will have to provide chairs. The folding type that can be hired are the easiest solution; they can be used to seat people during the ceremony and are then easily reassembled in small groups for lunch or supper while the guests are going through the receiving line. You'll also need small folding tables on which they can put their plates. At a four o'clock wedding, chairs aren't absolutely necessary as the food isn't that elaborate. Guests can stand during the relatively short ceremony, and afterward stroll about with drink in hand as they would at a cocktail party.

*Help:* The help you'll need at a home wedding is much the same as you would need at any large party, except that you and your husband, as hostess and host, have other roles to play as the parents of the bride, and it's unlikely that either of you will have time to greet guests as they arrive. But if you live in the suburbs or the country, you'll probably need someone to help with the parking; another person should be there to open the door and take the coats, and if you're not having ushers and are having chairs for the ceremony, you may want someone else to show guests to their seats. Someone must also be responsible for setting out the food on the buffet table after the ceremony, and circulating the sandwiches and canapés; you'll need others to open and serve the champagne, set up the tables and rearrange the chairs while you and your husband are in the receiving line.

In making plans for a home wedding, keep in mind that there are no hard and fast rules about any of it. Some of the traditions that have grown in regard to weddings, such as serving champagne or having a receiving line, are ways of enriching the sense of celebration and as such are nice, but there is no reason why they have to be followed. In all forms of entertainment, but particularly at something as personal as a wedding, you have all the latitude in the world to do what you like as long as it pleases the bride and groom.

# 16

# Holiday
# Entertaining

Holidays are a time to preserve traditions, to be with one's family and friends and, in drawing up a guest list, to make a point of including people who may be alone. But however much we enjoy these special occasions, they can also mean a lot of work. Ways of cutting corners have been discussed elsewhere in this book; on holidays you can still do this but continue to keep the rituals and traditions that give these days their significance.

## Christmas

In some way every family which observes Christmas has its own traditions. One of these might be making an occasion of decorating the Christmas tree; reading "The Night Before Christmas" or Dickens's *A Christmas Carol* on Christmas Eve; it might be a traditional midnight supper that you give every year on Christmas Eve after church; a huge breakfast on Christmas morning (before or after giving presents), or a big Christmas dinner in the late afternoon or in the evening. Some of these are times when you will want to share your family celebration. And basically these are the occasions for the same kinds of parties you might give at other times: a buffet supper on Christmas Eve, a breakfast or brunch on Christmas morning, a seated dinner any time between three and eight o'clock on Christmas Day. But with a difference. You will probably devote more loving attention to decorating your house or apartment and a lot of extra time on baked goodies and other foods either to give away as presents or to serve yourself.

*Decorations:* It's nice to go out and gather greens and make your own decorations. And if you live in the country this is probably what you would do. For city-dwellers, this may be one corner they choose to cut; instead they will buy their greenery.

To make a wreath for your front door, open up a coat hanger and join it at the ends; cover it with clipped pine boughs or pine cones and lady apples, attached with the hangers made for Christmas tree decorations. Ground pine has a nice effect looped over a mantel or a door frame, or used to enliven the forbidding features of your great-great-grandfather's portrait. Try stringing the Christmas cards you receive on narrow red or green ribbons hung from the top of a bookcase and make them part of your décoration. Think of a Christmas tree decorated entirely with homemade things: pastry crescents tied with red string, pomander balls made from small oranges studded with cloves, gingerbread men and gilded walnuts, with chains of popcorn looped over the tree. You will have other ideas of your own, and many to choose from the magazines that abound in them at this season.

One of your traditions may be a treasured tablecloth to cover the dining table, or it might be a special centerpiece: a set of Swedish candle chimes surrounded by holly, a crèche (packed away carefully from year to year), or a miniature sleigh with "eight tiny reindeer." Whatever it is, it's presence evokes memories of past Christmases and gives added meaning to the one you are celebrating.

A *Cooperative Buffet Supper:* If you've invited a group of family and close friends to come in for Christmas Eve, and still have to produce a Christmas dinner the next day, you might very well make this a cooperative party where, under your direction, each person brings a dish. As the hostess, one if your jobs is to see that there are no duplications and that the combined effort produces a festive, well-balanced board. For instance, an aunt by marriage, who makes a delicious avgolemono soup, might be asked to bring that (supplying the finishing touches in your kitchen). And if you have another relative or friend who suggests that she bring along her pumpkin soup, you will have to ward her off by saying something like "What we'd really like are those marvelous scalloped oysters you make." This way, you mastermind the menu without having to do much more work in the kitchen than provide the after-dinner coffee—and clean up afterward.

A cooperative dinner is also a great way of entertaining with friends at any time during the year, especially if the friends are gourmets who enjoy cooking. It saves the time and expense of one person having to produce an entire dinner alone, and the fun of a joint venture adds to the enjoyment of the party.

In working out and assigning the dishes on your Christmas Eve menu, remember to avoid poultry because of the traditional goose or turkey that many people serve on Christmas Day. Along with Aunt

Mary's soup, you might ask someone to bring a roasted leg of pork (fresh ham) with the rind left on so that those who like "cracklin'" can enjoy that. Cumberland sauce, made with currant jelly and madeira, makes a good accompaniment, with carrots and artichoke hearts and perhaps a spinach ring with creamed mushrooms as the vegetables. You might be the one to provide the dessert, which could be a homemade lemon sherbet in contrast to all these rich goodies to come on Christmas day. See pp. 267–74 for more menus and recipes.

For wine, you might serve a Beaujolais or a medium-bodied dry white wine such as Pouilly-Fuissé.

A nice touch at a cooperative party is to write out copies of the menu beforehand, listing the name of the person who has contributed each dish and put them with the place cards. If you're having a buffet supper rather than a seated dinner, make up a larger single copy of the menu, put it in an inexpensive standing frame and place it on the buffet table. If you want to go even further in publicizing your cooks, get their recipes and copy them out for distribution to the guests.

*A Carol-Singing Party:* One of the nicest traditions on Christmas Eve is to get a group of friends together and go carol-singing in the neighborhood after dinner. So why not ask them to come back afterward for a hot toddy (made with whiskey) or negus (made with sherry or port) or a mug of hot buttered rum? Decide in advance on one kind of hot drink (too many varieties can get complicated) and set up your bar earlier in the day with the necessary glasses or mugs (an old-fashioned glass for a hot toddy, goblets for negus, mugs for hot-buttered rum.) Get ready supplies of cube and finely granulated sugar, lemon peel and the necessary spices. You will also need a kettle of hot water and a warming tray, or better still, an electric kettle that you can plug in near the bar.

The food you serve could be anything from Christmas cookies and coffee cakes to the more substantial fare you would serve at a cocktail buffet. It all depends on what you feel up to and how hungry you think your guests will be only a few hours after dinner.

At this kind of impromptu get-together, you will probably not have more than twelve guests, and since some are likely to be young people let them be the ones to sit on the floor.

# The New Year

*Open House:* In Scotland, this is *the* important day, when open house is the traditional way of saying "Happy New Year." In the rush of holiday parties, it's better to issue written invitations, so that your guests will have something to remind themselves with. You might combine the invitation with a Christmas greeting. Decide how long you want your open house to be, and indicate on the card the hours when you expect people to drop in. It might begin in the late morning and last until late afternoon. Or it might be an entirely afternoon affair, beginning at one and lasting until five. It all depends on your stamina and perhaps too on how many other parties will be going on within your group of friends.

*Drink:* A New Year's open house is a good time to abandon the Bloody Marys, vodka and tonics and other drinks that require a bar and perhaps someone to tend it. Instead, get out (or rent) a punch bowl and glasses, and plan to serve a champange or wine punch, or something even stronger like a fish-house punch. Or choose the more traditional eggnog. All of these can be made ahead early on the day of the party except for the final addition of champagne, soda water or egg whites.

Punch glasses can be taken out and washed and recycled for the next influx of guests. However, it helps to have an emergency supply of plastic glasses for those times when everyone seems to come at once.

*Help:* At a party like this, the most useful help you can have is a resourceful teenager experienced in both dishwashing and baby-sitting. During the holidays, especially at a daytime party, many parents really have to bring along their children (indeed, you may have invited them to), so make the most of your helper, and if the assemblage of youngsters reaches an unmanageable point, ask her to take them to an area away from the grown-ups, and see that there is enough equipment in the way of games, toys, jump ropes, coloring books, etc., to keep them entertained. There is nothing that says you have to do this, but it does make a better party for everyone concerned.

The food you serve at an open house is similar to what you would have at a cocktail party, with some additional holiday trimmings, such as fruit cake, cookies, perhaps a homemade pâté someone has given you for Christmas, and an assortment of sweet holiday breads.

# Passover

One of the most significant holidays observed by the Jewish people is the Passover Seder. This celebration takes place on the first two nights of the Passover to mark the liberation of the Jews from Egyptian bondage over three thousand years ago. It is a holy and joyous occasion with family and friends as well as strangers not fortunate enough to have a Seder of their own, gathered together to share in a ritual ceremony and meal.

Everyone at the table, beginning with the youngest reader, takes turns reading from the Haggadah, which tells the story of the deliverance. Passages are explained and discussed in terms that even the youngest participants can understand and relate to themselves. The form of the ceremony varies somewhat between Sephardic and Ashkenazic Jews, but in general it is celebrated the same way on the same two nights of the year by Jews all over the world—as it has been throughout Jewish history.

*Setting the Seder Table:* It goes without saying that you will want your table to look as beautiful as possible with your best china, linen and tableware. Many families have traditional objects connected with the ritual and service of the Seder that are brought out each year for this occasion alone. For instance, you might own a small brass pitcher hinged above a brass bowl for the father, or whoever is the "leader" of the services, in which he can ritually wash his hands before the Passover service; or you might have an embroidered bag to hold the matzos, or a traditional Passover plate divided into compartments for the various foods that are passed around and blessed in the explanation during the service. One family we know has among its treasures a small china egg and spoon that is filled with salt water to be sprinkled on the bitter herbs during the meal, and thimble-sized cups from a great-great-grandmother, given to small children in the family to drink from so that they can have the ritual four glasses of wine without getting pixillated. Or, you may be fortunate enough to possess a silver cup for service to Elijah which, filled with wine, is traditionally kept on the table throughout the Seder in the hope that the prophet will appear as a messenger from the Lord and announce the coming of the Messiah. The children watch that wine cup carefully during the prayers to see whether in fact the level of the wine goes down.

Candles are placed on the table to be lighted by the mother of the house to symbolize the beginning of Passover. A glass of wine goes in the usual place at each table setting. A blessing is pronounced at the drinking of the first glass. Four glasses are drunk in all during the course of the Seder, signifying the four expressions of the Lord's promise to deliver the children of Israel. At each place is a copy of the Haggadah ("the telling"), which contains the complete Seder ceremonies in their prescribed order.

On the table is the Seder tray on which are placed three matzot, representing the unleavened bread hastily prepared by the Jews be-for their flight from Egypt. Also on the tray is the *z'roah,* a roasted shank bone that represents the ancient sacrifice of the Paschal lamb. To its left is a hard-boiled egg symbolizing the festival offering in the Temple, as well as being the Jewish symbol of mourning for the loss of the Temple.

In the center of the tray are the *maror* or bitter herbs (usually horseradish), which stand for the suffering of the Jews. Below the maror is another bitter herb—the *charosseth*—next to which is placed the *karpas,* a piece of parsley or lettuce signifying the meager diet of the Jews in bondage.

*Menu:* If you are giving a Passover dinner, whether or not you are an Orthodox observant Jew, this is a time when you will want to think of guests and older family members who abide by the Kosher rules, and observe carefully the dietary restrictions for this meal. For instance, you would not serve dairy products, or use butter in the preparation of the food or put it on the table, or serve cream with the coffee, although nowadays some families do serve nondairy commercial "cream."

In addition to the foods set out on the Seder tray and served in a prescribed order as part of the ritual of the Seder, gefilte fish is often served—usually as a first course. The next course is often a chicken broth with either matzo balls or the traditional small soup nuts, called *mandlen.* The main course is usually a large fowl or a roast, or both, with a vegetable stew traditionally made with sweet potatoes, carrots, nuts, raisins and prunes. Dessert is often a compote of stewed fruit served with cakes that have been made without leavening or ordinary flour.

*Wine:* Passover wine is traditionally heavy and sweet simply because that used to be the only type available. Now it is possible to get much drier wines that are far more palatable, but you'll also want to have some of the traditional type which older guests are accustomed to and which young children, who are allowed to have a tiny sip, prefer.

*Seating:* This is one occasion where the *pater familias,* or other person who is to conduct the service, always sits at the head of the table. The children, as well as the strangers you've invited, are the guests of honor and are placed near him in the old-fashioned way. And it is he who sets the pace of the service as well as the meal, who brings to the occasion the spirit that gives it its tone and beauty.

*Avoiding Pitfalls:* A Seder is not only a dinner but a prescribed ritual with uncertain timing. It is certainly an occasion when you'll want to talk to family members the day before about who will do what. For instance, who will carve, which one of you will pour the wine, and who will take away the dishes?

Keep your menu as simple as you can, without too many accompaniments to clutter the table. And since it's hard to figure out how long the reading of the first part of the Haggadah will take, it's a good idea to have your meats ready in a warming oven or other device when you sit down at the table.

Try to find wineglasses with good stable bottoms. You'll be glad you did, for the way things go, with children at the table, grown-ups juggling the Haggadahs, groping for their eyeglasses, or leaning over to pat a grandchild, a lot of wine can be spilled at this meal.

In order to have the reading of the Haggadah go smoothly, be sure that everyone has copies of the same translation; otherwise, everyone gets lost. You can get these free from one of the companies that puts them out as a public service. Avoid those big elaborate gift copies that are heavy to hold and easy to spot with wine or food.

Sometimes there's a problem with a child of reading age who doesn't read very well or isn't too confident about doing so. In this case, it's a good idea to alert the person who is conducting the service so that he can gracefully pass over the child and ask someone else to read next.

People outside the family, invited to the Seder often want to contribute to the meal. If you have a guest who kindly volunteers to "bring dessert" and offers to bake a cake, make sure that that person knows it must be a cake especially prepared for Passover according to the dietary restrictions. Otherwise, you may be in for an embarrassing moment, and not be able to serve it.

# Fourth of July

For the "Glorious Fourth," depending on where you live, you might think of organizing a sailing picnic to watch the fireworks on the shore. In this case, you won't be doing any cooking on the site, so basically all you need to bring along is something like a roasted bird and a bottle, with a couple of cold salads, a big thermos jug of coffee and plenty of split buttered French bread to piece out the menu. If you wanted to be fancier and also to follow the traditional *pièce de résistance* for a Fourth of July menu, you could bring, packed in a picnic refrigerator, a beautiful cold poached salmon with a cucumber sauce.

Alternatively, rural landlubbers could invite a group of friends to a barbecue (grilled salmon steaks are a possibility) before going on to watch the local fireworks (See Chapter 12). And even if you're a city-dweller there's no reason why you can't have sparklers and celebrate the Fourth with a cocktail buffet (see Chapter 6) or even a sit-down dinner in your apartment (see Chapter 8). And if you're fortunate enough to have a balcony, why not set up a trestle table with folding campstools for the seating, and have your guests dine there? In case of rain, you'll be a lot better off than the sailing picnickers, because at the last minute you can always set things up inside.

# Other Celebrations

If you really enjoy entertaining you won't wait for national holidays to find a reason to celebrate something. You might have a spur-of-the-moment impulse just before May Day to call up a dozen friends to come to a party. Or it might be Shrove Tuesday, or the first day of spring, or the mid-autumn Chinese Festival of the Living where you ask everyone to come in Chinese dress and offer mooncakes to the old man in the moon. Or it might be a "charette," the kind of party given by architectural students when they've finished a long period of hard work. The possibilities are endless, and the occasion described below is one you may not have thought of.

*Midsummer's Eve:* This night, which falls at the time of the summer solstice (on June 21) is a vastly neglected opportunity for celebration if you live in the country or a place where you can entertain out of doors. It is a night filled with magic and a little madness with a certain staginess, as we all know from *A Midsummer's Night Dream.* And since here we won't even think of, let alone discuss, the possibility of rain, set your stage for the outdoor festivities as they do in the Southwest, with a dozen or more candles set in heavy paper bags filled with sand and arranged about the lawn, or use kerosene flares or railwayman lanterns. And find some Japanese lanterns to decorate your porch or deck.

Since Midsummer's Eve lends itself to fancy, if you are any good at this kind of thing, you might send your invitations in rhyme. If not, steal a line or two from Shakespeare. But do try to find a delicate and unusual card that expresses the mood of your party. A pressed flower or bit of fern taped to a plain card is one possibility. And begin the party late—at nine or even ten; you want to have everyone feeling their best at the midnight hour. To further the mood, you might ask guests to come wearing a hat or headress of their own design. At midnight, everyone switches hats—and personalities. Or plan a mini-treasure hunt and let your guests draw picture-puzzle parts (preselected by you) which, fitted together, indicate who is to partner whom.

*Drink:* Wine is the best drink to serve on an occasion like this where the party spirit comes from the fun of putting aside one's everyday self and not from six to eight ounces of hard liquor consumed in an evening. And for those who don't drink you would have the usual fruit juice and soft drinks.

*A Midnight Supper:* If you have the space to arrange a sit-down supper to be served at midnight on your porch or deck, or out on the lawn, that's much the nicest way of doing things. Two picnic tables with seats attached make a splendid banqueting table. They can be made to look very elegant with two matching flowered sheets as tablecloths and small bunches of wildflowers set at intervals down the center. Use placecards and if you have a treasure hunt, make sure that each person has a new partner at dinner even if it means (as it undoubtedly will) some last-minute switching of the seating arrangements. During dinner, encourage fanciful toasts to help create the feeling of a banquet.

*Food:* To follow out the mood of the party, keep the menu simple but elegant and one that can be entirely prepared ahead of time —you want to have as much fun at this party as your guests. However, this is the night to make sure that the food is elegantly presented. You might have a chilled yogurt soup with sprigs of mint floating on the surface, followed by a handsomely decorated cold poached bass. This and a colorful vegetable salad are all you really need before the presentation of a dramatic dessert, such as cherries jubilee, or a lasciviously rich and beautifully decorated cake. If your guests are too many for a sit-down affair you could, of course, serve this menu as a buffet supper, using a tureen for the soup, perhaps skipping the cherries and settling for the cake alone.

*Music:* This is a must for Midsummer's Eve, even if it's only your trusty record player. Choose records that reinforce the light and fanciful feeling of your party. Madrigals and other Elizabethan music would be pretty during dinner, especially if you intersperse them with more contemporary music later. And if someone you know is a good guitarist (or an expert on the dulcimer) he might be the first person you invite to this party. Encourage people to sing, in fact, to perform in any way they like—even a spontaneous solo dance would be charming. Keep in mind that what you're giving is a children's party for grown-ups.

# 17

# Wines and Spirits

The drinks served at a party depend on what kind of a party it is, the number of people invited and (if you know most of them well) what they like to drink.

At a small gathering of friends it's simple: you know for example that Arthur drinks Scotch, Nancy likes martinis straight up, Roger drinks white wine and Alice doesn't drink at all, and you plan accordingly.

At a large cocktail party, the standard procedure is to set up a basic bar that includes the makings of a few popular drinks, mixers (including fruit juices) that can also be served plain to nondrinkers, and red and white wine (jug wine is fine).

Frozen daiquiris, piñas coladas, brandy Alexanders and other such extravaganzas are all within the capacity of a restaurant or hotel but nothing you'd want to try to do at a private party. If you're asked for something like this, feel perfectly comfortable in saying "Sorry, we're not set up for that; what else would you like?"

*The Basic Bar:* The basic bar for a cocktail party of sixty to seventy-five people would include: three quarts of Scotch, one quart of rye or blended whiskey, one quart of bourbon, three quarts of vodka, and two of gin, one bottle of dry vermouth and one of sweet, and one gallon each of white and red wine.

Depending on the region where you live and the tastes of your friends, you may want to add rum or, particularly if you live in the South, sour mash as well as regular bourbon. And you may want to alter the proportions of what you have on hand: if your particular friends are big on scotch and bourbon and don't care for rye, you could omit that. And it's always a good idea to have plenty of beer around.

These variations in taste from region to region and from person to person are the chief reason why it's not very practical to go by the available statistics on how much liquor serves how many people. We know, for instance, that the average person drinks from three to four drinks during a cocktail party, and that a quart of liquor provides twenty drinks of one-and-a-half ounces each, but these figures aren't much use because they don't tell us what those three or four drinks are going to be. However, one thing you can be sure of: for any given party it's better to have more than you need than run out. Most liquor stores will take back unopened bottles (although if you entertain often it makes more sense to keep them for another party), unopened mixers will keep almost forever in a cool place and leftover fruit juice can always be served for breakfast or turned into a gelatin dessert.

*Mixers:* You'll need seven to eight quarts of club soda, seven to eight of tonic water (in summer it's safer to make it eight), a bottle of lime juice, a quart of cola, a quart of ginger ale and an ample supply (at least three large cans each) of tomato and grapefruit juice. You'll also need a pitcher of cold water and another of prepared frozen orange juice.

*Equipment:* You'll want one-and-a-half-ounce shot glasses for gin, whiskey and vodka; a sixteen-ounce mixing glass for martinis; a metal shaker and strainer for manhattans, etc.; a long-handled stirring spoon; eight-ounce highball glasses; five-and-a-half-ounce all-purpose wineglasses for wines, cocktails and sours; a small cutting board and paring knife, as well as a large ice bucket and tongs.

*Arrangement:* You may want to arrange things differently, but the setup that seems to work best for professional bartenders is: ice and glasses to the left, liquors and mixes to the right, with the most popular liquors nearest the worker, and garnishes directly in front of the working space.

*Tips to the Bartender:* Most popular drinks are easy to make. If you're having untrained help at the bar it's a good idea to have a list of recipes pinned up above it for quick reference. Mixes are best chilled—you use less ice that way—and it's nice to use fresh ice in each repeat. In mixing drinks, always put the ice in first to chill the liquids as they are poured. One and a half ounces of liquor is enough for any one drink.

*Glassware:* For a large cocktail party, only two kinds of glasses are necessary: tall ones, for highballs, coolers and nonalcoholic soft drinks, and short ones, five-ounce straight-sided glasses, for cocktails, wine and fruit juice. And if you're renting glasses or using the plastic throwaway kind, there's no need to complicate matters by introducing other sizes and shapes. However, for a smaller gathering, where you're using your own glasses, why not serve cocktails as well as wine in stemmed, balloon-shaped glasses? They're pretty, and they have a practical advantage—a stemmed glass doesn't drip the way a straight-sided glass does, so there's no need for coasters.

*Pre-Dinner Drinks:* At any kind of party, especially one in the middle of the day, you may want to serve aperitif wines. The aperitif, so called by the French because it is said to stimulate the appetite, is a wine fortified with additional alcohol. Although milder than hard liquor, it is somewhat stronger than a table wine. Sherry and vermouth are both aperitifs, as are Dubonnet, Madeira, and Campari. These are usually served straight, but some, particularly Dubonnet and vermouth, are also served on the rocks with soda. The aperitif is a good choice for a luncheon party when most people prefer a mild drink.

An all-purpose wineglass will do nicely for an aperitif that is served straight. If you're serving it on the rocks, or with soda, choose a five-ounce, straight-sided glass.

*After-Dinner Drinks:* Traditionally, these are brandy, cordials (or liqueurs), port (a fortified wine) and the eaux de vie, which are similar to the cordials but without their sticky sweetness.

Brandy is basically a concentrated wine—that is, one that is further distilled to increase the flavor and alcoholic content. The French brandies are considered the best, and cognac, named for the region where it is made, the star among them. Armagnac is another excellent French brandy, and there are those who prefer it to cognac. As you shop in your liquor store you will see various kinds of cognacs, at various prices, most of them relatively expensive, and marked with three stars or four, or the letters V.S.O.P. and V.S.E.P. (very superior old pale and very superior extra pale). In each case, the latter designation means the finest—and the most expensive.

Cordials are rich, sweet alcoholic drinks made from liquor and fruit juices, with other flavorings added. Some popular types are mint-flavored crème de menthe, coffee-flavored Kahlúa, and the orange-flavored liqueur, Grand Marnier. B&B is a combination of an old French aromatic liqueur (Benedictine) and brandy. For wine drinkers, port, a fortified wine from Portugal, is a pleasant drink to serve after dinner with fruit and nuts. And Scotch lovers have their liqueur too, Drambuie, similar to brandy except that it is distilled from Scotch.

The eaux de vie (which means "water of life") differ from the cordials in that they are not sweet. However, they are equally high in alcoholic content. Kirsch (made from cherries), framboise (made from raspberries) and the Scandinavian aquavit (distilled from grain or potatoes) all belong to this category. Brandy, cordials and some of the eaux de vie are good served over ice cream or with fruit desserts, as well as with after-dinner coffee.

Brandy is traditionally served in a balloon-shaped brandy glass to bring out the aroma, but it can be served just as well in the one-ounce glass reserved for cordials and eaux de vie.

*Table Wines:* These wines, so called to distinguish them from forti-fied wines such as port and sherry, fall into four categories: the reds, the whites, the rosés and the sparkling wines—champagne, sparkling burgundy and the like.   ,

*What Goes with What:* The old rule about serving red wine with red meat, and white wine with chicken, fish or veal still holds, but there are exceptions. With a chicken dish made with red wine, or veal in a tomato sauce (osso bucco, for example), a red wine tastes better. And although turkey and goose are traditionally served with a white wine, duck goes best with red. If the fish is simply broiled or cooked in a white wine sauce, then white wine is the best choice. But if you're serving, say, a baked striped bass in red wine sauce, then serve a red wine with it. With ham, you might well serve a rosé—although a full-bodied white or red are both good, too.

Rosé is a good wine to serve at a summer luncheon or buffet supper, perhaps because it seems to go especially well with dishes like cold chicken and seafood, and salads.

Champagne is usually reserved for festive occasions although there are some domestic champagnes that are inexpensive enough for everyday parties), and theoretically can be served throughout the meal. It's the perfect choice for a buffet, or a Thanksgiving or Christmas dinner, with turkey or goose. However, it really mates best with dishes that are usually served with a white wine. If you're serv-ing a standing rib roast or rack of lamb, a red wine is the better choice. Sparkling burgundy is considered another festive wine, although quite a few people dislike it for its heavy fruity flavor. If you enjoy it, it's not a bad choice for a buffet where you're serving a variety of dishes.

*The Reds:* There are, of course, many kinds of wine within each category. Among the reds there are the rich, full-bodied types—Bur-gundy or claret, or the California equivalent, Pinot Noir and Cabernet Sauvignon; the lighter reds, Beaujolais, Italian Bardolino and their American counterparts, and the rugged, Chianti-type reds. Your own preference will help you decide which of these wines you want to serve with what, but a good general guide is that the first two cate-gories go well with steaks, chops and rich meat stews, and the simpler, more rugged types with pasta, pizza and family-style dishes.

*The Whites:* The whites divide up into the full-bodied Sauternes and Graves and their California equivalents—Semillon and Sauvignon Blanc. They vary in their degree of dryness. Then there are the lighter dry whites—Pouilly Fuissé and Pouilly Fumé, Chablis, the Italian Soave,

Rhine wine, Moselle and their domestic counterparts. Again, it's a matter of taste, but the heavier whites seem to go well with richer dishes such as pork, turkey, goose, and the dry ones compliment more delicate dishes such as veal, chicken and fish.

*Becoming An Expert:* The information above only begins to scratch the surface. Experts have spent a lifetime learning about wine, the varieties available from different countries, and the mysteries of different vineyards and vintages.

Other than taking a course or reading a book on the subject, the most convenient way of learning more about wines is to find a reliable wine shop or liquor store that specializes in them and make friends with the proprietor. Tell him you're having a dinner party, what you are serving and let him advise you. And don't hesitate to tell him what you can afford. One hostess, accustomed to serving good, but relatively inexpensive wines, suddenly found herself entertaining a well-known wine and food authority. She explained the situation to her dealer who said, enthusiastically, that he had just the right wine. And indeed he did. The wine and food authority was suitably impressed. It was not until the hostess got the bill that she realized that the wine was fourteen dollars a bottle.

On the other hand, a knowledgeable wine dealer can also save you from excesses. As in the case of the young woman who was giving a pizza party for her friends in the office and looking uncertainly among the imported wines. "Forget them," her wine dealer said, and kindly steered her to a shelf of American jug wines.

There are good or at least adequate wines to be had for as low as three dollars a bottle, and from many countries, including our own. Ultimately, the wines you choose to serve will be the wines you like best. And this is something you learn by trial and error, with a wine dealer to help you.

*Wine Service:* White wines and rosés are served slightly chilled, sparkling wines chilled and red wines at room temperature (or about 60F.) White and sparkling wines are usually served from the bottle, wrapped in a napkin. The rule used to be that red wines should be opened three or four hours before serving to allow them to "breathe." Red wines are served either from the bottle or from a decanter. The latter is an especially good idea if you wish to dress up (or conceal) a modest jug wine.

The custom is for the host (or, if there isn't one, the hostess) to be served first. This, of course, presuming that there is a helper on hand to pour. A little wine is poured into the host's glass, he tastes it, and if he approves, his glass is filled and wine is then served to the rest of the guests. There is a point to this ritual: if the wine is "corked" or has a vinegary taste, the bottle can be taken away and another opened. If the host is serving the wine himself, it's still worth doing, although the testing could take place in the kitchen, at the sideboard, or wherever else the bottle is being uncorked.

*Glassware:* Wineglasses are available in many shapes and sizes, stemming from the European custom of having a special glass for each kind of wine. However, today things are simpler and the wine experts agree that an eight-ounce, tulip-shaped glass is right for every kind of table wine. As an alternative, you can also use the eight-ounce balloon-shaped glass that's traditionally used for the great Burgundies, and which can also be used as a cocktail glass. The usual serving of wine is five ounces, and it's customary to fill glasses about two-thirds full—so the eight-ounce size works nicely.

Champagne, contrary to what you may have seen in old movies, should not be served in hollow-stemmed glasses—the bubbles escape too quickly. A better choice, according to the wine experts, is a tall, flute-shaped glass or even the all-purpose tulip-shape. This applies as well to other sparkling wines.

# Menus
## and Recipes

# Cocktail Parties

### GARLIC COCKTAIL OLIVES

1 jar (7 oz) pitted green olives,
   drained
1 jar (7 oz) pitted ripe olives,
   drained
1 tablespoon chopped parsley

1 clove garlic, crushed
3 tablespoons olive oil
¼ teaspoon salt
Dash pepper

1. In medium bowl, combine all ingredients; toss until well blended.
2. Refrigerate, covered, several days, to develop flavor.
Makes about 2½ cups.

### PICKLED MUSHROOMS

1 tablespoon salt
1 lb fresh button mushrooms
½ cup chopped onion
1 clove garlic, finely chopped
¼ cup chopped parsley
2 bay leaves

⅛ teaspoon pepper
½ teaspoon dried thyme leaves
2 cups white wine
2 cups white vinegar
½ cup olive or salad oil
2 tablespoons lemon juice

1. Add salt to 6 cups cold water. Wash mushrooms in this; drain.
2. Combine remaining ingredients in large saucepan. Add mushrooms; bring to boiling point.
3. Then reduce heat, and simmer, covered, 8 to 10 minutes, or until mushrooms are tender. Cool.
4. Refrigerate, covered, at least 1 hour, or until ready to use.

## TOASTED ANCHOVY ROLLS

**Anchovy Filling**
2 pkg (3-oz size) cream cheese,
   softened
1 can (2 oz) smoked anchovy
   fillets, drained and chopped
2 tablespoons chopped
   pimiento

2 tablespoons sour cream
⅛ teaspoon pepper

16 slices white sandwich
   bread
½ cup butter or margarine,
   melted

1. Make Anchovy Filling: In small bowl, combine cream cheese, anchovy, pimiento, sour cream, and pepper; beat until well blended. Refrigerate until needed.
2. Trim crusts from bread. Place slices on a moist towel, and flatten each with a rolling pin. Remove from towel.
3. Spread each slice with 1 tablespoon filling, and roll up, jelly-roll fashion. Cut each in half crosswise.
4. To freeze: Place rolls, seam side up, in shallow plastic freezer containers with tight-fitting lids, or in foil pans. Brush with melted butter; turn over; brush other side. Wrap pans with foil or plastic film; seal; label, and place in freezer.
5. To serve: Remove rolls from freezer. Let stand at room temperature 1 hour. Unwrap; broil, 4 inches fom heat, turning often, until hot and golden-brown—3 to 4 minutes.
Makes 32.

## MUSHROOM TURNOVERS

*Rich Pastry, below*

**Mushroom Filling**
2 tablespoons butter or
   margarine
½ cup finely chopped onion
1 cup finely chopped fresh
   mushrooms (¼ lb); or 1 can
   (3 oz) chopped mushrooms,
   drained

1 teaspoon flour
½ teaspoon seasoned salt
¼ teaspoon dried thyme leaves
Dash cayenne

1 egg yolk

1. Make Rich Pastry, and refrigerate as directed.
2. Make Mushroom Filling: In hot butter in skillet, sauté onion

until golden—about 3 minutes. Add mushrooms, and sauté 3 minutes. Remove from heat.

3. Stir in flour, salt, thyme, and cayenne until well blended. Cook, stirring, 1 minute, or just until thickened. Turn into small bowl.

4. Refrigerate, covered, until completely cool—about 1 hour.

5. Divide pastry in half. On lightly floured surface, roll out half of pastry into an 11-inch square. Cut into 16 rounds, using 2½-inch scalloped or plain cookie cutter.

6. Place 1 teaspoon filling on half of each round. Fold other half over filling, and press edge with fork to seal. Repeat with other half of dough.

7. To freeze: Arrange turnovers in shallow plastic freezer containers with tight-fitting lids, or in foil pans. Wrap with foil or plastic film; seal; label, and place in freezer.

8. To serve: Preheat oven to 400F. Beat egg yolk with 1 tablespoon water. Unwrap frozen turnovers, and place on ungreased cookie sheet; brush with egg yolk. Bake 20 minutes, or until golden-brown. Makes 32.

**Rich Pastry**
1 pkg piecrust mix

*¼ cup butter or regular*
*margarine, softened*

1. Make piecrust mix as package label directs. Shape into a ball.

2. On lightly floured surface, roll out pastry into a 12-by-16-inch rectangle. Spread with butter, ½ inch from edges. Fold lengthwise into thirds; press edges together to seal. Then, starting at one end, fold into thirds. Wrap in waxed paper.

3. Refrigerate 1 hour (the butter should be firm), or until ready to use.

## ROQUEFORT-CHEESE SPREAD

*½ lb Roquefort cheese*
*1 pkg (8 oz) cream cheese*
*¼ teaspoon Worcestershire*
*  sauce*

*Dash salt*
*¼ cup brandy*

1. Let cheeses warm to room temperature.

2. Combine with Worcestershire, salt, and brandy in large bowl of electric mixer. Beat at high speed until thoroughly combined and smooth. Store in refrigerator.

Makes 2 cups.

## GUACAMOLE DIP

1 medium tomato, peeled
2 ripe avocados (about 1½ lb)
¼ cup finely chopped onion
2 tablespoons finely chopped
    canned green chile peppers
1½ tablespoons white vinegar
1 teaspoon salt

Chilled cauliflowerets
Crisp celery sticks
Green onions
Radishes
Cherry tomatoes
Cucumber sticks

1. In medium bowl, crush tomato with potato masher.

2. Halve avocados lengthwise; remove pits and peel. Slice avocados into crushed tomato; then mash until well blended.

3. Add onion, chile pepper, vinegar and salt; mix well. Refrigerate, covered.

4. To serve: Place guacamole in bowl. Surround with chilled vegetables.

Makes about 2 cups.

## CHEDDAR-BEER SPREAD

½ lb mild Cheddar cheese,
    grated
½ clove garlic, crushed
Dash cayenne

1 tablespoon Worcestershire
    sauce
½ teaspoon dry mustard
½ cup beer

1. Combine cheese, garlic, cayenne, Worcestershire, mustard, and beer in medium bowl.

2. Mix until very smooth.

3. To store: Fill crock, and seal top with melted paraffin. Keep refrigerated several weeks. Then serve as a cocktail spread, or wrap as a gift. Remove from refrigerator ½ hour before serving.

Makes 1½ cups.

## TRICONAS
### (Hot Cheese Pastries)

**Filling**
2 pkg (8-oz size) cream cheese,
  softened
½ lb Greek cheese (feta),
  crumbled
1 egg
3 tablespoons butter or
  margarine, melted

1 pkg (1 lb) prepared phyllo-
  pastry or strudel-pastry
  leaves
1 cup butter or margarine,
  melted

1. Make filling: In small bowl of electric mixer, combine cream cheese, Greek cheese, egg and 3 tablespoons butter; beat at medium speed until well blended and smooth.

2. Preheat oven to 400F.

3. Place two leaves of phyllo pastry on board; brush with melted butter. Cut lengthwise into strips about 2 inches wide.

4. Place 1 heaping teaspoon filling at end of a strip. Fold over one corner to opposite side, to make a triangle. Continue folding, keeping triangle shape, to other end of strip. Arrange on brown-paper-lined cookie sheets. Repeat with remaining strips.

5. Repeat with other pastry leaves.

6. Bake 20 minutes, or until golden-brown.

7. Cool on wire rack. Arrange in single layer on tray. Freeze. When frozen hard, remove from tray; freezer wrap. Freeze until serving.

8. To serve: Preheat oven to 350F. Arrange frozen pastries on brown-paper-lined cookie sheets. Bake 10 minutes, or until heated through. Serve at once.

Makes about 7 dozen.

## MEXICAN MEATBALLS WITH CHILI SAUCE

**Meatballs**
3 slices fresh white bread
¼ cup milk
1 lb ground chuck
1 lb ground pork
2 teaspoons salt
¼ teaspoon pepper
1 teaspoon chili powder
½ teaspoon dried oregano
   leaves
2 eggs, slightly beaten

**Chili Sauce**
2 tablespoons olive or salad oil
½ cup finely chopped onion
1 clove garlic, crushed
1½ tablespoons chili powder
1 teaspoon salt
¼ teaspoon dried oregano
   leaves
¼ teaspoon ground cumin
1 can (8 oz) tomato sauce

1. Make meatballs: In medium bowl, soak bread in milk.

2. Mash bread with fork. Add remaining meatball ingredients; mix well with hands to combine.

3. With moistened hands, shape mixture into meatballs, 1¼ inches in diameter. Place meatballs in a 13-by-9-by-2-inch baking pan.

4. Make chili sauce: In hot oil in medium saucepan, sauté onion and garlic, stirring, until golden—about 5 minutes.

5. Add rest of sauce ingredients; mix well. Bring mixture to boiling, stirring. Reduce heat; simmer, covered, 15 minutes, or until sauce has thickened. Preheat oven to 350F.

6. Add 1¼ cups water to sauce; return to boiling. Spoon sauce over meatballs in baking pan. Cover pan tightly with foil. Bake 30 minutes.

7. To freeze: Cool meatballs in sauce. Cover tightly with foil, and freeze until ready to use.

8. To serve: Place pan of frozen meatballs in 350F oven 30 minutes, or until heated through. Serve at once.

Makes 50 cocktail-size meatballs.

## RUMAKI

16 chicken livers
½ cup soy sauce
¼ cup cream sherry

16 slices bacon, halved
   crosswise

1. Wash chicken livers; dry well on paper towels.

2. Cut each liver in half, removing any stringy portion. Turn livers into a large bowl.

3. Combine soy sauce and sherry; mix well. Pour over chicken livers; toss lightly to mix well. Let marinate, refrigerated, 1 hour.

4. Wrap each halved chicken liver with half a bacon slice; secure with wooden pick. Arrange on broiler rack in broiler pan. Brush each side with soy mixture.

5. Broil, 3 inches from heat, 2 or 3 minutes on each side, turning once or twice, until bacon is crisp and livers are cooked through.

6. Drain on paper towels. Then arrange in single layer on foil tray. Freezer-wrap. Freeze until ready to serve.

7. To reheat: Preheat oven to 350F. Unwrap; bake (still frozen) on tray 10 minutes, or until heated through. Serve at once.

Makes 32.

### HOT CHEESE PUFFS

*¾ lb sharp natural Cheddar
   cheese, grated
4½ tablespoons unsifted all-
   purpose flour
½ teaspoon salt
¼ teaspoon pepper*

*5 egg whites
½ cup packaged dry bread
   crumbs
Shortening or salad oil for deep-
   frying*

1. Combine cheese, flour, salt, and pepper; mix thoroughly.

2. In large bowl, beat egg whites until stiff peaks form when beater is slowly raised. Gently fold in cheese mixture until well combined.

3. Shape into balls, using level tablespoon of mixture for each. Roll in crumbs on waxed paper.

4. Meanwhile, slowly heat shortening or salad oil (at least 2 inches deep) to 375F on deep-frying thermometer.

5. Deep-fry balls until golden—about ½ minute. Lift out with slotted spoon; drain on paper towels. Serve hot.

Makes about 30.

*To do ahead:* Fry puffs; cool; wrap in foil; freeze or refrigerate. Unwrap; reheat on cookie sheet at 350F for 10 to 15 minutes, or until heated through. Serve at once.

―――――

## STEAK TARTARE

2 lbs ground beef round
½ cup finely chopped onion
½ cup capers, drained
8 anchovy fillets, finely chopped
4 egg yolks
1 teaspoon salt

⅛ teaspoon pepper
¼ cup finely chopped watercress

Unsalted saltine crackers or small
   rounds of rye bread

1. In large bowl and using 2 forks, lightly toss all ingredients, except crackers, until well combined.
2. Shape into a mound on a serving platter.
3. Refrigerate, covered, until ready to serve—2 to 3 hours.
4. Surround with crackers or rye bread.
Makes 20 servings.

―――――

## EGGPLANT APPETIZER

1 large eggplant
½ cup plus 2 tablespoons olive or
   salad oil
2½ cups sliced onion
1 cup diced celery
2 cans (8-oz size) tomato sauce
¼ cup red-wine vinegar

2 tablespoons sugar
2 tablespoons drained capers
½ teaspoon salt
Dash pepper
12 pitted black olives, cut in
   slivers
Toast rounds

1. Wash eggplant; cut into ½-inch cubes.
2. In ½ cup hot oil in large skillet, sauté eggplant until tender and golden-brown. Remove eggplant, and set aside.
3. In 2 tablespoons hot oil in same skillet, sauté onion and celery until tender—about 5 minutes.
4. Return eggplant to skillet. Stir in tomato sauce; bring to boiling. Lower heat, and simmer, covered, 15 minutes.
5. Add vinegar, sugar, capers, salt, pepper, and olives. Simmer, covered and stirring occasionally, 20 minutes longer.
6. Refrigerate, covered, overnight.
7. To serve: Turn into serving bowl. Surround with toast rounds.
Makes 6 to 8 appetizer servings.

## MARINATED ARTICHOKES

2 pkg (9-oz size) frozen artichoke
   hearts
½ cup tarragon vinegar
¼ cup olive oil

4 teaspoons sugar
2 teaspoons finely cut fresh
   tarragon or 1 teaspoon dried
   tarragon leaves

1. Cook artichoke hearts as the label directs. Drain, and turn into medium bowl.

2. In small bowl, combine vinegar, oil, sugar, and tarragon; stir until sugar dissolves. Pour over artichoke hearts.

3. Refrigerate, covered, overnight or several days. Carefully turn artichoke hearts occasionally.

4. To serve: Arrange in shallow serving dish, and garnish with sprigs of fresh tarragon, if desired. Pass hors-d'oeuvre picks.

Makes 12 hors-d'oeuvre servings.

## CAVIAR–CREAM-CHEESE BALL

2 pkg (8-oz size) cream cheese
1 jar (4 oz) red caviar, slightly
   drained

Party pumpernickel slices

1. Let cream cheese stand at room temperature, to soften—about 1 hour. Then, on serving tray, shape into a mound about 5 inches in diameter; flatten top. Refrigerate, covered.

2. To serve: Spoon caviar over top of cream cheese, letting a little drizzle over side. Surround with pumpernickel.

Makes 30 servings.

# Low-Calorie Recipes

## MARINATED SCALLOPS AND SHRIMP

1 lb sea scallops, halved
1 lb fresh shrimp (about 22),
   shelled and deveined
¼ cup finely chopped onion
1 bay leaf, 1 teaspoon salt
¼ teaspoon white pepper
1 lb fresh mushrooms (about 80),
   thickly sliced right through
   stem

Lemon Dressing
½ cup lemon juice
2 tablespoons olive or salad oil
2 teaspoons salt
½ teaspoon white pepper
½ to 1 teaspoon dried tarragon
   leaves
Chopped parsley

1. In medium saucepan, combine scallops, shrimp, onion, bay leaf, 1 teaspoon salt and ¼ teaspoon pepper. Add water to cover.

2. Bring to boiling; remove from heat; cover; let the mixture stand for 5 minutes.

3. With slotted spoon, remove scallops, shrimp and onion to a shallow baking dish. Add sliced mushrooms; toss with shellfish mixture.

4. Make lemon dressing: Combine well all dressing ingredients except parsley. Pour over shellfish; toss to mix well. Refrigerate, covered, overnight.

5. Just before serving, toss well; turn into serving dish; sprinkle with parsley. Serve with picks.

Makes about 36 servings; 12 calories per shrimp, 15 calories per scallop half.

## HERB-MARINATED VEGETABLES

Herb Marinade, below
Fresh green beans, ends trimmed
Green and red peppers, cut into
   strips ½ inch wide
Fresh cauliflower, separated into
   1-inch flowerets
Fresh okra, ends trimmed
Eggplant, cut into 1-inch cubes,
   skin on
Fresh mushrooms, stems on,
   thickly sliced

Fresh broccoli, separated into
   1-inch flowerets with stems
Frozen brussels sprouts, thawed
Carrots, pared and cut into
   5-inch sticks
Frozen artichoke hearts, thawed
Fresh zucchini, diagonally sliced
   ¼-inch thick
Radish roses, stems on
Fresh snow peas
Cherry tomatoes

1. Make Herb Marinade.

2. Wash and prepare an assortment of vegetables from the list above.

3. To blanch vegetables: Pour boiling water to cover over green beans, red- and green-pepper strips and cauliflowerets; let stand 10 minutes; drain. Pour boiling water to cover over okra; let stand 3 minutes; drain. Pour boiling water to cover over eggplant; let stand 7 minutes; drain. The other vegetables need not be blanched.

4. Arrange vegetables in single layer in shallow baking dish or plastic container. Pour marinade over them, tossing gently to coat well. Refrigerate, covered, overnight, spooning marinade over vegetables four or five times.

5. To serve, drain vegetables; arrange on attractive platter.

About 3 calories each, according to vegetable, with marinade: green beans, 3 calories each; peppers, 2 calories; cauliflowerets, 3 calories; okra, 3 calories; eggplant, 2 calories; mushroom slices, 1 calorie or less; broccoli, 3 calories; carrots, 3 calories; artichoke hearts, 2 calories; zucchini, 2 calories; radishes, 2 calories; snow peas, 2 calories; cherry tomatoes, 2 calories.

**Herb Marinade**
*1 bottle (8 oz) low-calorie Italian-style or herb-and-garlic salad dressing*

*2 teaspoons snipped fresh dill*
*¼ cup lemon juice*
*½ teaspoon salt*

Combine dressing, dill, lemon juice and salt; mix well. Refrigerate. Makes 1 cup, enough to marinate 2 pounds assorted vegetables—about 16 calories per tablespoon of marinade.

## SEVICHE

*1 lb red snapper, halibut or sole (see Note), boned and skinned*
*2 medium onions, thinly sliced*
*½ lb cherry tomatoes, halved and seeded*

*½ green pepper thinly sliced*
*1½ teaspoons salt*
*¼ teaspoon coarsely ground black pepper*
*½ cup lime juice*

1. Cut fish fillets crosswise into ½-inch strips. Turn into a large bowl. Add onion, tomatoes, green pepper, salt and pepper; toss lightly to mix well.

2. Turn into a shallow baking dish. Sprinkle with lime juice. Refrigerate, tightly covered, overnight, tossing several times.

3. Drain; serve with wooden picks.

Makes 23 servings (2 pieces of fish); about 40 calories per serving.
*Note:* Number of calories depends on fish; halibut is higher in calories than sole or snapper.

---

## TERIYAKI

2-lb flank steak (see Note)
½ cup chopped onion
2 cloves garlic, crushed
4 tablespoons soy sauce
2 tablespoons salad or peanut oil
2 tablespoons brown sugar

½ tablespoon crushed black
  pepper
2 tablespoons dry sherry
2 cans (8½-oz size) water
  chestnuts, drained
Scallion Flowers, below

1. Wipe steak with damp paper towels. Trim off any excess fat. Cut steak in half lengthwise. Slice across the grain in very thin slices, no more than ¼ inch thick.

2. In small bowl, mix well rest of ingredients, except water chestnuts and Scallion Flowers, for marinade.

3. Wrap each chestnut in a steak slice; fasten with wooden pick. Dip in marinade.

4. Arrange in shallow glass baking dish. Pour rest of marinade over steak, coating well. Let stand, covered, in refrigerator about 2 hours. Turn after 1 hour to marinate other side.

5. Place on ungreased rack in broiler pan. Broil four inches from heat, about 2 to 3 minutes on each side. Do not overcook. Arrange on warm platter; garnish with Scallion Flowers. Sprinkle with salt, if desired.

Makes 50; 43 calories each.

*Note:* If you partially freeze flank steak, it will be easier to slice thinly.

---

## SCALLION FLOWERS

Use the white part, 2 to 3 inches long, of 16 scallions. Make several crosscuts, ½ inch deep, in each end. Place in bowl of ice water; ends will open and curl. It will take about 1½ hours.

## STUFFED MUSHROOMS

16 small mushrooms
(about 1/5 lb)
1 tablespoon butter or margarine
3 tablespoons finely chopped
green pepper

3 tablespoons finely chopped
onion
1 teaspoon salt
⅛ teaspoon pepper

1. Preheat oven to 350F.
2. Wipe mushrooms with damp cloth. Remove stems and chop stems finely; set aside.
3. Heat butter in large skillet. Sauté mushroom caps, on bottom side only, 2 to 3 minutes; remove. Arrange, rounded side down, in shallow baking pan.
4. In same skillet, sauté chopped stems, green pepper and onion until tender—about 5 minutes.
5. Remove from heat. Stir in seasonings. Use to fill mushroom caps, mounding mixture high in center.
6. Bake 15 minutes. Serve warm from tray or chafing dish.
Makes 16 servings; about 2 calories each.

## SHRIMP-STUFFED TOMATOES

1 cup finely chopped, deveined,
cooked shrimp
¼ cup finely chopped onion
½ teaspoon salt
¼ teaspoon pepper

2 tablespoons low-calorie
mayonnaise
1 tablespoon lemon juice
1 box (1 lb) cherry tomatoes
Parsley sprigs

1. In small bowl, combine shrimp, onion, salt, pepper, mayonnaise and lemon juice; mix well. Refrigerate, covered, several hours to chill well.
2. Wash and dry tomatoes; refrigerate to chill well.
3. About 1 hour before serving, slice tomatoes across top to remove stem; scoop out some of seeds. Mound a little shrimp filling on top of each. Decorate each with parsley sprig. Arrange on tray. Refrigerate, covered, until serving time.
Makes 38; 17 calories each.

## CUCUMBER CANAPÉS

2 medium cucumbers                    Parsley sprigs
1 jar (4 oz) red caviar

1. Pare cucumbers, leaving a small amount of green skin on. Slice crosswise into rounds ¼ inch thick, making about 50 rounds.
2. Arrange on tray; spoon ¼ teaspoon red caviar in center of each round; top each with a parsley sprig.
Makes 50; 15 calories each.

## LOW-CALORIE ONION-SOUP DIP

1 cup (8 oz) plain yogurt             ¼ teaspoon chili powder
1 cup skim-milk cottage cheese        Chopped parsley
3 tablespoons dry onion-soup mix

1. In medium bowl, combine yogurt and cottage cheese until well blended. Stir in soup mix and chili powder.
2. Refrigerate dip, covered, 3 hours, to chill well and to let flavor develop.
3. Arrange on tray with an assortment of crisp vegetables. Sprinkle dip with some chopped parsley.
Makes 2 cups dip; 13 calories per tablespoon.

## YOGURT-DILL DIP

1 cup (8 oz) plain yogurt             2 tablespoons snipped fresh dill
½ cup low-calorie mayonnaise          ¼ teaspoon salt
2 tablespoons grated onion

1. In small bowl, combine yogurt with rest of ingredients; mix well. Refrigerate, covered, several hours or overnight, or until the dip is thoroughly chilled.
2. Serve with an assortment of raw vegetables for dipping.
Makes 1½ cups dip; 11 calories per teaspoon.

# Cocktail Buffets

## Menu for 10 to 12

Party Brioche \*
Hot Cheese Puffs \* or
Curried-Crabmeat Balls \*
Pickled Shrimp \*
Steak Tartare \*
Unsalted Saltine Crackers
Bowl of Crisp Assorted Vegetables
on Ice
(Cauliflowerets, cucumber sticks,
radishes, carrot rounds,
ripe olives)

### PARTY BRIOCHE

**Brioche Dough**
½ cup warm water (105 to 115F)
1 pkg active dry yeast
¼ cup sugar
1 teaspoon salt
1 teaspon grated lemon peel
1 cup butter, softened
6 eggs, at room temperature
4½ cups sifted \* all-purpose flour

\* Sift before measuring.

**Filling**
4 cans (4½-oz size) liver pâté
¼ cup packaged dry bread
  crumbs
1 teaspoon instant minced onion
6 pitted ripe olives, drained and
  sliced

1 egg yolk

1. Make Brioche Dough: If possible, check temperature of warm water with thermometer. Sprinkle yeast over water in large bowl of electric mixer; stir until dissolved.

2. Add sugar, salt, lemon peel, butter, 6 eggs, and 3 cups flour. Beat, at medium speed, 4 minutes, occasionally scraping side of bowl with rubber scraper.

3. Add remaining flour. Beat, at low speed, 2 minutes longer, or until smooth.

4. Cover bowl with waxed paper, then with a damp towel. Let rise in warm place (85F), free from drafts, until double in bulk—1 to 1½ hours. Refrigerate, covered, overnight.

5. Next day, butter well a 1½-quart brioche mold (8¾ inches wide, 3 inches deep).

6. Make Filling: In medium bowl, combine ham with bread crumbs, onion, olives; mix well. Set aside.

7. Using a floured knife, cut off about one fourth of dough for the top. On lightly floured pastry cloth, shape this into a ball, rolling over to coat well with flour.

8. Then remove about one eighth of dough to cover filling; set aside.

9. Turn out remaining dough onto lightly floured pastry cloth. With palms of hands, flatten dough into a circle 6 inches in diameter. Gently press into prepared mold so that dough comes up side of mold (should be 1 inch from top), with a depression in center.

10. Fill center with filling. Flatten dough reserved for covering into a 6-inch circle. Place over filling; press edge of covering and bottom together, to seal in filling all around.

11. With finger, make slight indentation in center, 2 inches wide. Fill with large ball of dough.

12. Cover with damp towel; let rise in warm place (85F), free from drafts, until side of dough rises to top of pan—about 1 hour.

13. Meanwhile, preheat oven to 350F. Combine egg yolk with 2 teaspoons water; mix well. Use to brush top of brioche only (do not let mixture run to edge of pan).

14. Bake 20 minutes, or until deep golden-brown. Cover top lightly with foil; bake 60 minutes longer, to cook center.

15. Let stand in pan on wire rack 30 minutes. Carefully loosen side from pan with small spatula. Turn out on serving plate.

16. Serve warm, cut into wedges.

Makes 16 servings.

*To make ahead:* Bake and cool Party Brioche. Foil-wrap; freeze. To serve: Let stand at room temperature until completely thawed—several hours; then reheat, still foil-wrapped, 1 hour at 350F, or until heated through. Serve warm.

## CURRIED-CRABMEAT BALLS

*1 can (7½ oz) king-crab meat*
*¼ cup butter or margarine*
*¼ cup unsifted all-purpose flour*
*1 cup milk*
*1 teaspoon salt*
*¼ teaspoon pepper*
*1 teaspoon Worcestershire sauce*
*1 teaspoon curry powder*

*⅛ teaspoon Tabasco*
*Flour*
*1 egg, beaten*
*¾ cup packaged dry bread*
*  crumbs*

*Salad oil or shortening for*
*  deep-frying*

1. Drain and flake crabmeat, removing any cartilage. Set aside.

2. Melt butter in medium saucepan; remove from heat. Stir in ¼ cup flour; then gradually add milk, stirring until smooth.

3. Bring to boiling, stirring constantly; reduce heat, and simmer 1 minute longer.

4. Remove from heat. Add salt, pepper, Worcestershire, curry powder, and Tabasco; mix well.

5. Stir in crabmeat. Refrigerate until completely cooled.

6. Shape mixture into balls, using 1 tablespoon of mixture for each. Roll in flour to coat lightly.

7. Dip each into beaten egg in shallow dish; then roll in crumbs on waxed paper to coat completely.

8. Slowly heat salad oil (at least 1½ inches) in deep skillet, electric skillet, or deep-fat fryer to 370F on deep-frying thermometer.

9. Deep-fry balls until golden-brown—about 1 minute. Lift out with slotted spoon; drain on paper towels. Serve hot.

Makes about 24.

*To do ahead:* Cook completely; cool. Freezer-wrap; then store in freezer until ready to use. Unwrap; reheat at 350F for 10 to 15 minutes, or until hot. Serve at once.

## PICKLED SHRIMP

3 lbs shrimp, shelled and
   deveined
2 cups cider vinegar
1 cup lemon juice
1 cup salad oil
2 tablespoons sugar
6 bay leaves
1 teaspoon crushed black pepper

1 teaspoon dill seed
½ teaspoon dried tarragon leaves
1 teaspoon celery salt
1 teaspoon dry mustard
1 teaspoon salt
1 cup chopped onion

Chopped parsley

1. Bring 6 cups water to boiling in large saucepan. Add shrimp; bring to boiling. Reduce heat; simmer, uncovered, 3 minutes. Drain; set aside.

2. In same saucepan, combine all ingredients, except onion and parsley; bring to boiling. Reduce heat; simmer, uncovered, 10 minutes.

3. Add shrimp; simmer 3 minutes longer. With slotted spoon, lift out shrimp.

4. In large, shallow dish, place a layer of shrimp; cover with a layer of onion. Repeat with rest of shrimp and onion. Pour on hot marinade; let stand until cool.

5. Refrigerate, covered and stirring occasionally, at least 48 hours before serving.

6. To serve: Drain shrimp, and turn into shallow serving dish. Sprinkle with parsley.

Makes 10 to 12 servings.

# Menu for 20

Marinated Mushrooms *
Chile con Queso with Raw Vegetables *
Stuffed Eggs *
Swedish Meatballs *
Cherry Tomatoes with Garlic Salt
Dry-Roasted Assorted Nuts

## MARINATED MUSHROOMS

*3 lbs small mushroom caps*

**Marinade:**
*2¼ cups salad oil*
*2¼ cups red-wine vinegar*
*¾ cup finely chopped onion*
*¾ cup finely chopped parsley*
*6 cloves garlic, crushed*

*3 teaspoons salt*
*3 teaspoons sugar*

*Boston-lettuce leaves*
*Watercress sprigs*

1. Wash mushroom caps well. Dry on paper towels.
2. Make Marinade: In large bowl, combine all marinade ingredients.
3. Toss mushroom caps with marinade, coating well.
4. Refrigerate, covered, at least 1½ hours.
5. To serve: Arrange lettuce and watercress on large platter or in wooden salad bowl. With slotted spoon, remove mushroom caps from marinade; mound in center of platter. Pour over remaining marinade, if desired.

Makes 18 to 24 servings.

## CHILE CON QUESO WITH RAW VEGETABLES

*½ cup butter or margarine*
*1 cup finely chopped onion*
*2 cans (1 lb size) tomatoes,*
  *undrained*
*3 to 4 cans (4-oz size) green*
  *chiles (see Note), drained and*
  *chopped*

*1 teaspoon salt*
*2 lbs Monterey Jack cheese,*
  *cubed*
*1 cup heavy cream*

1. In hot butter, in medium skillet, sauté onion until tender. Add tomatoes, chiles and salt, mashing tomatoes with fork. Simmer, stirring occasionally, 15 minutes.
2. Add cheese cubes, stirring until cheese is melted. Stir in cream. Cook, stirring constantly, 2 minutes.
3. Remove from heat, and let stand 15 minutes. Serve warm, in a casserole over a candle warmer, as a dip with carrot sticks, celery hearts, cucumber sticks and large corn chips.

Makes 20 to 24 servings.

*Note:* Use larger amount of green chiles, if you like this really hot.

## STUFFED EGGS

12 hard-cooked eggs
8 oz smoked salmon, finely
    chopped (1 cup)
½ cup mayonnaise or cooked
    salad dressing
2 tablespoons chopped parsley

4 teaspoons prepared mustard
½ teaspoon salt
Dash pepper
Black olives, drained
Pimiento, drained

1. Halve eggs lengthwise. Remove yolks to a small bowl. Reserve whites.

2. Mash yolks with fork. Add salmon, mayonnaise, parsley, mustard, salt, and pepper; mix well.

3. Fill each white with yolk mixture, mounding it high. Garnish with crescent-shape pieces of olive and bits of pimiento.

4. Refrigerate, covered, at least 1 hour before serving. Makes 24.

## SWEDISH MEATBALLS

4 eggs, slightly beaten
2 cups milk
1 cup packaged dry bread
    crumbs
4 tablespoons butter or
    margarine
1 cup finely chopped onions
2 lbs ground chuck
½ lb ground pork
Salt

Dill weed
¼ teaspoon allspice
¼ teaspoon nutmeg
¼ teaspoon ground cardamom
⅓ cup flour
¼ teaspoon pepper
2 cans (10½-oz size) condensed
    beef broth, undiluted
1 cup light cream

1. In a large bowl, combine the eggs, milk, and dry bread crumbs.

2. In 2 tablespoons hot butter in large skillet, sauté chopped onion until soft—about 5 minutes. Lift out with slotted spoon. Add to bread-crumb mixture, along with ground meats, 3 teaspoons salt, ½ teaspoon dill weed, the allspice, nutmeg, and cardamom. With a wooden spoon or your hands, mix well to combine.

3. Refrigerate, covered, for 1 hour.

4. Shape meat mixture into 60 meatballs.

5. Preheat the oven to 325F.

6. In remaining hot butter, sauté meatballs, about one-third at a

time, until browned all over. Remove as browned to two 2-quart casseroles.

7. Remove the skillet from heat. Pour off all but ¼ cup drippings; stir in flour, ½ teaspoon salt, and the pepper. Gradually stir in beef broth. Bring to boil, stirring constantly. Add cream and 1 teaspoon dill weed. Pour over meatballs in casseroles.

8. Bake, covered, 30 minutes. Garnish top of meatballs with fresh dill sprigs, if desired.

Makes 20 servings.

# The Buffet Dinner

## Menu I

Senegalese Soup *
Breast of Chicken in Madeira Sauce *
Buttered Rice and Peas
Salad of Fresh Greens and Avocado
Warm French Bread
Assorted Fruit Tarts *
or
Chocolate Mousse *
Chilled White Wine        Coffee

### SENEGALESE SOUP

1 medium onion, chopped
1 medium carrot, pared and
   diced
1 stalk celery, sliced
3 tablespoons butter or
   margarine
2 tablespoons curry powder
1½ tablespoons flour
1 tablespoon tomato paste

2 cans (10½-oz size) condensed
   chicken broth
1 tablespoon almond paste
1 tablespoon red-currant jelly
10 whole cloves
1 cinnamon stick
1½ cups heavy cream
2 tablespoons shredded coconut

1. In large saucepan, sauté onion, carrot, and celery in hot butter until golden—about 5 minutes. Remove from heat.

2. Stir in curry powder and flour until well blended. Add tomato paste; cook, stirring, 1 minute.

3. Gradually stir in undiluted chicken broth and 2 cups water; bring to boiling, stirring constantly. Stir in almond paste and jelly; add cloves and cinnamon stick; simmer, uncovered and stirring occasionally, ½ hour.

4. Strain; cool. Then refrigerate until very well chilled—several hours or overnight.

5. When ready to serve, skim off any fat from surface. Blend in cream. Serve in bouillon cups. Top each serving with coconut.

Makes 8 to 10 servings.

——————

## BREAST OF CHICKEN IN MADEIRA SAUCE

*1½ cups raw long-grain white rice*
*Salt*
*4 whole chicken breasts*
  *(about 3 lbs)*
*¼ cup butter or margarine*
*2 shallots, sliced*
*½ lb fresh mushrooms, washed*
  *and cut in half lengthwise*
*1 teaspoon dried thyme leaves*

*Dash pepper*
*1½ cups dry Madeira wine*
*1 teaspoon cornstarch*
*1 cup light cream*
*½ cup heavy cream*
*1 cup grated natural Swiss*
  *cheese*
*2 tablespoons chopped parsley*

1. Cook rice with ½ teaspoon salt and 3½ cups water as package label directs.

2. Wipe chicken breasts with damp paper towels. Cut breasts in half; with sharp knife, carefully remove skin and bone, keeping chicken breast intact.

3. In hot butter, in large skillet, cook shallots several minutes. Add chicken breasts; brown well over medium heat, about 10 minutes on each side.

4. Add mushrooms, thyme, 1½ teaspoons salt and pepper; cook about 3 minutes.

5. Preheat oven to 375F.

6. Turn rice into a lightly buttered, 2-quart shallow casserole. Arrange chicken breasts, overlapping slightly, down center of casserole. Arrange mushrooms around chicken.

7. In same skillet, pour wine into drippings; stir to dissolve browned bits in pan.

8. Meanwhile, dissolve cornstarch in 2 tablespoons light cream.

9. Add heavy cream, rest of light cream and cornstarch to wine mixture; bring just to boiling, stirring. Remove from heat; add cheese.

10. Spoon half of sauce over chicken; bake in oven 10 to 12 minutes; then run under broiler several minutes to brown slightly. Sprin-

kle with parsley. Reheat rest of sauce; serve along with casserole.
Makes 8 servings.

## FRUIT TARTS

**Tart Shells:**
*½ cup butter or regular*
  *margarine, softened*
*¼ cup sugar*
*¼ teaspoon salt*
*1 egg white*
*1½ cups sifted * all-purpose flour*

*\* Sift before measuring.*

*Rum Cream, below*
*Fruits: whole strawberries,*
  *blueberries, red raspberries,*
  *sliced bananas, seedless green*
  *grapes, apricot halves, black*
  *cherries (fresh, frozen, or*
  *canned), canned small*
  *pineapple rings or tidbits*
*Apricot Glaze or Currant-Jelly*
  *Glaze, below*

1. Make Tart Shells: In medium bowl, with fork, blend butter, sugar, salt, and egg white until smooth and well combined.
2. Gradually stir in flour, mixing until smooth.
3. For each tart, use 2 teaspoons dough. Press evenly into 2½- to 3-inch tart pans of assorted shapes and sizes. Set pans on cookie sheet.
4. Refrigerate 30 minutes.
5. Preheat oven to 375F. Bake tart shells 12 to 15 minutes, or until light golden. Cool in pans on wire rack a few minutes; then turn out, and cool completely before filling.
6. To fill tarts: Spoon several teaspoons of Rum Cream into each shell. Refrigerate.
7. Top with fruit. (Drain fruit very well before using.) Brush yellow or light fruit with warm Apricot Glaze and red or dark fruit with Currant-Jelly Glaze.
8. Refrigerate until ready to serve.
Makes 1½ dozen.
*Note:* If desired, make Tart Shells and Rum Cream day before. Then assemble tarts several hours before serving.

**Rum Cream**
*1 teaspoon unflavored gelatine*
*2 tablespoons granulated sugar*
*2 tablespoons flour*
*Salt*
*1 egg yolk*
*½ cup milk*

*2 tablespoons rum*
*1 egg white, stiffly beaten*
*½ cup heavy cream*
*1 tablespoon confectioners' sugar*
*1 inch vanilla bean, scraped, or*
  *½ teaspoon vanilla extract*

1. In small saucepan, mix gelatine, granulated sugar, flour, and dash salt; mix well.

2. Beat egg yolk with milk and rum. Add to gelatine mixture; cook over medium heat, stirring constantly with wire whisk, until mixture is thickened and comes to boiling.

3. Pour into medium bowl; set bowl in pan of ice and water; let stand, stirring occasionally, until mixture begins to set—about 8 to 10 minutes. Fold in beaten egg white.

4. Beat cream with confectioners' sugar; fold into gelatine mixture. Stir in vanilla. Refrigerate until ready to use—at least 30 minutes.

Makes about 1½ cups.

**Apricot Glaze**
*½ cup apricot preserves*

1. In small saucepan, over medium heat, stir apricot preserves until melted. (If preserves seem too thick, thin with ½ to 1 tablespoon hot water.)

2. Strain. Use warm, on tarts.

**Currant-Jelly Glaze**              *1 tablespoon kirsch*
*½ cup red-currant jelly*

1. In small saucepan, over moderate heat, stir currant jelly until melted. Remove from heat.

2. Stir in kirsch. Use warm, on tarts. (If glaze becomes too thick, reheat gently, and add a little hot water.)

## CHOCOLATE MOUSSE

*8 eggs*                                    *¼ cup cognac or brandy*
*2 cups semisweet chocolate*                *Whipped cream*
   *pieces*                  *Candied violets*
*10 tablespoons sweet butter*

1. One or two hours before serving, separate eggs, turning whites into a large bowl. Let whites warm to room temperature.

2. In top of double boiler, over hot, not boiling, water, melt chocolate and butter; stir to blend. Remove from hot water.

3. Using wooden spoon, beat in egg yolks, one at a time, beating well after each addition. Set aside to cool. Stir in cognac.

4. When the chocolate mixture has cooled, beat egg whites with

rotary beater just until stiff peaks form when beater is slowly raised.

5. With rubber scraper or wire whisk, gently fold chocolate mixture into egg whites, using an under-and-over motion. Fold only enough to combine—there should be no white streaks.

6. Turn into an attractive, 6-cup serving dish. Refrigerate overnight.

7. To serve, decorate with whipped cream and candied violets.

Makes 12 servings.

*Note:* For 6 servings, use 4 eggs, 1 pkg (6 oz) semisweet chocolate pieces, 5 tablespoons sweet butter and 2 tablespoons cognac or brandy. Make as directed above, using a 3-cup serving dish. Decorate as above.

# Menu II

A Celebration Buffet Menu
(Planned for 24)
Crabmeat Bisque *
Beef Bourguignon * With New Potatoes
or Beef Stroganoff* With
Wild and White Rice
or Coq au Vin With Mushrooms *
and Fluffy White Rice
Vegetable-Salad Platter *
Green Mayonnaise *
Crisp French Bread        Butter
Royal Meringue Dessert *
Chablis        Burgundy Wine
Coffee

## CRABMEAT BISQUE

| | |
|---|---|
| 5 cans (11-oz size) tomato bisque | Nutmeg |
| 4 cups light cream | 1 cup very dry sherry |
| ½ cup milk | 1 can (5 oz) crabmeat, drained |

1. In large saucepan or kettle, combine soup, cream, milk, ½ teaspoon nutmeg. Stir to combine. Heat slowly just to boiling—about 10 minutes.

2. Add sherry and crabmeat, stirring; heat until thoroughly hot; do not boil.

3. Serve in individual soup cups. Sprinkle top of each with a little nutmeg.

Makes 24 (½-cup) servings.

## BEEF BOURGUIGNON

*Butter or margarine*
*5 lb boneless beef chuck, cut into*
   *1½-inch cubes*
*6 tablespoons brandy*
*1 lb small white onions,*
   *peeled (24)*
*1 lb small fresh mushrooms*
*½ cup potato starch*
*5 teaspoons meat-extract paste*
*¼ cup tomato paste*

*3 cups Burgundy*
*1½ cups dry sherry*
*1½ cups ruby port*
*1 can (10½ oz) condensed beef*
   *broth, undiluted*
*¼ teaspoon pepper*
*2 bay leaves*
*24 small new potatoes*
*Chopped parsley*

1. Day before: Slowly heat an 8-quart Dutch oven with tight-fitting lid. Add 4 tablespoons butter; heat—do not burn.

2. In hot butter, over high heat, brown beef cubes well all over (about a fourth at a time—just enough to cover bottom of Dutch oven).

3. Lift out beef as it browns. Continue until all beef is browned, adding more butter as needed. Then return beef to Dutch oven.

4. In small saucepan, heat 4 tablespoons brandy just until vapor rises. Ignite and pour over beef. As flame dies, remove beef cubes; set aside.

5. Add 2 tablespoons butter to Dutch oven; heat slightly. Add onions; cook over low heat, covered, until onions brown slightly. Then add mushrooms; cook, stirring, 3 minutes. Remove from heat.

6. Stir in flour, meat-extract paste and tomato paste until well blended. Stir in Burgundy, sherry, port and beef broth.

7. Preheat oven to 350F.

8. Bring wine mixture just to boiling, stirring; remove from heat. Add beef, pepper and bay leaves; mix well.

9. Bake, covered and stirring occasionally, 45 minutes, adding remaining brandy little by little. Bake with sheet of waxed paper placed over Dutch oven and lid placed on top. Discard any liquid collecting on top of paper.

10. Meanwhile, scrub potatoes, leaving skins on. Cook, covered, in small amount of lightly salted, boiling water 10 minutes. Drain. Add potatoes to beef mixture, spooning liquid over potatoes.

11. Let cool; refrigerate, covered, overnight.

12. To serve: Heat gently, covered, about 1 hour, stirring in a little

more wine, if necessary, to thin sauce. Sprinkle with parsley.

Makes 12 servings.

*Note:* For 24 servings, you will need to make this recipe twice. This is easier than doubling the recipe and making it all at once.

## BEEF STROGANOFF

2 (2-lb size) flank steaks or 4 lb
   boneless beef sirloin, ½ inch
   thick
Instant unseasoned meat
   tenderizer
¼ to ⅓ cup butter or margarine
2 cups chopped onion
2 cloves garlic, finely chopped
1 lb fresh mushrooms, sliced
   ¼ inch thick
¼ cup flour

2 tablespoons tomato paste
4 teaspoons meat-extract paste
1 teaspoon salt
⅛ teaspoon pepper
1 can (10½ oz) condensed beef
   broth, undiluted
⅓ cup dry white wine
1½ tablespoons snipped fresh dill
3 cups dairy sour cream
¼ cup snipped fresh dill or
   parsley (optional)

1. Day before: Wipe beef with damp paper towels. Place in freezer 15 minutes; it will be easier to slice. With sharp knife, slice steak ¼ inch thick, across the grain. Sprinkle cut surface lightly with meat tenderizer.

2. Slowly heat a large heavy skillet. Melt 2 tablespoons butter. Add just enough beef strips to cover skillet bottoms. Over high heat, sear quickly on all sides. With tongs, remove beef as it browns. Brown rest of beef, adding more butter as needed.

3. Pour drippings from skillet into 5-quart Dutch oven. Add onion, garlic and mushrooms; sauté until onion is golden—about 5 minutes. Remove from heat.

4. Stir in flour, tomato paste, meat-extract paste, salt and pepper until well blended. Gradually stir in broth; bring to boiling, stirring constantly. Reduce heat and simmer 5 minutes.

5. Stir in wine and 1½ tablespoons dill until well combined. Remove from heat; stir in meat. Refrigerate, covered, overnight.

6. About 1 hour before serving, bring beef mixture to boiling over medium heat. Remove from heat. Gradually stir in sour cream; cook over low heat until hot but not boiling.

7. Keep warm in chafing dish. Garnish with snipped fresh dill. Serve with wild and white rice, cooked according to package directions.

Makes 12 servings.

*Note:* For 24 servings, make recipe twice.

## COQ AU VIN WITH MUSHROOMS

10 whole chicken breasts
  (12-oz size)
¾ lb bacon, chopped coarsely, or
  ¾ lb salt pork, cut up
  (see Notes)
20 small onions
6 tablespoons Cognac
6 shallots
Bouquet garni (see Notes)
1 glove garlic, pressed

¾ lb fresh mushrooms, sliced
1 bottle dry red wine
  (about 3½ cups)
2 teaspoons salt
¼ teaspoon pepper
2 teaspoons sugar
½ teaspoon nutmeg
6 tablespoons flour
¼ cup dry sherry
3 tablespoons chopped parsley

1. Day before: Cut chicken breasts in half; wipe well with damp paper towels.

2. In large skillet, heat bacon. Add onions; sauté over medium heat until golden. Lift out onions and bacon with slotted spoon.

3. Add chicken breasts, skin side down; sauté, turning, until golden-brown on each side—about 5 minutes.

4. Heat Cognac slightly; pour over chicken; ignite. Remove chicken with liquid to 6-quart Dutch oven.

5. Add shallots, bouquet garni, garlic and mushrooms to skillet. Simmer, covered, over low heat 20 minutes.

6. Meanwhile, in large saucepan, reheat bacon; add ¾ of the red wine; bring to boiling; pour over chicken. Add salt, pepper, sugar, and nutmeg; and stir to mix well. Bring to boiling; reduce heat and simmer, covered, 30 minutes. Add onions during last 20 to 25 minutes of cooking.

7. Combine rest of wine with flour, to make a smooth mixture; stir into liquid in Dutch oven; bring to boiling; sauce will be slightly thickened. Remove; discard bouquet garni. Refrigerate, covered, overnight.

8. To serve: Add sherry and reheat gently, covered, 30 minutes; if sauce seems too thick, add a little more wine. Arrange the coq au vin on a serving platter, and sprinkle with chopped parsley. Serve with fluffy white rice.

Makes 12 servings.

Notes: For 24 servings, make recipe twice.

If you are using bacon, you may want to use half the amount of salt called for in recipe.

To make a bouquet garni, tie a large sprig of fresh parsley, ½ teaspoon dried thyme leaves and a bay leaf in a square of cheesecloth to make a small bag.

## VEGETABLE-SALAD PLATTER

**Marinade**
3 cups salad oil
1 cup white-wine vinegar
1 tablespoon salt
1 tablespoon sugar
1 teaspoon cracked black pepper

1 lb fresh young green beans
Salt
Boiling water
1 head cauliflower (2½ to 3 lbs)

1½ lb zucchini
2 lbs small, thin carrots
3 pkg (10-oz size) frozen broccoli
    spears
2 cans (15-oz size) white
    asparagus, drained
6 medium-size ripe tomatoes,
    cut in half with scallop cutter
3 heads Boston lettuce, washed
    and crisped
Green Mayonnaise, below

1. Day before, marinate vegetables: For marinade, combine oil, vinegar, 1 tablespoon salt, the sugar and black pepper in large jar with a tight-fitting cover. Shake to mix well. Refrigerate until ready to use.

2. Prepare vegetables: Wash beans under cold, running water; drain. Trim ends of beans. Place in a 2½-quart saucepan. Add 1 teaspoon salt and boiling water to measure 1 inch. Bring to boiling; boil green beans gently, covered, 12 minutes, or just until tender-crisp; drain. Arrange in shallow baking dish or roasting pan. Pour some of marinade over hot beans, to coat well.

3. Wash cauliflower thoroughly; cut into flowerets. Cook, covered, in 1 inch lightly salted boiling water just until tender—about 10 minutes; drain well. Arrange in baking dish with beans; pour some of marinade over hot cauliflower.

4. Wash zucchini; cut into 3-inch fingers. In medium skillet with tight-fitting cover, bring ⅛ cup water with ½ teaspoon salt to boiling. Add zucchini; cook, covered, over medium heat 6 to 8 minutes, or just until tender, not mushy. Drain well. Arrange in baking dish with other vegetables. Pour some of marinade over hot zucchini.

5. Wash carrots; pare. Cut in half lengthwise; pare each half to look like a small whole carrot. Place in large saucepan; add 1 teaspoon salt and enough boiling water to cover. Bring to boiling; simmer gently, covered, 15 minutes, or until tender. Drain. Arrange in baking dish with other vegetables; pour some of marinade over hot carrots.

6. Cook broccoli as package label directs; drain; cool. Remove stems, leaving flowerets. Add to baking dish. Pour some of marinade over broccoli flowerets.

7. Arrange drained asparagus and tomato halves, cut again into quarters, in baking dish. Pour marinade over them.

8. Turn vegetables to coat well with marinade. Refrigerate, covered, overnight.

9. Several hours before serving, arrange drained vegetables, in rows, on two large platters, lined with crisp lettuce leaves. Refrigerate until serving time. Serve very well chilled, with Green Mayonnaise.

Makes 24 servings.

**Green Mayonnaise**
3 cups mayonnaise
6 tablespoons lemon juice
6 tablespoons chopped parsley

3 tablespoons chopped chives
3 tablespoons chopped
    watercress

1. Day before: In a large bowl, combine mayonnaise, lemon juice, parsley, chives and watercress; mix well.

2. Refrigerate, covered, overnight. Mix well before serving.

Makes 3¾ cups; 24 servings.

## ROYAL MERINGUE DESSERT

6 egg whites (1 cup)
½ teaspoon cream of tartar
½ teaspoon salt
1½ cups granulated sugar
¼ cup chopped pecans

Assorted fruits: 2 large navel

oranges, sectioned; ¾ cup
drained canned pineapple
chunks; ¾ cup seedless green
grapes; 1 banana, sliced and
dipped in orange juice
2 cups heavy cream
½ cup confectioners' sugar

1. In a large bowl, let the egg whites warm to room temperature—about 1 hour.

2. With electric mixer at high speed, beat egg whites with cream of tartar and salt until soft peaks form when beater is slowly raised. Gradually beat in granulated sugar, 2 tablespoons at a time, until very stiff peaks form. Mixture should be moist and shiny.

3. Preheat oven to 275F. Lightly butter and flour two large cookie sheets. Drop meringue by tablespoonfuls, using rubber scraper to push meringue from spoon, to form mounds, 1 inch apart. There should be 40 to 50. Sprinkle each with a little of the chopped pecans. Bake about 1 hour, or until crisp and very light golden color. Cool on wire rack.

4. Drain fruit; save juice for another time.

5. Beat cream with confectioners' sugar until stiff. Fold in three fourths of drained fruit.

6. Arrange some of meringues on round serving platter to form a

9-inch round layer. Spoon some of whipped-cream mixture on center of meringues, mounding. Arrange more meringues around and on top of whipped-cream mixture.

7. Continue to make a pyramid with meringues and whipped-cream mixture (you will need about 40 meringues in all). Fill in spaces between meringues with more fruit. Decorate side with rest of fruit.

8. Place one meringue on top. Sprinkle with chocolate curls or shaved chocolate, if desired.

9. Refrigerate to chill well—4 hours or overnight.

Makes 10 to 12 servings. Make two separate meringue desserts to serve 24.

*Note:* Meringues may be baked several days ahead, if desired, and stored in a cool, dry place until ready to assemble dessert.

# Menu III

═══

Eggplant Appetizer *
or Melon with Prosciutto *
Lasagna *
or Manicotti *
Italian-Style Salad Bowl
Whole Wheat and White Italian Bread
Cassata *
or Peaches in Marsala *
with Amaretti Cookies *
Valpolicella or Chianti Red Wine
Café Expresso

═══

## EGGPLANT APPETIZER

| | |
|---|---|
| 1 large eggplant | 2 tablespoons sugar |
| ½ cup plus 2 tablespoons olive or salad oil | 2 tablespoons drained capers |
| 2½ cups sliced onion | ½ teaspoon salt |
| 1 cup diced celery | Dash pepper |
| 2 cans (8-oz size) tomato sauce | 12 pitted black olives, cut in slivers |
| ¼ cup red-wine vinegar | Toast rounds |

1. Wash eggplant; cut into ½-inch cubes.

2. In ¼ cup hot oil in large skillet, sauté eggplant until tender and golden-brown. Remove eggplant, and set aside.

3. In 2 tablespoons hot oil in same skillet, sauté onion and celery until tender—about 5 minutes.

4. Return eggplant to skillet. Stir in tomato sauce; bring to boiling. Lower heat, and simmer, covered, 15 minutes.

5. Add vinegar, sugar, capers, salt, pepper, and olives. Simmer, covered and stirring occasionally, 20 minutes longer.

6. Refrigerate, covered, overnight.

7. To serve: Turn into serving bowl. Surround with toast rounds.

Makes 6 to 8 appetizer servings.

---

## MELON WITH PROSCIUTTO

¼ lb sliced prosciutto (Italian
   ham) or baked Virginia ham
1 (2½ lb) honeydew melon,
   well-chilled

1 lemon
1 lime

1. Cut prosciutto into 1-inch strips.

2. Cut melon in half; scoop out seeds and fibers. Cut half into six wedges; remove rind.

3. Roll each melon wedge in strip of ham. Serve garnished with lemon and lime wedges.

Makes 6 servings (2 wedges per person).

---

## LASAGNA

1 lb sweet or hot Italian sausage
   (5 links)
½ lb ground beef
½ cup finely chopped onion
2 cloves garlic, crushed
2 tablespoons sugar
1 tablespoon salt
1½ teaspoons dried basil leaves
½ teaspoon fennel seed
¼ teaspoon pepper
¼ cup chopped parsley
4 cups canned tomatoes,
   undrained; or 1 can (2 lb, 3 oz)

Italian-style tomatoes
2 cans (6-oz size) tomato paste
1 tablespoon salt
12 curly lasagna noodles
   (¾ of 1-lb pkg)
1 container (15 oz) ricotta or
   cottage cheese, drained
1 egg
½ teaspoon salt
¾ lb mozzarella cheese,
   thinly sliced
1 jar (3 oz) grated Parmesan
   cheese (¾ cup)

1. Remove sausage meat from outer casings; chop the meat. In 5-quart Dutch oven, over medium heat, sauté sausage, beef (break up beef with wooden spoon), onion and garlic, stirring frequently, until well browned—20 minutes.

2. Add sugar, 1 tablespoon salt, the basil, fennel, pepper and half of parsley; mix well.

3. Add tomatoes, tomato paste and ½ cup water, mashing tomatoes with wooden spoon. Bring to boiling; reduce heat; simmer, covered and stirring occasionally, until thick—1½ hours.

4. In 8-quart kettle, bring 3 quarts water and 1 tablespoon salt to boiling. Add lasagna, 2 or 3 at a time. Return to boiling; boil, uncovered and stirring occasionally, 10 minutes, or just until tender. Drain in colander; rinse under cold water. Dry lasagna on paper towels. Preheat oven to 375F.

5. In medium bowl, mix well ricotta, egg, remaining parsley and salt.

6. In bottom of 13-by-9-by-2-inch baking dish, spoon 1½ cups sauce. Layer with 6 lasagna, lengthwise and overlapping, to cover. Spread with half of ricotta mixture; top with third of mozzarella. Spoon 1½ cups sauce over cheese; sprinkle with ¼ cup Parmesan.

7. Repeat layering, starting with 6 lasagna and ending with 1½ cups sauce sprinkled with Parmesan. Spread with remaining sauce; top with rest of mozzarella and Parmesan.

8. Cover with foil, tucking around edge. Bake 25 minutes; remove foil; bake, uncovered, 25 minutes longer, or until bubbly. Cool 15 minutes.

9. To serve: With sharp knife, cut in squares. Use wide spatula to serve.

Makes 8 servings.

## BAKED MANICOTTI WITH CHEESE FILLING

**Sauce**
⅓ cup olive or salad oil
1½ cups finely chopped onion
1 glove garlic, crushed
1 can (2 lb, 3 oz) Italian
    tomatoes, undrained
1 can (6 oz) tomato paste
2 tablespoons chopped parsley
1 tablespoon salt
1 tablespoon sugar
1 teaspoon dried oregano leaves
1 teaspoon dried basil leaves
¼ teaspoon pepper

**Filling**
2 lb ricotta cheese
1 pkg (8 oz) mozzarella cheese,
    diced
⅓ cup grated Parmesan cheese
2 eggs
1 teaspoon salt
¼ teaspoon pepper
1 tablespoon chopped parsley

¼ cup grated Parmesan cheese

**Manicotti**
6 eggs, at room temperature
1½ cups unsifted all-purpose flour
¼ teaspoon salt

1. Make sauce: In hot oil in 5-quart Dutch oven, sauté onion and garlic 5 minutes. Mix in rest of sauce ingredients and 1½ cups water, mashing tomatoes with fork. Bring to boiling, and reduce heat. Simmer mixture, covered and stirring occasionally, 1 hour.

2. Make manicotti: In medium bowl, combine 6 eggs, the flour, ¼ teaspoon salt and 1½ cups water. With electric mixer, beat just until smooth. Let stand ½ hour or longer.

3. Slowly heat an 8-inch skillet. Pour in 3 tablespoons batter, rotating the skillet quickly to spread batter evenly over bottom. Cook over medium heat until top is dry but bottom is not brown.

4. Turn out on a wire rack to cool. Continue cooking until all of batter is used. As manicotti cools, stack with waxed paper between them. Preheat oven to 350F.

5. Make filling: In large bowl, combine ricotta, mozzarella, ⅓ cup Parmesan, the eggs, salt, pepper and parsley; beat with wooden spoon to blend well.

6. Spread about ¼ cup filling down the center of each manicotti, and roll up.

7. Spoon 1½ cups sauce into each of two 12-by-8-by-2-inch baking dishes. Place eight rolled manicotti, seam side down, in single layer; top with five more. Cover with 1 cup sauce; sprinkle with Parmesan. Bake, uncovered, ½ hour, or until bubbly.

8. To freeze: Line baking dish with large piece of foil; assemble as directed. Fold foil over to seal, and freeze in dish. When frozen, remove dish.

9. To serve: Unwrap; place in baking dish, and let stand 1 hour to thaw. Bake, covered, 1 hour in 350F oven.

Each dish makes 6 generous servings.

## PEACHES IN MARSALA

2 cans (1-lb, 14-oz size) peach       1 cup cream Marsala
  halves                              2-inch cinnamon stick

1. Drain the peach halves, reserving 2 tablespoons of the peach syrup.

2. In medium bowl, combine peaches, Marsala, cinnamon stick, and reserved syrup.

3. Refrigerate, covered, until the peaches are very well chilled—at least 2 hours.

4. To serve: Turn peaches and liquid into individual dessert dishes. Makes 8 servings.

## AMARETTI

**Cookie Dough**                      2 egg whites
½ cup granulated sugar
½ cup confectioners' sugar            ⅓ cup finely chopped blanched
¼ cup unsifted all-purpose flour        almonds
⅛ teaspoon salt                       Candied red or green cherries,
1 can (8 oz) almond paste               halved

1. Preheat oven to 300F. Lightly grease two large cookie sheets.

2. Make cookie dough: Sift granulated and confectioners' sugars with flour and salt; set aside.

3. Using a fork, break almond paste into small pieces in medium bowl. Add egg whites; beat with electric mixer at medium speed until well blended and smooth. With wooden spoon, stir in flour mixture until well blended.

4. Using slightly rounded teaspoonfuls, roll dough between hands into balls about 1 inch in diameter; then roll in almonds.

5. Place 2 inches apart on prepared cookie sheets. Lightly press into rounds 1½ inches in diameter. Press a candied-cherry half into top of each.

6. Bake 20 to 25 minutes, or until golden. Remove to wire rack; cool. Store several days in tightly covered container, to mellow.

Makes about 2½ dozen.

―――

## CASSATA ALLA SICILIANA

Spongecake, below

**Rum Syrup**
1¼ cups granulated sugar
4 orange slices
2 lemon slices
⅔ cup golden rum

**Cheese Filling**
1 lb ricotta cheese
½ cup confectioners' sugar

½ cup semisweet-chocolate
pieces, chopped
1 jar (4 oz) mixed candied fruit,
finely chopped
1 tablespoon golden rum
2 tablespoons semisweet-
chocolate pieces, melted
⅓ cup seedless raspberry jam
1½ cups heavy cream
2 tablespoons confectioners'
sugar
Candied cherries

1. Make Spongecake.

2. Make rum syrup: In small saucepan, combine granulated sugar, 1 cup water and the orange and lemon slices. Bring to boiling, stirring until sugar is dissolved. Boil gently, uncovered, 20 minutes. Discard fruit slices. Stir in ⅔ cup rum; set aside.

3. Make cheese filling: In medium bowl, combine ricotta and ½ cup confectioners' sugar; beat with electric mixer until well combined —about 3 minutes. Stir in ½ cup chopped chocolate pieces, the candied fruit and rum.

4. For chocolate-cheese filling: Remove 1 cup cheese filling to small bowl, and stir in melted chocolate until well blended. Refrigerate both fillings until ready to assemble cake.

5. To assemble cake: Split each spongecake layer in half, to make four layers in all. Place a layer, cut side up, on serving plate. Drizzle with ½ cup of the rum syrup. Then spread with half of the plain cheese filling.

6. Spread cut side of second layer with half of the raspberry jam. Place, jam side down, over cheese layer. Drizzle with ½ cup syrup. Spread with all the chocolate-cheese filling.

7. Add third layer, cut side up. Drizzle with ½ cup syrup. Spread with remaining plain cheese filling. Spread remaining jam over cut side of fourth layer. Place, jam side down, over cheese layer. Drizzle on remaining syrup.

8. Beat cream with confectioners' sugar until stiff. Use to frost side

and top of cake. If desired, place some of cream in pastry bag with rosette tip, and use to decorate cake. Garnish with candied cherries.

9. Refrigerate at least 4 hours, or until serving time.

Makes 10 servings.

**Spongecake**
4 eggs
1 cup sifted * cake flour
¾ teaspoon baking powder

¼ teaspoon salt
¼ teaspoon cream of tartar
1 cup sugar
1 teaspoon vanilla extract
1 teaspoon lemon juice

* Sift before measuring.

1. Separate eggs, whites in large bowl, yolks in small bowl. Let whites warm to room temperature—1 hour.

2. Preheat oven to 350F.

3. Sift flour, baking powder and salt.

4. Add cream of tartar to egg whites. With electric mixer at medium speed, beat whites until foamy. Gradually beat in ½ cup sugar, a tablespoonful at a time. Continue beating until stiff, glossy peaks form when beater is raised.

5. With same beater, beat egg yolks until thick and lemon-colored. Gradually beat in remaining sugar, a tablespoonful at a time. Beat until thick and light—2 minutes.

6. In measuring cup, combine ¼ cup water, the vanilla and lemon juice.

7. At low speed, blend flour mixture, one third at a time, into egg-yolk mixture, alternately with water mixture. Beat 1 minute.

8. With wire whisk or rubber scraper, fold into egg-white mixture.

9. Pour batter into two ungreased 8-inch layer-cake pans.

10. Bake 25 to 30 minutes, or just until surface springs back when lightly pressed with fingertip.

11. Invert pans, setting rims on two other pans. Cool 1½ hours.

12. Loosen around edge. Tap inverted pan on counter top, to loosen.

Makes two (8-inch) layers.

# Menu IV

Stuffed Grape Leaves *
Moussaka *
Fresh Spinach Salad Bowl *
Basket of Assorted Breads
Oranges Orientale *
Chocolate-Dipped Butter Cookies *
or Almond Crescents *
Carafes of Red and White Wine
Coffee

## STUFFED GRAPE LEAVES

**Filling**
2 tablespoons butter or
   margarine
2 tablespoons chopped onion
2 cups fluffy cooked rice
2 tablespoons olive or salad oil
1 teaspoon salt

⅛ teaspoon pepper
2 tablespoons chopped parsley
1 jar (16 oz) vine leaves, drained
   and separated
2 tablespoons lemon juice
1 cup tomato juice

1. Make Filling: In hot butter in small skillet, sauté onion until golden. Add remaining filling ingredients; mix well.

2. Lay vine leaves, shiny side down, on flat surface. Place 1 teaspoon rice mixture on each.

3. Fold sides of each leaf over filling, then roll up, starting from narrow end. Place stuffed leaves, seam side down, close together, in bottom of medium skillet.

4. Pour lemon and tomato juices over them. Set a heavy plate or pie plate on top, to keep rolls in place during cooking.

5. Bring to boiling: reduce heat, and simmer, covered, 20 minutes. Remove from heat. Cool to room temperature. Refrigerate rolls until they are cold.

6. To serve: Lift out of liquid with slotted utensil. If desired, brush with olive oil, to make leaves shiny.

Makes 48.

## MOUSSAKA

**Meat Sauce**
2 tablespoons butter or
  margarine
1 cup finely chopped onion
1½ lb ground chuck or lamb
1 clove garlic, crushed
½ teaspoon dried oregano leaves
1 teaspoon dried basil leaves
½ teaspoon cinnamon
1 teaspoon salt
Dash pepper
2 cans (8-oz size) tomato sauce

2 eggplants (1-lb, 4-oz size),
  washed and dried
Salt

½ cup butter or margarine,
  melted

**Cream Sauce**
2 tablespoons butter or
  margarine
2 tablespoons flour
½ teaspoon salt
Dash pepper
2 cups milk
2 eggs

½ cup grated Parmesan cheese
½ cup grated Cheddar cheese
2 tablespoons packaged dry
  bread crumbs

1. Make meat sauce: In 2 tablespoons hot butter in 3½-quart Dutch oven, sauté onion, chuck and garlic, stirring, until brown—10 minutes. Add oregano, basil, cinnamon, 1 teaspoon salt, dash pepper and the tomato sauce; bring to boiling, stirring. Reduce heat; simmer, uncovered, ½ hour.

2. Halve unpared eggplant lengthwise, then slice crosswise, ½ inch thick. Place in bottom of broiler pan; sprinkle lightly with salt; brush lightly with ½ cup melted butter. Broil, 4 inches from heat, 4 minutes on each side, or until golden.

3. Make cream sauce: In medium saucepan, melt butter. Remove from heat; stir in flour, salt and pepper. Add milk gradually. Bring to boiling, stirring until mixture is thickened. Remove from heat.

4. In small bowl, beat eggs with wire whisk. Beat in some hot cream-sauce mixture; return mixture to saucepan; mix well. Preheat oven to 350F.

5. To assemble casserole: In bottom of a shallow, 2-quart baking dish (12 by 7½ by 2 inches), layer half of eggplant, overlapping slightly; sprinkle with 2 tablespoons each grated Parmesan and Cheddar cheeses.

6. Stir bread crumbs into meat sauce; spoon evenly over eggplant in casserole; then sprinkle with 2 tablespoons each Parmesan and Cheddar cheeses.

7. Layer rest of eggplant slices, overlapping. Pour cream sauce over

all. Sprinkle top with remaining cheese.

8. Bake 5 to 40 minutes, or until golden-brown and top is set. If desired, brown top a little more under broiler—1 minute. Cool slightly to serve. Cut in squares.

Makes 12 servings.

## FRESH SPINACH SALAD

**White-Wine French Dressing**
¼ cup white-wine vinegar
¼ cup lemon juice
1 cup salad oil
2 teaspoons salt
¼ teaspoon pepper
1 teaspoon sugar
1 teaspoon dry mustard
1 clove garlic (optional)

**Salad**
1½ lbs tender young spinach
6 green onions, thinly sliced
   (¾ cup)
1 cup sliced radishes
1 medium cucumber, pared and
   thinly sliced

1. Make White-Wine French Dressing: Combine all dressing ingredients in jar with tight-fitting lid; shake vigorously. Refrigerate until ready to use.

2. Make Salad: Wash spinach, and remove stems. Tear leaves in bite-size pieces into salad bowl.

3. Arrange the other vegetables in groups on spinach. Refrigerate, covered, about 2 hours.

4. To serve: Remove garlic from dressing, and shake vigorously. Pour dressing over salad; toss until spinach is well coated. Serve at once.

Makes 12 servings.

## ORANGES ORIENTALE

12 large navel or Temple oranges
2¼ cups sugar
2¼ cups light corn syrup

Red food color (optional)
½ cup lemon juice
½ cup Cointreau

1. With sharp paring knife, remove peel from 6 oranges in 1½-inch-long strips. Remove any white membrane from strips; cut each into ⅛-inch-wide pieces. (Or, if desired, remove peel with a coarse grater.)

2. Peel remaining oranges; remove any white membrane from all

oranges. Place oranges, whole or cut in half, in large bowl; set aside.

3. In small saucepan, combine prepared peel with 3 cups cold water. Bring to boiling, covered. Remove from heat; drain. Reserve peel.

4. In large saucepan, combine sugar and corn syrup with a few drops red food color and 2¼ cups water; bring to boiling, over high heat, stirring until sugar is dissolved. Cook, uncovered and over medium heat, 15 minutes. Add reserved peel.

5. Continue cooking 30 minutes longer, or until syrup is slightly thickened. Remove from heat; stir in lemon juice and Cointreau.

6. Pour hot syrup over oranges in bowl. Refrigerate, covered, at least 8 hours; turn oranges occasionally.

7. Serve chilled oranges topped with some of the syrup and candied peel. Decorate, if desired, with candied violets. Serve with dessert forks and fruit knives.

Makes 12 servings.

---

## CHOCOLATE-DIPPED BUTTER COOKIES

2⅓ cups sifted (see Note)
  all-purpose flour
¼ teaspoon salt
1 cup butter or regular
  margarine, softened
⅔ cup sugar
1 egg yolk
1 teaspoon vanilla extract
1 cup finely chopped unblanched
  almonds

**Chocolate Dip**
1 pkg (6 oz) semisweet chocolate
  pieces
3 tablespoons butter or
  regular margarine
1 tablespoon hot water
Chopped almonds, chocolate
  shot or multicolor nonpareils

1. Sift flour with salt; set aside.

2. In large bowl, with wooden spoon or electric mixer at medium speed, beat butter, sugar, egg yolk and vanilla until light and fluffy.

3. Gradually stir in flour mixture and 1 cup almonds, mixing until well blended.

4. With hands, shape dough into two rolls 1½ inches in diameter. Wrap in foil or plastic wrap. Refrigerate until firm—about 2 hours.

5. Preheat oven to 350F. Lightly grease cookie sheets. With sharp knife, cut into slices ¼ inch thick. Place cookies, 1 inch apart, on prepared cookie sheets.

6. Bake 8 to 10 minutes, or until lightly browned. Remove to rack; cool.

7. Make chocolate dip: In small saucepan, over low heat, melt chocolate and butter; add hot water.

8. Dip half of each cooled cookie in chocolate mixture. Sprinkle with chopped almonds, chocolate shot or multicolor nonpareils.

Makes 6 dozen.

*Note:* Sift flour before measuring.

## ALMOND CRESCENTS

1. Follow recipe for Butter Cookies, above. Using rolling pin, crush ¾ cup sliced unblanched almonds. Using palms of hands, roll dough into four rolls ½ inch thick. Cut off 2-inch pieces; roll in crushed almonds.

2. Place, 2 inches apart, on lightly greased cookie sheet; curve each to make a crescent. Bake as directed for Butter Cookies. Remove to wire rack; cool completely.

Makes 4½ dozen.

# The Seated Dinner

## Menu I

Royal Consommé Madrilène *
Rack of Lamb, Provençale *
New Potatoes with Lemon Butter *
Buttered Peas and Mushrooms
Salad of Bibb Lettuce and Watercress
French Bread
Apricot Soufflé *
Coffee     Cabernet Sauvignon

### ROYAL CONSOMMÉ MADRILÈNE

**Royal Custard:**
1 egg
⅓ cup light cream
¼ teaspoon salt
Dash white pepper

2 cans (13-oz size) consommé
    madrilène
½ cup dry sherry or Madeira
1 tablespoon lemon juice

1. Preheat oven to 300F. In small bowl, with rotary beater, beat egg, cream, salt, and pepper until well blended but not foamy.

2. Strain into a buttered 2-cup custard cup. Set custard cup in shallow pan on oven rack. Pour hot water into pan to ½-inch level. Cover custard cup with piece of waxed paper.

3. Bake 25 to 30 minutes, or until knife inserted in center comes out clean. Remove custard cup from water. Cool; then refrigerate until well chilled.

4. Just before serving: In medium saucepan, heat madrilène just to boiling.

5. Cut chilled custard into ⅓-inch cubes. Place cubes in 6 consommé cups, dividing evenly.

6. Stir sherry and lemon juice into madrilène. Ladle over custard cubes in consommé cups.

Makes 6 servings.

## RACK OF LAMB, PROVENÇALE

4- to 5-lb rack of lamb (12 chops)
1 cup fresh bread crumbs
¼ cup chopped parsley
1 clove garlic, crushed
1 teaspoon salt

¼ teaspoon pepper
2 tablespoons Dijon mustard
¼ cup butter or margarine,
  melted

1. Preheat oven to 375F. Wipe lamb with damp paper towels; trim off all fat. Place lamb, using ribs as rack, in shallow, open roasting pan.

2. Roast, uncovered, 15 minutes for each pound.

3. Remove roast from oven; let cool about 15 minutes.

4. Combine bread crumbs, parsley, garlic, salt, and pepper.

5. Spread mustard over top of lamb. Pat crumb mixture into mustard, pressing firmly. Drizzle with butter. Insert meat thermometer into center of middle chop.

6. Roast 20 minutes, or until thermometer registers 175F. Garnish with parsley, if desired.

Makes 6 servings.

## NEW POTATOES WITH LEMON BUTTER

3 lbs small new potatoes
Boiling water
Salt
½ cup butter or margarine

3 tablespoons lemon juice
2 tablespoons finely snipped
  chives, parsley or mint

1. Scrub potatoes. Pare a strip of skin, about ½ inch wide, around center of each potato. Place in medium saucepan; add boiling water to measure 2 inches and ½ teaspoon salt.

2. Bring to boiling; boil gently, covered, 20 minutes, or until potatoes are tender. Drain. Return to heat several minutes, to dry out.

3. Melt butter in small saucepan. Stir in lemon juice, chives, and ½ teaspoon salt. Pour over potatoes, turning to coat well.

4. Turn into serving dish.

Makes 6 to 8 servings.

## APRICOT SOUFFLÉ

8 egg whites, unbeaten
2½ cups dried apricots
¼ teaspoon almond extract
Butter
Granulated sugar
¼ teaspoon cream of tartar

⅛ teaspoon salt
1 cup cold heavy cream
2 tablespoons confectioners'
    sugar
⅛ teaspoon almond extract

1. In large bowl of electric mixer, let egg whites warm to room temperature—about 1 hour.

2. Meanwhile, in 3½ cups water, simmer apricots, covered, about ½ hour, or until very tender. Then press apricots, with cooking liquid, through sieve or food mill, or mix in electric blender, to make purée.

3. To 2 cups of apricot purée add ¼ teaspoon almond extract; then refrigerate.

4. About 1 hour before dessert time, preheat oven to 325F.

5. Lightly butter 2-quart casserole; then sprinkle with a little granulated sugar.

6. Beat egg whites until foamy throughout; add cream of tartar and salt; continue beating to form soft peaks. Gradually add ½ cup granulated sugar, 2 tablespoons at a time, beating after each addition until whites form stiff peaks.

7. Gently fold apricot purée into whites until thoroughly combined; turn into prepared casserole; set in pan of hot water. Bake 45 minutes.

8. At dessert time, whip the heavy cream until stiff; add confectioners' sugar and almond extract.

9. Serve soufflé at once with the whipped cream.

Makes 6 to 8 servings.

# Menu II

Homemade Noodles with Pesto Sauce *
Roman Veal Scallopini *
Buttered Green Beans
Tossed Green Salad
Crusty Whole-Wheat Italian Bread
Coffee Tortoni *
Café Espresso    Chilled White Wine

### HOMEMADE NOODLES WITH PESTO SAUCE

*3 cups unsifted all-purpose flour*          *2 tablespoons lukewarm water*
*Salt*                                       *Pesto Sauce, below*
*4 eggs*

1. Sift flour with ½ teaspoon salt into medium bowl.

2. Make a well in center. Add eggs and water; beat with fork until well combined. Dough will be stiff.

3. On wooden board, knead dough until smooth and elastic—about 15 minutes. Cover with bowl; let rise at least 30 minutes.

4. Divide dough into four parts. Keep covered with bowl until ready to roll out.

5. On lightly floured pastry cloth or board, roll each part into a 16-by-14-inch rectangle. Dough should be about $\frac{1}{16}$ inch thick. Rectangle need not be perfect in shape. Work quickly, as dough will dry out.

6. Starting with long side, roll loosely as for jelly roll. With thin sharp knife, cut roll into ⅛-inch-wide strips for fine noodles, ⅓-inch-wide strips for broad noodles. Unwind noodles, and stretch a little bit; then wind loosely around fingers. Arrange on ungreased cookie sheets. Let dry overnight before cooking. Makes about 1 pound noodles.

7. Next day, make Pesto Sauce.

8. To cook noodles: Cook half the noodles (8 ounces) for 6 servings. In large kettle, bring 3 quarts water and 1 tablespoon salt to rapid boil. Add noodles. Bring back to boiling; cook, uncovered, stirring occasionally with long fork to prevent sticking, just until tender— 7 to 10 minutes. Do not overcook. Drain well in colander. Do not rinse. Serve with Pesto Sauce.

*Note:* Store dried noodles in a covered glass jar in cool place.

**Pesto Sauce**
¼ cup butter or margarine,
  softened
¼ cup grated Parmesan cheese
½ cup finely chopped parsley
1 clove garlic, crushed

1 teaspoon dried basil leaves
½ teaspoon dried marjoram
  leaves
¼ cup olive or salad oil
¼ cup chopped pine nuts or
  walnuts

1. Cream ingredients in bowl with spoon or with mortar and pestle. Blend butter with Parmesan, parsley, garlic, basil and marjoram. Gradually add oil, beating constantly. Add nuts; mix well.

2. Add to noodles in heated dish; toss until well coated.

Makes enough Pesto Sauce for 8 ounces cooked noodles, 6 servings.

## ROMAN VEAL SCALLOPINI

8 tablespoons butter or
  margarine
¾ lb mushrooms, sliced
1 small onion, finely chopped
1 clove garlic, peeled
3 cups coarsely chopped, peeled
  fresh tomatoes (about 2 lbs)

⅔ cup dry white wine
Salt
¼ teaspoon dried tarragon leaves,
  crushed
12 thin veal scallops (1½ lb)
⅛ teaspoon pepper
Grated Parmesan cheese

1. In 5 tablespoons hot butter in skillet, sauté mushrooms until golden-brown—about 5 minutes. Add onion and garlic; cook until onion is golden.

2. Add tomatoes, wine, ¾ teaspoon salt and tarragon; stir until well blended. Reduce heat; simmer, covered and stirring occasionally, 30 minutes.

3. Meanwhile, wipe veal with damp paper towels. Sprinkle with ½ teaspoon salt and the pepper.

4. Heat 3 tablespoons butter in another skillet. Add veal, a few pieces at a time, and cook until lightly browned on both sides— about 5 minutes. Remove and keep warm.

5. Return veal to skillet. Remove garlic from sauce. Pour sauce over veal; simmer, covered, 5 minutes. Sprinkle with Parmesan cheese.

Makes 6 servings.

## COFFEE TORTONI

*2 egg whites, at room*
  *temperature*
*2 tablespoons instant coffee*
*¼ teaspoon salt*
*¼ cup granulated sugar*
*2 cups heavy cream*

*½ cup confectioners' sugar*
*2 teaspoons vanilla extract*
*2 teaspoons almond extract*
*½ cup coarsely chopped toasted*
  *almonds*

1. In medium bowl, with portable electric mixer, beat egg whites until foamy. Beat in coffee and salt; beat in granulated sugar, a little at a time. Beat until stiff peaks form when beater is slowly raised.

2. Also, beat cream in medium bowl (use clean beaters) with confectioners' sugar just until stiff.

3. With wire whisk or rubber scraper, gently fold whipped cream into egg whites, along with vanilla and almond extracts.

4. Use to fill ten paper tortoni cups; sprinkle top of each with chopped toasted almonds. Freeze until firm—overnight. Let stand 5 minutes at room temperature before serving. (If storing in freezer longer, freezer-wrap.)

Makes 10 servings.

# Menu III

Shrimp Bisque
Roast Cornish Hens *
with Turkish Pilaf *
Green Salad Bowl
Hot Rolls
Fresh Pears in Port *
Chilled White Wine    Coffee

## ROAST CORNISH HENS

6 Cornish hens (see Note),
  about 1¼ lb each
¾ cup butter or margarine
¾ cup dry white wine
7 tablespoons dried tarragon
  leaves

Salt, pepper
6 cloves garlic, peeled
Garlic salt
2 tablespoons flour
Turkish Pilaf, below

1. Wash hens under cold running water; drain.

2. Make basting sauce: Melt butter in saucepan; stir in wine and 1 tablespoon tarragon.

3. Sprinkle inside of each hen with ¼ teaspoon salt, ⅛ teaspoon pepper and 1 tablespoon tarragon. Place one clove of garlic inside each. Sprinkle outside of each liberally with garlic salt. Refrigerate.

4. About 1 hour before serving, preheat oven to 450F. Place hens in a shallow roasting pan without a rack. Roast, basting often with sauce, 1 hour, or until hens are browned and tender.

5. Place hens on platter; keep warm.

6. Gravy: Dissolve flour in 1 cup water; stir into drippings in pan. Bring to boiling, stirring until thickened.

7. To serve: Turn Turkish Pilaf into center of platter; arrange hens on top.

Makes 6 servings.

Note: If frozen, let thaw overnight in refrigerator.

**Turkish Pilaf**
2 cups cracked wheat
2 cans (13¾-oz size) chicken
  broth

¼ teaspoon pepper
¼ cup butter or margarine
1 can (3 oz) chow-mein noodles,
  crumbled

1. In medium saucepan, combine cracked wheat and chicken broth. Cover; bring to boiling; reduce heat and simmer 20 minutes. Remove from heat; let stand 10 minutes longer, or until all liquid is absorbed.

2. Add pepper, butter and chowmein noodles; toss gently to combine.

Makes 6 to 8 servings.

## FRESH PEARS IN PORT

*6 fresh pears,\* peeled and cored*    *1 cup sugar*
*(about 3 lbs)*    *1 cup port wine*
   *\* Or substitute 6 drained*    *½ cup orange juice*
*canned pear halves; omit water*    *Grated peel of 1 orange*
*and sugar; add pear halves in*
*step 2*

1. In large saucepan, drop pears into ½ cup water and sugar; simmer, covered, until soft, about 30 minutes.

2. Remove from heat and add wine, orange juice, and grated orange peel. Mix gently. Chill, if desired.

Makes 6 servings.

# Menu IV

Cream-of-Butternut-Squash Soup *
Steak with Marrow Sauce *
Salsify Provençal *
Stuffed Mushrooms *
Tossed Green Salad Bowl
French Bread     Water Biscuits
Platter of Assorted Cheeses
Fresh Fruit Bowl
(Ripe Pears, Grapes, Apples)
Burgundy or Bordeaux     Coffee

## CREAM-OF-BUTTERNUT-SQUASH SOUP

*1 butternut squash (about 3 lbs)*    *Dash white pepper*
*2 cans (10½-oz size) condensed*    *1 cup heavy cream*
   *chicken broth, undiluted*    *¼ teaspoon nutmeg*
*¼ teaspoon salt*

1. Preheat oven to 400F. Bake whole squash about 1 hour, or until tender when pierced with a fork.

2. Let squash cool slightly. Cut in half lengthwise; discard seeds.

With a spoon, scoop squash pulp from the skin.

3. In electric blender, combine half of squash pulp and 1 can broth; blend at low speed until well combined, then at high speed until smooth. Turn into bowl. Repeat with remaining squash and broth. Stir in salt and pepper.

4. Refrigerate soup, covered, overnight.

5. At serving time, heat squash mixture just to boiling. Gradually stir in ½ cup cream; cook slowly until heated through. Taste for seasoning, adding more salt and pepper if necessary.

6. Meanwhile, beat remaining cream just until stiff.

7. Serve soup very hot. Garnish each serving with a spoonful of whipped cream; sprinkle with nutmeg.

Makes 6 servings.

———

## STEAK WITH MARROW SAUCE

2½ lb round steak, 1½ inches
  thick * or 3 lb boneless sirloin
  steak
Freshly ground pepper

Marrow Sauce:
2 large marrowbones
  (about 1½ lb)
3 tablespoons butter or
  margarine
  * Use Prime or Choice quality
meat. If desired, you may use unseasoned meat tenderizer as
package label directs on round
steak.

6 shallots, chopped
1½ tablespoons flour
1½ cups red wine
1 tablespoon chopped parsley
½ teaspoon dried thyme leaves
½ teaspoon salt

2 tablespoons butter or
  margarine
1 shallot, chopped
1 teaspoon chopped parsley
½ teaspoon salt
Watercress

1. Wipe steak with damp paper towels. Sprinkle both sides with pepper, pressing in well. Let stand 30 minutes.

2. Make Marrow Sauce: In large saucepan, bring 1 quart water to boiling. Add marrowbones; bring back to boiling; reduce heat; simmer, uncovered, 10 minutes. Remove bones; cool. Scoop out marrow; chop finely.

3. In 3 tablespoons hot butter in small saucepan, sauté 6 chopped shallots, stirring, until transparent—about 5 minutes. Remove from heat; stir in flour. Cook over low heat, stirring 1 minute. Slowly add wine, stirring constantly. Add 1 tablespoon parsley, the thyme, and ½ teaspoon salt. Simmer gently 10 minutes. Stir in marrow. Keep

warm over very low heat while cooking steak.

4. In 2 tablespoons hot butter in heavy skillet, sauté 1 shallot and the parsley about 1 minute. Add steak; cook over medium heat 10 minutes, turning once. Steak will be quite rare. Cook 5 minutes longer for medium rare. Place on hot serving platter; sprinkle with salt.

5. Pour about ¼ cup marrow sauce into skillet; bring to boiling, stirring to loosen brown particles. Add to rest of sauce. Spoon a little of hot marrow sauce over steak. Garnish platter with watercress. Pass rest of sauce. To serve, slice steak very thinly, on the diagonal.

Makes 8 servings.

## SALSIFY PROVENÇAL

*2 jars (14-oz size) salsify strips*     *⅓ cup finely chopped parsley*
*¼ cup butter or margarine*     *1 teaspoon salt*
*1 clove garlic, finely chopped*     *⅛ teaspoon white pepper*

1. Drain salsify. Melt butter in skillet.

2. Add drained salsify, garlic, parsley, salt, and pepper; toss lightly.

3. Cook, covered, over medium heat until heated through—8 to 10 minutes.

Makes 6 servings.

## STUFFED MUSHROOMS

*12 to 16 fresh medium*     *1½ cups fresh-bread cubes*
  *mushrooms*     *(¼ inch)*
*½ cup butter or margarine*     *½ teaspoon salt*
*3 tablespoons finely chopped*     *⅛ teaspoon pepper*
  *green pepper*     *Dash cayenne*
*3 tablespoons finely chopped*
  *onion*

1. Preheat oven to 350F.

2. Wipe mushrooms with damp cloth. Remove stems, and chop stems fine; set aside.

3. Heat 3 tablespoons butter in large skillet. Sauté mushroom caps only on bottom side 2 to 3 minutes; remove. Arrange, rounded side down, in shallow baking pan.

4. Heat rest of butter in same skillet. Sauté chopped stems, green pepper, and onion until tender—about 5 minutes.

5. Remove from heat. Stir in bread cubes and seasoning. Use to fill mushroom caps, mounding mixture high in center.

6. Bake 15 minutes.

Makes 6 to 8 servings.

=====

### FRUIT AND CHEESE FOR DESSERT

The fruit must be nicely chilled, at its peak of ripeness, served with fruit knives. A fruit bowl arrangement might be: crisp, chilled apples, ripe pears, strawberries, peaches or nectarines, and grapes.

The cheese should be at room temperature, unless it is a fresh soft cheese, which should be slightly chilled. The soft, ripened type should be very "ripe," almost running.

On your cheese board, serve a selection of cheeses to give variety in flavor and texture. A combination might be: a creamy Gervais, Brie (everyone's favorite), a mild Bonbel, and the stronger Stilton, all served with plain crackers, French bread and sweet butter.

Wines might be a continuation of the white or red wine served at dinner or a port wine. Nuts in the shell are a nice addition.

# Menu V

=====

Asparagus Vinaigrette *
Fillets of Sole Bonne Femme *
Baked Tomato Casserole
Assorted Hot Rolls
Strawberries with Raspberry Sauce *
Chilled White Wine     Coffee

=====

### ASPARAGUS VINAIGRETTE

| | |
|---|---|
| 2 to 2½ lb fresh asparagus | 2 tablespoons olive oil |
| Boiling water | ½ teaspoon sugar |
| Salt | Dash pepper |
| 3 tablespoons cider vinegar | 1 hard-cooked egg, chopped |
| ¼ cup salad oil | 2 sweet gherkins, chopped |

1. Break or cut off tough ends of asparagus stalks. Wash asparagus well with cold water; if necessary, use a soft brush to remove grit. With vegetable parer or paring knife, remove scales and skin from lower part of stalks.

2. Tie stalks into a bunch with string. Stand upright in deep saucepan. Add boiling water, to depth of 2 inches, and 1½ teaspoons salt.

3. Bring to boiling; cook, covered, 15 to 20 minutes, or just until tender. Drain well. Lay stalks in shallow baking dish.

4. In jar with tight-fitting lid, combine vinegar, oils, 2 tablespoons salt, the sugar, and pepper; shake well.

5. Pour dressing over asparagus. Refrigerate 1 hour, turning stalks several times.

6. Arrange asparagus on platter. Sprinkle with egg and pickle.
Makes 6 servings.

## FILLETS OF SOLE FEMME

*4 tablespoons butter or*
   *margarine*
*2 shallots, chopped*
*6 sole,, haddock, or flounder*
   *fillets (about 2½ lb)*
*½ lb fresh mushrooms, sliced*

*1 teaspoon salt*
*⅛ teaspoon pepper*
*1 cup white wine*
*1 tablespoon chopped parsley*
*1½ tablespoons flour*

1. Melt 2 tablespoons butter in large skillet. Add shallots, and sauté 2 minutes.

2. Wash fillets; dry on paper towels. Arrange fish over shallots, and top with mushrooms. Sprinkle salt and pepper over all. Add wine.

3. Bring to boiling; reduce heat, and simmer, covered, 10 minutes. Add parsley; cook 5 minutes longer, or until fish flakes easily with fork.

4. Drain fish well, reserving 1 cup liquid. Arrange fish and mushrooms in 12-by-8-by-2-inch baking dish.

5. Melt remaining butter in same skillet; remove from heat. Stir in flour until smooth. Gradually stir in reserved fish liquid.

6. Cook over medium heat, stirring, until thickened. Pour over fish. Run under broiler 3 to 5 minutes, or until top is golden-brown.
Makes 6 servings.

## STRAWBERRIES WITH RASPBERRY SAUCE

*2 pint boxes fresh strawberries*          *1 pkg (10 oz) frozen raspberries, partially thawed*

1. Gently wash strawberries in cold water; drain; hull.
2. Mound in shallow serving dish. Refrigerate.
3. Make Raspberry Sauce: Press raspberries through sieve, or blend in electric blender, covered, about 1 minute.
4. To serve, spoon sauce over strawberries.
Makes 6 servings.

# Quick Dinners

## Menu I

Sirloin Steak with Red Wine *
Pâté-Stuffed Mushrooms *
Baked Tomato Halves *
Chilled Asparagus
with Mustard Dressing *
Poppy-Seed Rolls
Jewel Fruit Torte *
Red Wine      Coffee

### SIRLOIN STEAK WITH RED WINE

4½- to 5-lb sirloin steak
  (see Note) about 1½ inches
  thick
1 clove garlic, split
⅓ cup olive or salad oil
1½ teaspoons salt

½ teaspoon coarsely cracked
  pepper
1¼ teaspoons dried rosemary
  leaves
½ cup dry red wine
1 tablespoon butter or margarine

1. Preheat oven to 350F.

2. Wipe steak with damp paper towels. Rub each side with garlic; reserve garlic.

3. Heat oil in a large, heavy skillet until very hot.

4. Over high heat, brown steak very well on both sides—3 to 5 minutes per side.

5. Place steak on rack in shallow roasting pan. Sprinkle with salt, pepper, and rosemary; add garlic. Insert meat thermometer in side of

steak, making sure point is as close to center of meat as possible.

6. Bake in top part of oven 25 to 30 minutes, or until meat thermometer registers 130 degrees, for medium rare. Remove thermometer; place steak on hot platter.

7. Pour fat from roasting pan; discard garlic. Add wine to pan, and bring to boiling, stirring to loosen brown particles. Stir in butter. Pour 2 tablespoons sauce over steak; pass the rest.

8. To serve, slice thinly on the diagonal.

Makes 6 to 8 servings.

*Note:* Have steak at room temperature.

———

## PÂTÉ-STUFFED MUSHROOMS

*½ lb large fresh mushrooms*
*4 tablespoons butter or*
    *margarine*
*2 tablespoons dry sherry*

*2 cans (4¾-oz size) liver pâté*
*Dash pepper*
*1 tablespoon chopped parsley*

1. Wipe mushrooms with damp paper towels. Remove stems; refrigerate to use another time.

2. In hot butter in skillet, over medium heat, sauté mushroom caps just until tender—2 or 3 minutes. Sprinkle with 1 tablespoon sherry; set skillet aside.

3. In small bowl, combine pâté, 1 tablespoon sherry, the pepper, and half of parsley; mix well.

4. Spoon pâté mixture, or press through pastry bag with a number-5 star tip into mushroom caps, mounding high.

5. Reheat slightly in skillet just before serving. Arrange around steak; pour drippings from skillet over mushrooms. Sprinkle with remaining parsley.

Makes six servings.

———

## BAKED TOMATO HALVES

*6 medium tomatoes*
*6 teaspoons prepared brown*
    *mustard*
*3 cups small, fresh bread cubes*
*4 tablespoons butter or*
    *margarine, melted*

*¼ teaspoon salt*
*⅛ teaspoon pepper*
*1½ teaspoons Worcestershire*
    *sauce*
*2 dashes Tabasco*

1. Preheat oven to 375F.

2. Wash tomatoes; halve crosswise. Place in shallow baking dish. Spread each half with ½ teaspoon mustard.

3. In small bowl, toss bread cubes with butter, salt, pepper, Worcestershire, and Tabasco. Spoon about 2 tablespoons evenly over each tomato half.

4. Bake 20 to 25 minutes, or until just tender and crumbs are golden.

Makes 6 servings.

## CHILLED ASPARAGUS WITH MUSTARD DRESSING

1 can (15 oz) green asparagus
   spears, drained
1 can (15 oz) white asparagus
   spears, drained

½ cup bottled herb-garlic
   dressing
2 tablespoons prepared brown
   mustard

1. Place asparagus in freezer, to chill quickly.

2. Combine dressing and mustard; mix well. Refrigerate.

3. To serve: Arrange asparagus on small platter. Spoon dressing over it.

Makes 6 servings.

## JEWEL FRUIT TORTE

8-inch packaged spongecake
   layer
Light rum
¾ cup whipped cream cheese
1 tablespoon confectioners' sugar
1 can (1 lb, 14 oz) cling-peach
   halves, drained
1 can (1 lb, 1 oz) pear halves,
   drained

1 can (3¼ oz) mandarin-orange
   sections, drained
1 tablespoon preserves
¼ cup frozen berries
2 fresh strawberries
¾ cup apple jelly
¼ cup chopped toasted almonds

1. Place cake layer on strips of waxed paper (to keep plate clean) on serving plate. Sprinkle cake with 2 or 3 tablespoons rum, to moisten.

2. In small bowl, beat cream cheese with confectioners' sugar until smooth. Spread on cake.

3. Dry all fruit well on paper towels. Place a peach half, rounded side up, in center of cake. Arrange other peach halves, rounded sides

up, around it. Place a pear half between each two peach halves. Arrange mandarin-orange sections between peaches and pears.

4. Top center peach with preserves. Mound slightly thawed berries on preserves. Top with a strawberry. If desired, decorate with pieces of strawberry.

5. Melt jelly over low heat. Brush over fruit and around side of cake. Press chopped nuts around side of cake.

6. Carefully remove waxed-paper strips. Refrigerate cake (or place in freezer 10 minutes) until serving.

Makes 8 servings.

# Menu II

Pineapple-Glazed Baked Ham *
Scalloped-Potato Casserole *
Asparagus with Browned Butter
Onion-Twist Rolls *
Chilled Melon with Port
Thin Chocolate Cookies
White Wine or Rosé      Coffee

## PINEAPPLE-GLAZED BAKED HAM

1 can (2 lb) boneless ham
¼ cup dry white wine

Pineapple Glaze
½ cup pineapple preserves
½ teaspoon dry mustard
Dash ground cloves

1. Preheat your oven to 350F.

2. Place ham in small, shallow baking pan. Bake 10 minutes. Pour wine over ham; bake 20 minutes longer. Remove from oven.

3. Increase oven temperature to 450F.

4. Meanwhile, make Pineapple Glaze: In small bowl, combine preserves, mustard, and cloves; mix well. Spread on top and sides of ham.

5. Bake ham 15 to 20 minutes, or until glaze is slightly browned. Remove to serving platter.

Makes 6 servings.

## SCALLOPED-POTATO CASSEROLE

*1 pkg (5⅝ oz) scalloped potatoes*　　　*¼ cup chopped green onion*
*¼ cup ready-to-use crumbled*
　*bacon*

1. Preheat your oven to 350F.
2. Prepare potatoes as package label directs, adding bacon and onion; mix.
3. Bake, uncovered, 50 minutes.
Makes 6 servings.

## ONION-TWIST ROLLS

*½ cup dairy sour cream*　　　*1 pkg (8 oz) refrigerator crescent*
*½ env (1⅜-oz size) dry onion-soup*　*rolls*
　*mix*

1. Preheat oven to 375F.
2. In small bowl, combine sour cream and onion-soup mix.
3. Spread out one rectangular section of roll dough. Cut in half crosswise. Cut each half lengthwise into four strips. Repeat with other section of dough.
4. Spread each strip evenly with 1 teaspoon sour-cream mixture. Twist each strip loosely 5 times. Place on ungreased cookie sheet.
5. Bake 10 to 12 minutes, or until golden-brown. Serve hot.
Makes 16.

# Menu III

Hot Consommé Madrilène
Chicken Livers
en Brochette *
Mushroom Rice Pilaf *
Buttered Whole Green
Beans
Maple-Walnut Sundaes
(Vanilla Ice Cream,
Maple Syrup, Walnuts)
Chilled White Wine
Coffee

## CHICKEN LIVERS EN BROCHETTE

1½ lb chicken livers (about 18)
¾ teaspoon dried marjoram
  leaves
¾ teaspoon dried thyme leaves
¾ teaspoon salt
⅛ teaspoon pepper

12 large fresh mushrooms
9 slices bacon, halved crosswise
6 tablespoons butter or
  margarine, melted
¼ cup dry white wine

1. Rinse chicken livers; pat dry with paper towels.

2. In medium bowl, combine the marjoram, thyme, salt, and pepper. Add livers; toss to combine.

3. Remove stems from mushrooms; reserve for rice pilaf. Wipe mushroom caps with damp towels.

4. Wrap each liver in bacon. On each of 6 skewers, alternate 3 livers and 2 mushrooms. Arrange skewers on rack in broiling pan. Brush with half of butter.

5. Broil, 4 inches from heat, 5 minutes. Turn skewers; brush with remaining butter and the wine. Broil 5 to 7 minutes longer, or until bacon is crisp (livers should still be pink on inside).

6. Serve skewers on platter of Mushroom Rice Pilaf.
Makes 6 servings.

## MUSHROOM RICE PILAF

¼ cup butter or margarine
1½ cups raw converted white rice
2 chicken-bouillon cubes,
    crumbled
¾ teaspoon salt

¼ teaspoon pepper
1 cup chopped mushroom stems
3½ cups boiling water
Chopped parsley

1. Preheat oven to 375F.
2. Melt butter in flameproof casserole. Add rice, and sauté, stirring, until lightly browned—about 10 minutes.
3. Add bouillon cubes, salt, pepper, mushroom, and boiling water; mix well.
4. Bake, tightly covered, 40 minutes, or until rice is tender and liquid is absorbed.
5. To serve: Fluff up pilaf with a fork, and turn out on serving platter. Sprinkle with the chopped parsley.

Makes 6 servings.

# Menu IV

Antipasto Platter
Scampi *
Spaghetti with Butter and Cheese
Broccoli with Lemon
Bread Sticks
Quick Sicilian Cheesecake *
Italian White Wine      Coffee

## SCAMPI

2 lbs large raw shrimp
½ cup butter or margarine
1 teaspoon salt
6 cloves garlic, crushed

¼ cup chopped parsley
2 teaspoons grated lemon peel
2 tablespoons lemon juice

6 lemon wedges

1. Preheat oven to 400F.

2. Remove shells from shrimp, leaving shell on tail section only. Devein: wash under running water; drain on paper towels.

3. Melt butter in 13-by-9-by-2-inch baking dish in oven. Add salt, garlic, and 1 tablespoon parsley; mix well.

4. Arrange shrimp in a single layer in baking dish. Bake, uncovered, 5 minutes.

5. Turn shrimp. Sprinkle with lemon peel, lemon juice, and remaining parsley. Bake 8 to 10 minutes, or just until tender.

6. Arrange shrimp on heated serving platter. Pour garlic butter over all. Garnish with lemon wedges.

Makes 6 to 8 servings.

## QUICK SICILIAN CHEESECAKE

⅓ cup light rum
¾ cup candied mixed fruit
2 pkg (10¾- or 11-oz size) cheesecake mix
¼ cup sugar

⅔ cup butter or margarine,
melted
2 cups milk
1 teaspoon grated lemon peel
¾ cup ricotta cheese, well drained

1. In small bowl, combine rum and ½ cup candied fruit; let stand.

2. In medium bowl, combine graham-cracker crumbs from both packages of cheesecake mix, the sugar, and butter; mix well. Turn into 8-inch springform pan, patting evenly on bottom and 2 inches up side of pan. Refrigerate.

3. In small bowl, combine 2 envelopes cheesecake mix, the milk, and lemon peel. Drain rum from fruit; add rum to cheesecake mixture. With electric mixer, beat at low speed 1 minute, to blend; then at high speed 1 minute.

4. With mixer at low speed, gradually beat in ricotta; then beat at high speed 30 seconds, to blend.

5. Stir in rum-flavored candied fruit. Spoon cheesecake mixture into crumb-lined pan. Decorate cake with remaining candied fruit.

6. Chill in freezer 30 minutes before serving. (May also be chilled in refrigerator 1½ hours before serving.)

Makes 8 to 10 servings.

# One-Dish Meals

## Menu I

Liver Pâté en Gelée *
Beef à la Mode *
(with carrots, white turnips and peas)
Green Salad Bowl
Sesame Bread
Mincemeat Glacé *
Shortbread Fans *
Burgundy Wine      Espresso or Coffee

### LIVER PÂTÉ EN GELÉE

1½ teaspoons unflavored gelatine
1 cup canned condensed beef
   broth
4 canned whole mushrooms
1 can (4¾ oz) liver pâté

1 tablespoon butter or regular
   margarine
1 teaspoon brandy
Thin slices toast

1. In small saucepan, sprinkle gelatine over ¼ cup undiluted broth; let stand 5 minutes, to soften. Heat over low heat, stirring constantly, until gelatine dissolves. Remove from heat. Add remaining broth.

2. Place 1½-cup decorative mold in pan of ice and water. Spoon about 2 tablespoons gelatine mixture into mold. Let stand a few minutes, until almost set.

3. Cut mushrooms in half. Arrange, in a pattern, on set gelatine in mold. Add enough more gelatine mixture to cover mushrooms.

4. In small bowl, combine liver pâté, butter, brandy. With electric mixer or fork, beat until combined.

5. Turn mixture into empty liver-pâté can, making top even; invert onto waxed paper. With can opener, remove end of can. Lift can, and carefully push pâté, through can, onto center of set gelatine in mold, being careful to keep its shape.

6. Spoon remaining chilled gelatine mixture around and over pâté. Refrigerate, covered, 3 hours, or until firm.

7. To unmold: Run sharp knife around edge of mold. Invert over serving plate. Plate a hot, damp dishcloth over mold; shake gently to release. Lift off mold.

8. Remove crusts from toast; cut toast diagonally in quarters. Arrange triangles around mold. Or serve mold with crackers, if you wish.

Makes 8 servings.

═══

## BEEF À LA MODE

| | |
|---|---|
| 4 tablespoons chopped parsley | 2 whole cloves |
| 1 teaspoon seasoned salt | 1 bay leaf |
| ¼ lb salt pork | 1 teaspoon dried thyme leaves |
| 4- or 5-lb beef top- or bottom-round roast | 1 can (10½ oz) condensed beef consommé, undiluted |
| Flour | 1 cup dry red wine |
| 1½ teaspoons salt | ½ lb carrots, pared and cut in 1-inch pieces |
| ¼ teaspoon pepper | ½ lb white turnips, pared and cut in 1- inch cubes |
| ¼ cup salad oil | |
| ½ cup chopped onion | |
| 1 clove garlic, crushed | 1 pkg (10 oz) frozen peas |

1. Combine parsley and seasoned salt on waxed paper. Cut salt pork into strips 3 inches long; ¼ inch thick. Roll in parsley mixture.

2. Wipe roast with damp paper towels. Make cuts 3 to 4 inches deep, 1½ inches apart. Push salt-pork strips into cuts.

3. Mix ¼ cup flour, the salt, and pepper; use to coat roast. Save any remaining flour mixture.

4. In hot oil in Dutch oven, over medium heat, brown roast well on all sides—about 20 minutes in all. Add onion, garlic, cloves, bay leaf, thyme, consommé, and ½ cup wine.

5. Bring to boiling; reduce heat, and simmer, covered and turning roast several times, 2½ hours. Add carrots and turnips; simmer 20 minutes. Add peas; simmer 20 minutes longer, or until meat and vegetables are tender.

6. Remove roast to heated serving platter. Using slotted spoon, remove vegetables, and place around roast. Keep warm. Skim fat from pan juices.

7. Add enough flour to remaining flour mixture to make 6 tablespoons. Mix, in small bowl, with remaining wine until smooth. Stir into pan juices; bring to boiling, stirring. Reduce heat, and simmer 3 minutes. Pass with meat.

Makes 8 servings.

## MINCEMEAT GLACÉ

1 cup prepared mincemeat                1 quart soft vanilla ice cream
¼ cup slivered toasted almonds

1. Drain mincemeat well; mix with almonds.

2. With spatula or back of large spoon, press ¼ ice cream into bottom of 5-cup mold. Then press ¾ of mincemeat mixture irregularly to side of mold. Pack in rest of ice cream, filling in any crevices with remaining mincemeat mixture.

3. Place mold in freezer; freeze overnight, or until ice cream is firm.

4. To unmold, loosen edge with sharp knife. Invert mold on round of aluminum foil or serving platter. Place hot, damp cloth around mold, to melt ice cream slightly; then shake out ice cream. Store in freezer until serving time. (Freezer-wrap if to be stored longer than several hours.)

Makes 8 servings.

## SHORTBREAD FANS

1 cup butter, softened                2½ cups sifted all-purpose flour *
½ cup light-brown sugar, firmly
　　packed                                * Sift before measuring.

1. In large bowl, with portable electric mixer at medium speed, or wooden spoon, beat butter with sugar until light and fluffy.

2. With wooden spoon, stir in flour until smooth and well blended (dough will be stiff).

3. Refrigerate, covered, several hours.

4. Preheat oven to 300F. Divide dough in half; refrigerate one half until ready to roll out.

5. On lightly floured surface, roll out each half ⅛ inch thick. Make fan design from cardboard; cover with foil. Then lay pattern on dough, and cut around it. Or use 1½- or 2-inch fancy cookie cutters.

6. Place fans, 1 inch apart, on ungreased cookie sheets; bake 25 minutes, or until light golden. Remove to wire racks; cool.

7. To freeze: Place in freezer container. Or arrange in foil baking dishes or on paper plates, and wrap with freezer-wrapping material. Seal; label; place in freezer.

8. To serve: Cookies can be arranged on plate directly from freezer. Makes about 5 dozen.

# Menu II

Cold Ratatouille *
Cassoulet *
Leek Salad Platter*
Whole Wheat Casserole Bread *
Pear Tarte Tatin *
Beaujolais     Coffee

## COLD RATATOUILLE

| | |
|---|---|
| 1 medium green pepper | 1 clove garlic, crushed |
| 1½ medium zucchini (½ lb) | 2 medium tomatoes (¾ lb), peeled |
| ¼ lb medium mushrooms | and cut into wedges |
| ½ medium eggplant (½ lb) | 1 teaspoon salt |
| 6 tablespoons salad or olive oil | ⅛ teaspoon pepper |
| ½ cup thinly sliced onion | 2 tablespoons chopped parsley |

1. Wash pepper; halve. Remove ribs and seeds. Cut lengthwise into ¼-inch-thick slices.

2. Scrub zucchini. Cut on diagonal into ¼-inch-thick slices. Wash mushrooms; slice lengthwise, right through stems, ¼ inch thick.

3. Wash eggplant; do not peel. Cut lengthwise into quarters; then cut crosswise into ¼-inch slices.

4. In 2 tablespoons hot oil in medium skillet, sauté green pepper, mushrooms, onion, and garlic 5 minutes, or until onion is transparent. With slotted spoon, remove to medium bowl.

5. Add 2 tablespoons oil to skillet. In hot oil, sauté zucchini, turning frequently, until tender—about 10 minutes. With slotted utensil, remove from skillet to same bowl.

6. Add remaining oil to skillet. In hot oil, sauté eggplant, turning occasionally, until tender—5 minutes.

7. Return vegetables to same skillet. Layer half of tomato wedges on top. Sprinkle with salt, pepper, and ½ tablespoon parsley. Stir gently to mix.

8. Layer remaining tomato on top. Sprinkle with ½ tablespoon parsley.

9. Simmer mixture, covered, over low heat 10 minutes.

10. Remove cover; cook 5 minutes longer, basting occasionally with pan juices, or until liquid has evaporated.

11. Turn into large, shallow serving dish. Refrigerate, covered, until very well chilled—several hours.

12. Sprinkle with remaining parsley.

Makes 8 servings.

## CASSOULET

1½ lb Great Northern white beans
2 cans (10½-oz size) condensed chicken broth, undiluted
2 bay leaves
5 carrots, pared
6 onions, peeled
4 whole cloves
½ cup coarsely chopped celery leaves
1½ teaspoons salt
3 whole black peppers
3 cloves garlic, peeled and sliced
1½ teaspoons dried thyme leaves

1 teaspoon dried marjoram leaves
1 teaspoon dried sage leaves
¼ lb bacon (in one piece)
1 lb Polish sausage (whole)
4-lb roasting chicken, cut in 8 pieces
2 tablespoons butter or margarine
⅛ teaspoon pepper
1 can (1 lb) peeled tomatoes
2 tablespoons chopped parsley

1. In an 8-quart kettle, combine beans with 4½ cups water; let soak about 2 hours—no longer (they will burst easily in cooking). Do not drain beans.

2. Add chicken broth, bay leaves, 2 carrots cut into chunks, 5 onions, 1 onion studded with whole cloves, celery leaves, 1 teaspoon salt, the black pepper, garlic, thyme, marjoram and sage. Bring just to boiling; reduce heat and simmer, covered, 1 hour. Add remaining carrots; cook, covered, 15 minutes longer.

3. Meanwhile, cut bacon into 1-inch cubes. Sauté bacon until crisp, turning on all sides. Drain off fat.

4. Preheat oven to 350F.

5. Turn bean mixture into a 6-quart casserole. Add bacon. Bake, uncovered, 30 minutes.

6. Meanwhile, in large skillet, brown chicken in hot butter, turning to brown well—20 to 25 minutes; sprinkle with ½ teaspoon salt and the pepper. Add chicken and undrained tomatoes to beans. With sharp knife, cut 9 diagonal slashes, ⅛ inch deep, in top of sausage. Place sausage on top of chicken and vegetables.

7. Cover top with foil; bake 45 minutes, or until chicken is tender. Bake, uncovered, 10 minutes longer. Sprinkle with parsley.

Makes 8 servings.

*Note:* Cassoulet is even better made the day before and reheated at 300F, covered, 1 hour before serving. If necessary, add 1 cup broth or water to make it moister.

═══════

## LEEK SALAD PLATTER

**Dressing**
½ *cup salad or olive oil*
¼ *cup cider vinegar*
*1 tablespoon grated onion*
*1 tablespoon snipped chives*
*1 teaspoon salt*

¼ *teaspoon pepper*

*8 medium leeks*
*1 teaspoon salt*
*1 tablespoon chopped parsley*
*1 hard-cooked egg, chopped*

1. Make Dressing: In jar with tight-fitting lid, combine oil, vinegar, onion, chives, 1 teaspoon salt, and the pepper. Shake to blend well. Refrigerate until needed.

2. Trim root ends of leeks; trim green tops so leeks are about 7 inches long; discard trimmings. Wash leeks thoroughly.

3. In medium skillet, bring 1½ quarts water with 1 teaspoon salt to boiling. Add leeks; simmer, covered, 15 minutes, or until tender. Drain. Cool 30 minutes.

4. Arrange leeks in 10-by-8-by-2-inch dish. Pour dressing over them. Refrigerate, covered, 3 hours, or until well chilled.

5. To serve: Remove leeks and dressing to serving dish. Sprinkle with chopped parsley and egg.

Makes 8 servings.

## WHOLE WHEAT CASSEROLE BREAD

1 cup milk
¾ cup shortening
½ cup honey
2 teaspoons salt
2 pkg active dry yeast
¾ cup warm water (105 to 115F)

3 eggs, slightly beaten
4½ cups unsifted all-purpose
  flour
1½ cups whole-wheat flour
1 teaspoon soft butter or
  margarine

1. In small saucepan, heat milk until bubbles form around edge of pan; remove from heat. Stir in shortening, honey, and salt until shortening is melted. Cool to lukewarm.

2. Sprinkle yeast over warm water in large bowl; stir until yeast is dissolved. Stir in milk mixture and eggs.

3. Combine all-purpose and whole-wheat flours. Add two thirds flour mixture to yeast mixture; with electric mixer at low speed, beat until blended. Then beat at medium speed until smooth—about 2 minutes. With wooden spoon, gradually beat in remaining flour mixture. Then beat, stretching dough 20 to 30 times.

4. Cover with waxed paper and a towel. Let rise in warm place (85F), free from drafts, until double in bulk—about 1 hour.

5. Lightly grease a 2½- or 3-quart casserole or heatproof bowl. Punch down dough, and beat with spoon until smooth—about 30 seconds. Turn into casserole. Cover, and let rise until double in bulk— 20 to 30 minutes.

6. Preheat oven to 375F.

7. With a sharp knife, cut a 4-inch cross about ½ inch deep in top of dough.

8. Bake 45 to 50 minutes, or until bread is nicely browned and sounds hollow when rapped with knuckle.

9. Remove from casserole to wire rack. Rub butter over top of bread. Serve slightly warm. Cut in wedges.

Makes 1 round loaf.

## PEAR TARTE TATIN

2 cans (1-lb, 14-oz size) pear
  halves
1 cup sugar
1 tablespoon butter or margarine
½ pkg piecrust mix
  (pastry for 1-crust pie)

1 jar (9½ oz) marrons in syrup,
  drained (optional)
1 cup heavy cream, whipped and
  sweetened

1 Preheat oven to 450F.

2. Drain pears well. Cut each in half lengthwise; drain on paper towels.

3. To caramelize sugar: In large skillet, cook sugar over medium heat, stirring occasionally, until sugar melts and becomes a light-brown syrup.

4. Immediately pour into bottom of 8½-inch round baking dish. Arrange pears, rounded side down, spoke fashion, in caramelized sugar. Top with a second layer of pears, rounded side up, fitting pieces over bottom layer to fill open spaces.

5. Dot with butter. Bake, uncovered, 25 minutes, or just until caramelized sugar is melted.

6. Let stand in baking dish on wire rack until cooled to room temperature—about 1½ hours.

7. Meanwhile, prepare pastry, following package directions. On lightly floured surface, roll out to a 9-inch circle. Place on ungreased cookie sheet; prick with fork. Refrigerate 30 minutes.

8. Bake pastry at 450F for 10 minutes, or until golden-brown. Let stand on cookie sheet on wire rack until ready to use.

9. To serve: Place pastry circle over pears in baking dish. Top with serving plate; invert, and remove baking dish. Mound marrons in center. Serve with whipped cream.

Makes 8 servings.

# Menu III

Eggs Mayonnaise *
Spring Lamb Stew with Dill *
Bibb Lettuce and Endive Salad
Assorted Hot Rolls
Deep-dish Apple-Cider Pie *
Coffee      Cold Beer

## EGGS MAYONNAISE

1¼ cups mayonnaise or cooked
    salad dressing
⅓ cup chili sauce
1 teaspoon grated onion
1 tablespoon chopped parsley
Dash cayenne

2 tablespoons vinegar
1 teaspoon Worcestershire sauce
1 teaspoon prepared horseradish
3 cups shredded lettuce
6 hard-cooked eggs, chilled and
    halved

1. In medium bowl, with rotary beater, beat mayonnaise, chili sauce, onion, parsley, cayenne, vinegar, Worcestershire, and horseradish until well blended.

2. Refrigerate mixture, covered, until serving.

3. To serve: Arrange lettuce on 6 salad plates. Place 2 egg halves on each. Spoon some of mayonnaise mixture over each serving.

Makes 6 servings.

## SPRING LAMB STEW WITH DILL

2½ lb boneless lamb
2 tablespoons salad oil
12 small white onions, peeled
¾ cup tomato juice
2 teaspoons salt
¼ teaspoon pepper

6 medium carrots
6 new potatoes
¼ cup flour
1 pkg (10 oz) frozen peas
Fresh dill

1. Cut lamb in 1-inch pieces; trim off fat. In hot oil in Dutch oven, over medium heat, brown one third of meat at a time until browned on all sides. Remove as browned.

2. Add onions; brown on all sides. Remove. Pour all fat from pan.

3. Return lamb to pan. Add 2 cups water, the tomato juice, salt and pepper; bring to boiling. Reduce heat; simmer, covered, 30 minutes.

4. Meanwhile, scrape carrots; cut in half. Pare a band of skin, ½ inch wide, around center of each potato.

5. Add onions, carrots and potatoes to lamb mixture. Simmer, covered, 40 minutes longer, or until meat and vegetables are tender. Remove from heat; skim off fat.

6. Mix flour with 6 tablespoons water. Stir into lamb mixture. Add peas and 3 tablespoons snipped dill. Simmer, covered, 10 to 15 minutes longer, or until peas are tender.

7. Remove from heat; let stand 5 minutes; skim off any fat. Ladle stew into heated serving dish. Garnish with a fresh dill sprig.

Makes 6 servings.

## DEEP-DISH APPLE-CIDER PIE

**Filling**
*1½ cups apple cider*
*1 to 1¼ cups sugar*
*3 lbs tart cooking apples*
*2 tablespoons lemon juice*

*2 tablespoons butter or*
*margarine*

*Pastry for 1-crust pie*
*1 egg yolk*

1. Make filling: In large saucepan, combine cider and sugar; bring to boiling, stirring until sugar is dissolved. Boil, uncovered, 10 minutes.

2. Meanwhile, pare and core apples; slice thinly into large bowl. Sprinkle with lemon juice. Add to cider mixture; return to boiling over moderate heat, stirring several times. Lower heat; simmer, uncovered, 5 minutes, or just until apples are partially cooked.

3. With slotted spoon, lift apples out of syrup into a round, 8¼-inch shallow baking dish, mounding in center.

4. Return remaining syrup to boiling; boil, uncovered, 5 minutes. (Syrup should measure ½ cup.) Pour over apple slices; dot with butter.

5. Preheat oven to 400F.

6. On lightly floured surface, roll out pastry into an 11-inch circle. Fit over top of baking dish; flute edge. Make several slits in center for vents.

7. Beat egg yolk with 1 tablespoon water; brush over pastry. Bake 40 to 45 minutes, or until pastry is golden-brown and juice bubbles through slits.

8. Serve warm, with ice cream, light cream or hard sauce.
Makes 6 to 8 servings.

# Menu IV

Jellied Madrilène
Seafood au Gratin *
with Mashed Potato *
Petit Pois
Marinated Sliced Cucumbers
French Bread
Cold Strawberry Soufflé *
Chilled White Wine          Coffee

## SEAFOOD AU GRATIN

*10 medium-size flounder fillets*
*¾ teaspoon salt*
*¼ teaspoon white pepper*
*¼ cup lemon juice*
*¼ cup snipped fresh dill*
*¾ cup dry white wine*
*Butter or margarine*
*½ lb mushrooms, sliced*

**Sauce**
*¼ cup flour*
*Reserved fish broth*
*1 cup light cream*
*1 can (3 oz) baby shrimp,*
*drained*

**Mashed Potato, below**
*Fresh dill for garnish*

1. Preheat oven to 350F.
2. Rinse fillets under cold water; pat dry with paper towels.
3. Arrange fillets in a large, oven-proof (2-inch-deep) platter.
4. Sprinkle with salt, pepper, lemon juice and snipped dill. Add wine. Cut 2 tablespoons butter in small pieces, and place on top of fish.
5. Cover dish with foil. Bake 25 minutes.
6. Meanwhile, in 3 tablespoons hot butter in medium skillet, over low heat, sauté mushrooms until tender—about 10 minutes; remove from heat.
7. Remove fish from oven. Carefully drain off fish liquid. Drain fish very well. Liquid should measure 1½ cups.
8. Make sauce: Add flour to mushrooms. Stir until smooth. Stir in reserved fish broth and cream. Cook over medium heat, stirring constantly, until mixture comes to a boil; reduce heat and simmer 5 minutes, stirring. Add shrimp.

9. Pour sauce over fish. Prepare Mashed Potato.

10. With mashed potato in a pastry bag with a number-6 tube, make lattice pattern over the fish and around edge. Refrigerate if not serving soon.

11. When ready to serve, preheat oven to 350F.

12. Place in oven until bubbly and hot and mashed potato is lightly browned—about 40 minutes. Garnish with dill sprigs, as pictured.

Makes 8 servings.

## MASHED POTATO

| | |
|---|---|
| 3 lbs white potatoes | 1 teaspoon salt |
| ½ cup butter or margarine | ⅛ teaspoon white pepper |
| ⅓ cup hot milk | 1 egg yolk |

1. Pare potatoes; cut in quarters. Cook in 1 inch salted boiling water, covered, until tender—20 minutes. Drain very well; return to saucepan; heat slightly over low heat to dry out potatoes.

2. Beat, with portable electric mixer (or mash with potato masher), until smooth.

3. In saucepan, heat butter and milk until butter melts—don't let milk boil!

4. Gradually beat in hot milk mixture until potato is smooth. Beat in salt, pepper and egg yolk until potato is light and fluffy.

## COLD STRAWBERRY SOUFFLÉ

| | |
|---|---|
| 4 egg whites | 1 tablespoon lemon juice |
| 2 pkg (10-oz size) frozen | ⅛ teaspoon salt |
|    strawberries, thawed | ½ teaspoon vanilla extract |
| 1 envelope unflavored gelatine | ⅓ cup sugar |
| 4 egg yolks | 1 cup heavy cream |

1. Make a collar for a 1-quart, straight-side soufflé dish: Cut a strip of foil 6 inches wide and long enough to go around edge of soufflé dish. Fold foil twice. Place band of foil tightly around dish, so it extends above dish to form a 1½-inch-deep collar. Fasten securely with string.

2. Let egg whites stand, in large bowl of electric mixer, at room temperature—about 1 hour.

3. Meanwhile, drain strawberries, reserving ½ cup syrup. Set aside

a few large strawberries for garnish.

4. Sprinkle gelatine over reserved strawberry syrup in top of double boiler. Let stand 5 minutes to soften.

5. In small bowl, beat egg yolks with 3 tablespoons water. Stir into gelatine mixture.

6. Cook, stirring, over boiling water, until gelatine is dissolved and mixture is slightly thickened.

7. Remove from hot water. Stir in lemon juice, salt and vanilla to mix well. Refrigerate until mixture is cooled—about 20 minutes.

8. Press strawberries (except those reserved for garnish) through sieve to make a purée; this should measure about 1⅓ cups. Stir into gelatine mixture.

9. Beat egg whites, at high speed, just until soft peaks form when beater is slowly raised. Gradually beat in sugar; beat until stiff peaks form.

10. With rotary beater, beat cream until stiff.

11. Using rubber scraper or wire whisk, with an under-and-over motion, fold gelatine mixture and whipped cream into egg whites until well combined.

12. Turn evenly into prepared soufflé dish. Refrigerate until firm —about 4 hours.

13. To serve: Gently remove collar from soufflé. Garnish edge with reserved strawberries and more whipped cream, if desired.

Makes 8 servings.

# Breakfast, Brunch and Lunch

## Menu I: A Special Brunch for 8

———

Ella Brennan's Milk Punch *
Grilled Grapefruit with Kirsch *
or Fresh Fruits on Ice *
Omelets Made to Order *
Choice of Fillings *: Red Caviar and
Sour Cream; Chicken Liver
and Mushroom; Creamed Oyster;
Creamed Spinach;
Münster Cheese with Caraway
Basket of Crescent Rolls, Brioches, Blueberry Muffins *
Toasted English Muffins
Sweet-Butter Balls, Preserves
Coffee

———

### ELLA BRENNAN'S MILK PUNCH

*1½ cups bourbon or brandy*
*1½ pints half-and-half*
*1 teaspoon vanilla extract*

*2½ tablespoons confectioners'*
  *sugar*
*½ cup heavy cream*
*Nutmeg*

1. Combine bourbon, half-and-half, and vanilla. Stir in sugar until dissolved. Cover; refrigerate several hours, or until very well chilled.

2. Just before serving, whip cream until stiff. Pour bourbon mixture into punch bowl or glass serving bowl. Set bowl in a bowl of crushed ice, if desired.

3. Spoon whipped cream on punch. Sprinkle with freshly grated nutmeg.

Makes 8 or 9 (punch-cup) servings.

*Note:* Half-and-half is half milk and half cream.

## GRILLED GRAPEFRUIT WITH KIRSCH

*4 grapefruit, halved*         *1 cup kirsch*
*1 cup sugar*

1. Cut out centers and remove seeds from each grapefruit half. Cut around each section with grapefruit knife, to loosen.

2. Sprinkle each half with 2 tablespoons sugar, then with 2 tablespoons kirsch.

3. Broil, 4 inches from heat, about 5 minutes, or until bubbly and brown. Garnish with maraschino cherries and mint sprigs, if desired.

Makes 8 servings.

## FRESH FRUITS ON ICE

*2 pint boxes fresh strawberries*    *½ to ¾ cup granulated sugar*
*1 pint box fresh raspberries*      *1½ cups orange juice*
*1 pint box fresh blueberries*      *Crushed ice*

1. Wash all the berries; drain. Hull strawberries.

2. In a deep, glass serving bowl, place a layer of strawberries. Sprinkle strawberries generously with some of sugar.

3. Continue layering the remaining berries, sprinkling each layer generously with sugar.

4. Pour 1½ cups of orange juice over berries. Let stand at room temperature 1 hour.

5. Just before serving, cover berries with a thin layer of crushed ice.

Makes 8 servings.

―――――

## OMELETS MADE TO ORDER

**Basic Omelet**                    *Dash pepper*
*16 eggs*
*½ cup light cream*                 *Fillings, below*
*2 teaspoons salt*                  *½ cup butter or margarine*

1. Make Basic Omelet: In larger bowl, with electric mixer at low speed or with rotary beater, beat eggs with cream, salt, and pepper until well blended but not frothy. Refrigerate the mixture until you are ready to cook omelets.
2. Make the Fillings.
3. To cook omelet: Slowly heat an 8-inch skillet. Add 1 tablespoon butter, and heat until it sizzles briskly but does not brown.
4. Ladle about ½ cup egg mixture into skillet; cook over medium heat. As egg sets, run spatula around edge to loosen, and tilt pan to let uncooked portion run underneath. Continue loosening and tilting until the omelet is almost dry on top and golden-brown underneath.
5. Place your choice of filling on half of omelet. Fold other half over, and slide omelet onto heated serving plate.
Makes 8 omelets.

**Red-Caviar-and-Sour-Cream**        *1 cup (½ pint) dairy sour cream*
**Filling**
*1 jar (4 oz) red caviar*

1. Turn caviar and sour cream into small bowls.
2. Spread omelet, still in skillet, with 3 tablespoons sour cream.
3. Fold over omelet; slide onto serving plate, and top with a heaping teaspoonful of drained red caviar. Serve omelet at once.
Makes enough for 4 or 5 omelets.

**Chicken-Liver-and-Mushroom**       *1 teaspoon instant minced onion*
**Filling**                          *½ teaspoon seasoned salt*
*½ lb chicken livers*                *¼ teaspoon dried chervil leaves*
*3 tablespoons butter or*            *⅛ teaspoon pepper*
*    margarine*                      *⅓ cup dry sherry*
*¼ lb mushrooms, chopped*

1. Rinse chicken livers; pat dry with paper towels. Cut into small pieces.
2. In hot butter in medium saucepan, sauté mushrooms until golden-

brown—about 2 minutes. Add liver, onion, salt, chervil, and pepper; sauté until liver is browned—about 4 minutes. Add sherry; reduce heat, and simmer 5 minutes. Turn into attractive serving bowl; keep warm.

Makes enough for 4 to 6 omelets (about ⅓ cup each).

**Creamed-Oyster Filling**
1 can (8 oz) oysters
Milk
2 tablespoons butter or
    margarine

1 tablespoon chopped shallot or
    onion
3 tablespoons flour

1. Drain liquid from oysters into 1-cup measure; add milk to make 1 cup.

2. In hot butter in small saucepan, sauté shallot until tender—about 2 minutes. Remove from heat. Stir in flour until well combined. Gradually stir in milk mixture. Bring to boiling, stirring constantly; reduce heat, and simmer 1 minute.

3. Add oysters; return to boiling. Turn into serving bowl; keep warm.

Makes enough for 4 omelets (¼ cup each).

**Creamed-Spinach Filling**
1 pkg (10 oz) frozen leaf spinach
1 tablespoon butter or margarine

1 tablespoon flour
1 cup light cream
⅛ teaspoon nutmeg

1. Cook spinach as package label directs. Drain well; chop.

2. Melt butter in small saucepan; remove from heat. Stir in flour until smooth; gradually stir in cream; add nutmeg. Bring to boiling, stirring constantly; reduce heat, and simmer 1 minute. Stir in spinach. Turn into attractive serving bowl; keep warm.

Makes enough for 4 to 6 omelets (about ⅓ cup each).

**Munster-Cheese-with-Caraway**
**Filling**
½ cup grated Münster cheese

1 teaspoon caraway seed

Combine cheese and caraway in attractive serving bowl.
Makes enough for 4 omelets (2 tablespoons each).

## BLUEBERRY MUFFINS

2 cups sifted all-purpose flour
   (see Note)
1½ teaspoons double-acting
   baking powder
¼ teaspoon salt
½ cup butter or regular
   margarine, softened

1 cup sugar
2 eggs
1 teaspoon vanilla extract
½ cup milk
1 cup fresh or drained, thawed
   frozen blueberries

1. Night before: With paper liners, line 18 muffin-pan cups (2½ by 1¼ inches); or grease them well.

2. Sift flour with baking powder and salt.

3. In large bowl, with electric mixer at high speed, beat butter with sugar, eggs and vanilla until light and fluffy, occasionally scraping side of bowl with rubber scraper—about 4 minutes.

4. At low speed, beat in flour mixture (in fourths), alternately with milk (in thirds), beginning and ending with flour mixture. Beat just until smooth.

5. With rubber scraper, gently fold in blueberries just until combined.

6. Scoop about ¼ cup batter into each prepared muffin cup, to fill each about two thirds full. Refrigerate overnight.

7. To serve next day: Preheat oven to 350F. Bake 25 to 30 minutes, or until golden-brown and cake tester inserted in center comes out clean.

8. Remove muffins to wire rack; let cool slightly. Serve warm.

Makes 18 muffins.

*Note:* Sift before measuring.

# Brunch

## Menu II

Fresh Orange Spritzer *
Scrambled Eggs, Sunday Style *
( in Brioche )
Or Eggs Florentine *
Sautéed Canadian Bacon *
Toasted English Muffins
Assorted Preserves
Coffee

### FRESH ORANGE SPRITZER

2 cans (6-oz size) frozen orange-
 juice concentrate
1 bottle (1 pt, 12 oz) club soda,
 chilled

3 tablespoons lemon juice
Ice cubes

1. In large pitcher, combine orange-juice concentrate and 1 cup cold water; stir until orange juice is thawed.

2. Add soda, lemon juice, and 2 cups cubes.

Makes 6 tall servings.

## SCRAMBLED EGGS, SUNDAY STYLE
### (in Brioche)

4 individual brioches
  (from bakery)

**Scrambled Eggs**
7 eggs
¼ cup milk

½ teaspoon salt
Dash pepper
2 tablespoons butter or
  margarine
1 pkg (3 oz) chive cream cheese,
  cut in ½-inch cubes
Chopped parsley or chives

1. Preheat oven to 350F. Heat brioches on cookie sheet while preparing eggs.
2. Make scrambled eggs: In medium bowl, combine eggs, milk, salt and pepper; with rotary beater, beat just until combined.
3. Heat butter in a large skillet. Pour in egg mixture; cook over low heat. As eggs start to set on bottom, gently lift cooked portion with spatula to form flakes, letting uncooked portion flow to bottom of pan.
4. Add cheese; cook until eggs are moist and shiny but no longer runny.
5. Cut off tops of brioches; set aside. With fork, scoop soft inside from center of each brioche.
6. Spoon scrambled eggs into brioches; sprinkle with parsley; replace tops.
Makes 4 servings.

## POACHED EGGS

In shallow pan or skillet, bring water (about 1 inch deep) to boiling point. Reduce heat to simmer. Break each egg into a saucer; quickly slip egg into water. Cook, covered, 3 to 5 minutes. Lift out of water with slotted pancake turner or spoon. Drain well on paper towels.

## EGGS FLORENTINE

¼ cup butter or regular margarine
2 tablespoons finely chopped
   onion
¼ cup unsifted all-purpose flour
½ teaspoon salt
⅛ teaspoon pepper
Dash nutmeg
1½ cups milk

½ cup light cream
1 egg yolk
½ cup grated Swiss or Parmesan
   cheese
1 pkg (10 oz) frozen chopped
   spinach, thawed and drained
12 eggs
Grated Swiss or Parmesan cheese

1. In hot butter in medium-size, heavy saucepan, sauté onion, stirring, until golden—about 5 minutes. Remove from heat.

2. Add flour, salt, pepper and nutmeg; stir until smooth. Add all of the milk, then the cream, a small amount at a time, stirring after each addition. Return to heat.

3. Over medium heat, bring to boiling, stirring constantly; reduce heat and simmer 3 minutes, stirring. In small bowl, beat egg yolk with fork; stir in about ½ cup hot sauce; mix well. Return egg-yolk mixture along with ½ cup grated cheese to rest of sauce in saucepan, stirring constantly. Cook, stirring, over low heat until thickened and cheese is melted; do not boil. Cover and place over hot water.

4. Cook spinach as package directs; drain well.

5. Poach eggs as directed in recipe for Poached Eggs, above.

6. Layer spinach in bottom of six scallop baking shells or individual shallow baking dishes (1 cup). Place 2 eggs in each spinach-lined dish; cover with sauce; sprinkle each dish with 1 teaspoon grated cheese.

7. Arrange shells on cookie sheet. Broil, 6 inches from heat, 4 to 5 minutes, or until lightly browned.

Makes 6 servings.

## SAUTÉED CANADIAN BACON

2 tablespoons butter or
   margarine
1½ lbs Canadian bacon, sliced
   ¼ inch thick

½ cup white wine or cider or
   apple juice

1. In hot butter in large skillet, sauté bacon gently (half at a time in a single layer) 2 to 3 minutes on each side, to brown slightly. Remove as browned.

2. Return slices to skillet; pour wine over all. Simmer gently, covered, until heated through—about 5 minutes.

Makes 6 to 8 servings.

# Menu III

___

Frozen Tomato Frappés * or
Bloody Marys
Cheese-and-Spinach Roulade *
With Cheese Sauce *
Basket of Assorted Hot Rolls
Warm Streusel Coffeecake *
Butter     Preserves
Coffee     Chilled White Wine

___

### FROZEN TOMATO FRAPPÉS

| | |
|---|---|
| 1 tablespoon butter or margarine | ½ teaspoon Worcestershire sauce |
| ⅓ cup finely chopped onion | 1 can (1 qt, 14 oz) tomato juice |
| 2 teaspoons sugar | Lemon wedges |
| 1 teaspoon lemon juice | Crackers |

1. Night before: In hot butter, sauté onion until golden. Turn into blender; add sugar, lemon juice, Worcestershire and half of tomato juice.

2. Blend, at high speed, 1 minute, or until smooth. Turn into 13-by-9-by-2-inch metal pan. Stir in remaining tomato juice. Cover; freeze overnight.

3. One hour before serving, remove from freezer. Let stand at room temperature until it begins to melt.

4. Break up with a fork, and beat until no large pieces remain. Blend half at a time, at high speed, until smooth, not melted. Turn into sherbet glasses. Serve with lemon and crackers.

Makes 8 servings.

## CHEESE-AND-SPINACH ROULADE

**Cheese Roll**
7 eggs
Butter or regular margarine
6 tablespoons unsifted
 all-purpose flour
1½ teaspoons salt
Dash cayenne
1¼ cups milk
Grated Parmesan cheese
½ cup coarsely grated sharp
 Cheddar cheese
¼ teaspoon cream of tartar

**Spinach Filling**
2 pkg (10-oz size) frozen
 chopped spinach
2 tablespoons butter or
 margarine
¼ cup finely chopped onion
½ teaspoon salt
¼ cup grated sharp Cheddar
 cheese
½ cup sour cream

1. Night before, make cheese roll: Separate eggs, placing whites in one large bowl and yolks in another. Let whites warm to room temperature—1 hour.

2. Meanwhile, lightly grease bottom of 15½-by-10½-by-1-inch jelly-roll pan; then line bottom of pan with waxed paper.

3. Preheat oven to 350F. Melt 5 tablespoons butter in medium saucepan; remove from heat. Using a wire whisk or wooden spoon, stir in flour, 1 teaspoon salt and the cayenne until smooth. Gradually stir in milk. Bring to boiling, stirring constantly.

4. Reduce heat; simmer, stirring, until mixture is thick and leaves bottom and side of pan; remove from heat. Beat in ½ cup Parmesan cheese and ½ cup Cheddar cheese.

5. With wire whisk or wooden spoon, beat egg yolks. Gradually beat in cooked mixture.

6. At high speed of electric mixer, beat egg whites with ½ teaspoon salt and the cream of tartar until stiff peaks form when beater is slowly raised. With wire whisk, using an under-and-over motion, gently fold one third of whites into warm cheese mixture, to combine well.

7. Carefully fold in remaining egg whites just until combined. Turn into prepared jelly-roll pan. Bake 12 to 15 minutes, or until surface is puffed and feels firm when lightly pressed with fingertip.

8. Meanwhile, make spinach filling: Cook spinach gently in ½ cup boiling water just until thawed. Turn into sieve, and press to get all water out. In hot butter in medium skillet, sauté onion until golden and tender. Remove from heat. Add spinach, salt, Cheddar and sour cream; mix well.

9. Invert baked cheese roll on waxed paper that has been sprinkled lightly with Parmesan cheese; gently peel off waxed paper that lined pan. Spread evenly with spinach filling.

10. Starting with long side, roll up; place, seam side down, on wire rack to cool completely. Wrap in foil; refrigerate overnight.

11. To serve next day: Preheat oven to 350F. Remove foil from roulade. Place on greased ovenproof serving dish. Bake 40 minutes, or until heated through.

Makes 8 servings.

---

### STREUSEL COFFEECAKE

*1⅓ cups packaged biscuit mix*
*¾ cup granulated sugar*
*¾ cup milk*
*1 egg*
*3 tablespoons butter or regular*
  *margarine, softened*
*1 teaspoon vanilla extract*

**Topping**
*¼ cup light-brown sugar, packed*
*1 tablespoon butter or regular*
  *margarine, softened*
*1 tablespoon all-purpose flour*
*½ teaspoon ground cinnamon*
*¼ cup coarsely chopped walnuts*

1. Night before: Grease and flour an 8-by-8-by-2-inch baking pan.

2. In small bowl of electric mixer, combine biscuit mix, granulated sugar, ¼ cup milk, the egg, 3 tablespoons butter and the vanilla; beat at medium speed 1 minute, or just until smooth. Add remaining milk; beat ½ minute. Turn batter into prepared baking pan; refrigerate overnight.

3. To serve next day: Preheat oven to 350F. Bake 40 minutes, or until cake tester inserted in center comes out clean.

4. Meanwhile, make topping: Combine all topping ingredients in small bowl; mix well.

5. Spread topping evenly over baked coffeecake. Run under broiler, 4 inches from heat, for about 2 to 3 minutes, or until topping is bubbly and golden-brown. Serve warm, cut into squares.

Makes 9 servings.

# Menu IV

Bloody Marys
or Chilled Cantaloupe Soup *
Indivdual Cheese Soufflés in Patty Shells
with Lobster Sauce *
Buttered Oatmeal Toast          Bar-le-Duc
Coffee

## CHILLED CANTALOUPE SOUP

| | |
|---|---|
| 1 (3 lb) ripe cantaloupe | ¼ cup sugar |
| ½ cup dry sherry | 1 tablespoon lime juice |

1. Cut melon in half; scoop out seeds. Scoop out cantaloupe meat.
2. In blender, combine cantaloupe and rest of ingredients. Blend until smooth—several times if necessary. Refrigerate, covered, until very cold.
Makes 4 cups.

## INDIVIDUAL CHEESE SOUFFLÉS IN PATTY SHELLS WITH LOBSTER SAUCE

| | |
|---|---|
| 1 pkg (10 oz) frozen patty shells | Dash cayenne, ¼ cup milk |
| | 3 tablespoons coarsely grated |
| **Cheese Soufflés** | natural Cheddar cheese |
| 2 eggs | ¼ cup grated Parmesan cheese |
| 2 tablespoons butter or | Dash cream of tartar |
| margarine | |
| 2 tablespoons flour | Lobster Sauce, below |
| Salt | |

1. Bake patty shells as package label directs; cool. (These may be baked early in the day or day before.)
2. Make cheese soufflés: Separate eggs, placing whites in medium bowl, yolks in small bowl. Let whites warm to room temperature —about 1 hour.
3. Preheat oven to 375F. Melt butter in small saucepan; remove from heat. Stir in flour, ¼ teaspoon salt, and the cayenne until smooth. Gradually stir in milk.

4. Bring to boiling, stirring. Reduce heat, and simmer, stirring, until mixture becomes thick—about 1 minute. Remove from heat.

5. With wire whisk or wooden spoon, beat egg yolks. Gradually beat in cooked mixture. Add cheeses; beat until well combined.

6. Add ⅛ teaspoon salt and the cream of tartar to egg whites. With rotary beater, beat just until stiff peaks form when beater is slowly raised.

7. With rubber scraper, fold beaten egg whites into cheese mixture.

8. Use soufflé mixture to fill patty shells. Bake 15 minutes until soufflés are puffed and golden. Serve at once with Lobster Sauce. Makes 6 servings.

**Lobster Sauce**
1 pkg (11½ oz) frozen lobster
  Newburg

Heat lobster Newburg as label directs, adding a little sherry, if desired. Serve over cheese soufflés.

# Menu V

Piñas Coladas * or Orange-Lemon Mist *
Ham and Eggs in a Cloud *
Baked Cherry Tomatoes
Warm Blueberry-Coffeecake Squares*
Strawberry Crescents *      Coffee

## PIÑAS COLADAS

½ cup cream of coconut
  (see Note)
1 cup unsweetened pineapple
  juice, chilled

⅔ cup light rum
2 cups crushed ice

1. Refrigerate 6 cocktail glasses, to chill well—about 1 hour.

2. In electric blender, combine cream of coconut, pineapple juice, rum, and ice; cover, and blend at high speed ½ minute.

3. Pour into chilled glasses. If desired, serve with a pineapple spear. Makes 1 quart; 8 servings.

Note: Cream of coconut may be purchased as coconut-milk cream.

## ORANGE-LEMON MIST

*1 can (6 oz) frozen orange-juice*
   *concentrate, undiluted*
*¼ cup lemon juice*

*1 pint orange or lemon sherbet*
*Fresh mint sprigs*

1. In electric blender or drink shaker, combine undiluted orange juice, 3 juice cans cold water, lemon juice.
2. Blend, covered, at high speed, or shake very well until mixture is well blended and frothy.
3. Divide sherbet into 6 or 8 chilled old-fashioned glasses. Add orange mixture. Garnish with mint.
   Makes 8 servings.

## HAM AND EGGS IN A CLOUD

*1 lb sliced Canadian bacon or*
   *baked ham*
*6 slices white bread, toasted,*
   *buttered, and halved*

*10 eggs*
*Salt*
*½ teaspoon dry mustard*
*Dash pepper*

1. Preheat oven to 400F. Lightly grease a 14-by-9-by-2-inch baking dish. Arrange Canadian bacon, overlapping, against sides of dish. Cover bottom with toast, to keep bacon in place.
2. Separate eggs, placing whites in a large bowl and keeping each yolk in its half shell (place half shell back in egg carton for safekeeping). Use 8 yolks.
3. With electric mixer, beat whites with ½ teaspoon salt and the mustard until stiff. Turn into baking dish, mounding high. Make 8 depressions, spacing evenly. Bake, uncovered, 1 or 2 minutes, or until slightly set.
4. Place an egg yolk in each depression. Sprinkle each with a little salt and pepper. Bake, uncovered, 8 to 10 minutes, or until whites are slightly golden and yolks are set. Serve at once.
   Makes 8 servings.

## BLUEBERRY COFFEECAKE

1 egg
½ cup sugar
1¼ cups sifted (see Note)
  all-purpose flour
2 teaspoons double-acting
  baking powder
¾ teaspoon salt

⅓ cup milk
3 tablespoons butter or regular
  margarine, melted
1 cup fresh blueberries
2 tablespoons sugar
1 tablespoon butter or margarine

1. Night before: Lightly grease an 8-by-8-by-2-inch baking pan.

2. In medium-size bowl, with wooden spoon, beat egg; then gradually add ½ cup sugar, beating until well combined.

3. Sift together flour, baking powder and salt. Add to sugar mixture alternately with milk; beat well after each addition.

4. Add the melted butter and beat thoroughly. Then gently fold in blueberries.

5. Pour batter into prepared pan. Sprinkle top with 2 tablespoons sugar. Refrigerate overnight.

6. To serve next day: Preheat oven to 350F. Bake 35 minutes, or until top springs back when lightly touched with fingertip. Brush top with 1 tablespoon butter. Cut into squares; serve warm with butter.

Makes 9 servings.

*Note:* Sift before measuring.

## STRAWBERRY CRESCENTS

⅓ cup strawberry jam
2 tablespoons chopped walnuts
1 pkg (8 oz) refrigerator crescent
  rolls

½ cup confectioners' sugar
1 tablespoon butter or margarine
1 tablespoon milk

1. Combine jam and walnuts well.

2. Preheat over to 375F.

3. Unroll crescent-roll dough. Cut along perforations to make 8 pieces.

4. Spread each with jam-walnut mixture, dividing evenly. Roll up as package label directs.

5. Place, 2 inches apart, on a lightly greased cookie sheet; bake 10 to 15 minutes, or until golden.

6. Meanwhile, in small bowl, mix sugar, butter, and milk until smooth.

7. Remove crescents to wire rack. Spread tops with icing. Serve warm.

Makes 8 crescents.

# More Breakfast and Brunch Ideas

## CORNED-BEEF QUICHE

*1 can (15½ oz) corned-beef hash*
*¼ cup finely chopped onion*
*9-inch unbaked pieshell*
  *(see Note)*
*2 eggs*

*1 container (4 oz) whipped cream*
  *cheese with chives*
*1 cup cottage cheese*
*¼ teaspoon pepper*

1. Preheat oven to 350F.

2. Combine corned beef and onion; use to line bottom of pieshell.

3. In medium bowl, beat eggs until frothy. Add remaining ingredients; blend well. Pour over corned beef.

4. Bake 50 minutes. Serve warm.

Makes 6 to 8 servings.

*Note:* If using a frozen 9-inch prepared pieshell, let thaw and use only 1½ cups corned beef in bottom layer.

## DAY-BEFORE FRENCH TOAST

*6 slices Italian or French bread,*
  *¾ inch thick*
*4 eggs*
*1 cup milk*
*3 tablespoons granulated sugar*
*¼ teaspoon salt*
*1 teaspoon vanilla extract*

*3 tablespoons butter or*
  *margarine*
*Confectioners' sugar*
*Maple syrup or sour cream*
*Preserves or thawed, frozen*
  *berries*

1. Arrange bread in single layer in 9-inch-square baking dish.

2. In small bowl, with rotary beater, beat eggs, milk, granulated sugar, salt and vanilla until blended. Pour over bread; turn slices to coat evenly.

3. Refrigerate bread, covered, overnight.

4. In hot butter in skillet, sauté bread until golden—4 or 5 minutes

on each side. Sprinkle with confectioners' sugar and serve with syrup or sour cream and preserves or frozen, thawed strawberries.

Makes 4 servings.

———

## HAM-AND-CHEESE FRENCH TOAST

3 eggs
¾ cup milk
1 tablespoon sugar
¼ teaspoon salt

8 white-bread slices,
  lightly buttered
4 slices boiled ham
4 slices Swiss or American cheese
Butter or margarine

1. With rotary beater, beat eggs with milk, sugar and salt just to combine.

2. Make 4 sandwiches with bread, ham and cheese; cut into quarters diagonally. Place in single layer in shallow baking dish. Pour egg mixture over top, covering completely. Refrigerate overnight.

3. Next day, just before serving, in hot butter sauté sandwiches until golden on each side and cheese is slightly melted.

Makes 4 servings.

———

## PUFFY OMELET WITH CHERRY PRESERVES

6 egg whites
⅛ teaspoon cream of tartar
6 egg yolks
¾ teaspoon salt
Dash pepper
6 tablespoons milk

2 tablespoons butter or
  margarine
2 teaspoons salad oil

Confectioners' sugar
Cherry preserves

1. In large bowl of electric mixer, let egg whites warm to room temperature—about 1 hour.

2. At high speed, beat egg whites with cream of tartar just until stiff peaks form when beater is slowly raised.

3. In small bowl of electric mixer, using same beater, beat egg yolks until thick and lemon-colored.

4. Add salt, pepper, and milk gradually; beat until well combined.

5. With wire whisk or rubber scraper, using an under-and-over motion, gently fold egg-yolk mixture into egg whites just until combined.

6. Slowly heat a 9- or 10-inch heavy skillet with a heat-resistant handle, or an omelet pan. To test temperature: Sprinkle a little cold water on skillet; water should sizzle and roll off in drops.

7. Add butter and oil; heat until butter mixture sizzles briskly—it should not brown. Tilt pan to coat side with butter mixture.

8. Spread egg mixture evenly in pan; cook, over low heat and without stirring, until lightly browned on underside—about 10 minutes. Meanwhile, preheat oven to 350F.

9. Transfer skillet to oven; bake omelet 10 to 15 minutes, or until top seems firm when gently pressed with fingertip.

10. To serve: Fold omelet in half. Turn out onto heated serving platter. Sprinkle with sugar. Serve with cherry preserves.

Makes 4 to 6 servings.

## SCRAMBLED EGGS WITH OYSTERS

*⅓ cup butter or margarine*
*9 eggs*
*¼ teaspoon salt*

*Dash pepper*
*1 can (7 oz) oysters, rinsed and*
    *drained*

1. Melt butter in large skillet.

2. With rotary beater, beat eggs with salt and pepper until well combined but not frothy.

3. Pour egg mixture into skillet; cook, over medium heat, until eggs just start to set. Then stir lightly with a fork.

4. When eggs are partially cooked, add oysters; continue cooking, stirring, until eggs are soft and creamy. Serve hot, from a chafing dish.

Makes 6 servings.

## BRIOCHES

*½ cup warm water (105 to 115F)*
*1 pkg active dry yeast*
*¼ cup sugar*
*1 teaspoon salt*
*1 teaspoon grated lemon peel*

*1 cup butter or regular*
    *margarine, softened*
*6 eggs*
*4½ cups sifted all-purpose flour* *
*1 egg yolk*

*\* Sift before measuring.*

1. If possible, check temperature of warm water with thermometer. Sprinkle yeast over water in large bowl of electric mixer; stir until dissolved.

2. Add sugar, salt, lemon peel, butter, 6 eggs, and 3 cups flour; at medium speed, beat 4 minutes. Add remaining flour; at low speed, beat until smooth—about 2 minutes.

3. Cover bowl with waxed paper and damp towel; let rise in warm place (85F), free from drafts, until double in bulk—about 1 hour. Refrigerate, covered, overnight.

4. Next day, grease 24 (3-inch) muffin-pan cups.

5. Stir down dough with wooden spoon (dough will be soft). Turn out onto lightly floured board; divide in half. Return half to bowl; refrigerate until ready to use.

6. Working quickly, shape three fourths of dough on board into a 12-inch roll. With floured knife, cut into 12 pieces. Shape each into a ball; place balls in the prepared muffin cups.

7. Divide remaining fourth of dough into 12 parts; shape into balls. With finger, press indentation in center of each large ball; fill with small ball.

8. Cover with towel; let rise in warm place (85F), free from drafts, until double in bulk—about 1 hour.

9. Meanwhile, shape refrigerated half of dough, and let rise, as directed above.

10. Preheat oven to 400F.

11. Combine egg yolk with 1 tablespoon water; brush on brioches. Bake 15 to 20 minutes, or until golden-brown. Serve hot or cold.

Makes 24 brioches.

# Luncheons

## Menu I

Hot Consommé    Cheese Straws
Curried-Chicken Salad
in Avocado Halves *
Curry Accompaniments
( chutney, salted peanuts,
chopped cucumber, chopped tomato,
kumquats, coconut chips )
Hot Popovers
Peach Sherbet *
Coffee    Iced Tea

### CURRIED-CHICKEN SALAD IN AVOCADO HALVES

4 chicken breasts, split
  (about 3 lbs)
1 medium onion, sliced
1 stalk celery, cut in 1-inch pieces
2½ teaspoons salt
6 whole black peppers
1 bay leaf
1 small pineapple
1 cup mayonnaise or cooked
  salad dressing
½ cup heavy cream

¼ cup chutney
1 tablespoon chopped preserved
  ginger
1 tablespoon curry powder
1 cup thinly sliced celery
¼ cup thinly sliced green onion
4 large ripe avocados
2 tablespoons bottled Italian-
  style dressing
Watercress

1. In a large saucepan, combine chicken breasts, onion, celery pieces, 2 teaspoons salt, the whole peppers, bay leaf, and 4 cups water.

2. Bring to boiling over medium heat. Reduce heat; simmer 30 minutes, or until chicken is tender.

3. Remove from heat; let chicken cool in broth 1 hour, or until cool enough to handle.

4. Remove chicken breasts from broth; remove skin and bones, and discard. Refrigerate chicken, covered, 1 to 2 hours or overnight, until well chilled.

5. Pare and core pineapple; cut fruit into ¾-inch cubes. You should have about 2 cups.

6. In large bowl, combine mayonnaise, heavy cream, chutney, ginger, curry powder, and remaining ½ teaspoon salt until well blended.

7. Cut chicken into ¾-inch cubes. Fold into dressing with sliced celery and green onion. Cover. Refrigerate 2 hours.

8. To serve: Mix pineapple cubes into chicken mixture. Cut avocados in half lengthwise; remove pits. Brush cut surfaces with Italian-style dressing. Fill each half with about 1 cup chilled chicken salad.

9. Arrange around a pineapple on a large tray, or on individual salad plates. Garnish with watercress.

Makes 8 servings.

## PEACH SHERBET

| | |
|---|---|
| 1 env unflavored gelatine | 1 pkg (10 oz) frozen sliced |
| 4 cups milk |    peaches, undrained, puréed |
| 1⅓ cups sugar | 2 tablespoons lemon juice |
| ½ teaspoon salt | Food color (optional) |
| | Almond extract |

1. In small, heavy saucepan, sprinkle gelatine over ½ cup milk; let stand 5 minutes to soften.

2. In medium bowl, combine remaining milk, the sugar, salt and peach purée. Stir until sugar is dissolved. Add lemon juice, 3 drops yellow food color, 1 drop red food color, if desired and ⅛ teaspoon almond extract.

3. Heat gelatine mixture over low heat, stirring constantly until gelatine is dissolved. Remove from heat; slowly stir into mixture in bowl.

4. Turn into 9-by-9-by-1¾-inch square pan. Freeze until frozen 1 inch from edge.

5. Turn into chilled bowl; with electric mixer or rotary beater, beat mixture quickly until smooth but not melted. Return to pan.

6. Freeze several hours, or until firm.

7. To serve: Spoon into sherbet glasses. Return to freezer until ready to serve.

Makes 8 servings.

# Menu II

Salmon Poached in White Wine *
Green Mayonnaise *
Fresh Buttered Peas with Mushrooms
Hot Rolls
Strawberry Flan *
Dry White Wine    Coffee

## SALMON POACHED IN WHITE WINE

*4-lb piece fresh salmon or bass,
    scaled and boned*

**Court Bouillon**
*2 cups Chablis*
*1 cup chopped celery*
*1 small onion, peeled and sliced*
*4 parsley sprigs*
*4 lemon slices*
*1 bay leaf*

*2½ teaspoons salt*

*4 env unflavored gelatine*
*1 cup Chablis*
*Large unpitted ripe olives*

*Deviled eggs or sliced hard-
    cooked eggs*
*Watercress*

1. Day before serving: Wipe salmon inside and out with damp paper towel. Wrap in double thickness of cheesecloth.

2. Prepare Court Bouillon: In large roasting pan, combine 2 quarts water with 2 cups Chablis, the celery, onion, parsley, lemon, bay leaf, and salt. Add salmon to pan; cover tightly, using foil if necessary.

3. Bring to boiling over medium heat (use 2 burners for more even cooking). Reduce heat, and simmer 35 to 40 minutes. Remove roasting pan from heat.

4. Carefully remove 2 cups Court Bouillon from pan; strain through a triple thickness of cheesecloth. Refrigerate.

5. Using broad spatulas, carefully turn over salmon in pan. Cover

loosely with foil; let stand until completely cool. Then remove fish from liquid; discard cheesecloth and remaining Court Bouillon. Place fish on wire rack. Refrigerate, covered with plastic film, overnight.

6. Early next day: Sprinkle gelatine over 1 cup cold water; let stand to soften.

7. In large saucepan, combine 1 quart water, the reserved Court Bouillon, and 1 cup Chablis; bring to boiling. Add softened gelatine, stirring until gelatine is dissolved. Remove from heat.

8. Set aside 2 cups gelatine mixture for decorating fish. Pour the rest into a 13-by-9-by-2-inch baking dish. Refrigerate until the gelatine mixture is firm.

9. Now decorate fish: Using tip of sharp knife, carefully cut off outer black covering of olives, removing as little olive meat as possible. Cut olive meat into crescent or diamond shapes with aspic cutter.

10. Using tip of sharp knife, make two cuts the length of fish; begin about 3 inches apart, and taper to about 1 inch. Carefully remove skin and fatty layer between cuts. Set fish on wire rack on a tray.

11. Place some of reserved gelatine mixture over ice cubes; let stand, stirring occasionally, just until consistency of unbeaten egg white. Carefully brush over salmon, to make a thin glaze.

12. Decorate salmon with olive cutouts. Carefully spoon remaining thickened gelatine mixture over top and sides of salmon, to glaze evenly. Refrigerate until serving time.

13. To serve: Put gelatine mixture in baking dish through ricer. Arrange fish on serving tray; surround with riced gelatine. Garnish with deviled eggs and watercress.

Makes 8 servings.

---

## GREEN MAYONNAISE

*1½ cups mayonnaise or cooked*
*salad dressing*
*1 cup torn raw spinach*
*¼ cup parsley sprigs (no stems)*

*¼ cup watercress (no stems)*
*1 tablespoon chives*
*2 tablespoons dry white wine*

1. Day before serving: Place half of all ingredients in electric blender; cover; blend at high speed until smooth. Add remaining ingredients, and blend well.

2. Refrigerate, covered, overnight.

3. To serve: Spoon into bowl, and pass with Salmon Poached in White Wine.

Makes 1⅔ cups.

*Note:* If blender is not available, chop spinach, parsley, watercress, and chives very finely; then mix well with mayonnaise and wine.

---

## STRAWBERRY FLAN

**Flan Shell:**
¼ cup butter or regular
   margarine, softened
2 tablespoons granulated sugar
3 tablespoons almond paste
½ teaspoon grated lemon peel
1 egg white
¾ cup sifted all-purpose flour *

**Rum Cream:**
1 teaspoon unflavored gelatine
2 tablespoons granulated sugar

* *Sift before measuring.*

2 tablespoons flour
Salt
1 egg yolk
½ cup milk
2 tablespoons rum
1 egg white, stiffly beaten
½ cup heavy cream
1 tablespoon confectioners' sugar
1 inch vanilla bean, scraped

1½ pint boxes strawberries,
   washed and hulled
Currant-Jelly Glaze, below

1. Make Flan Shell: Grease and lightly flour an 8-by-1½-inch round layer-cake pan.

2. In a medium bowl, with electric mixer at medium speed, cream butter with 2 tablespoons granulated sugar, the almond paste, and lemon peel until well combined.

3. Add 1 egg white; beat at high speed until smooth. Gradually beat in ¾ cup flour until well blended. Turn into prepared pan; pat evenly over bottom and side. (If too soft to work with, refrigerate 10 minutes.) Refrigerate 1 hour or longer.

4. Preheat oven to 300F. Bake shell 50 minutes, or until golden-brown. Let cool in pan on wire rack 15 minutes; then gently turn out onto rack, and let cool completely.

5. Make Rum Cream: In small saucepan, mix gelatine, granulated sugar, flour, and dash salt; mix well.

6. Beat egg yolk with milk and rum. Add to gelatine mixture; cook over medium heat, stirring constantly with wire whisk, until mixture is thickened and comes to boiling.

7. Pour into medium bowl; set bowl in pan of ice and water; let stand, stirring occasionally, until mixture begins to set—about 8 to 10 minutes. Fold in beaten egg white.

8. Beat cream with confectioners' sugar; fold into gelatine mixture. Stir in scraped vanilla bean. Spread evenly over flan shell. Refrigerate 30 minutes.

9. Arrange berries on rum cream in shell; brush with Currant-Jelly Glaze. Refrigerate until serving.

Makes 8 servings.

**Currant-Jelly Glaze**                    *½ tablespoon kirsch*
*¼ cup red-currant jelly*

1. In small saucepan, over moderate heat, stir currant jelly until melted. Remove from heat.

2. Stir in kirsch. Use warm, on berries. (If glaze becomes too thick, reheat gently, and add a little hot water.)

# Menu III

Tomato Bisque
Warm Asparagus-and-Swiss-Cheese Tart *
Tossed Green Salad Bowl
Hot Rolls
Lime Sherbet *
Ladyfingers
Tea      Coffee

## ASPARAGUS-AND-SWISS-CHEESE TART

*1 pkg (11 oz) piecrust mix*          *¼ teaspoon nutmeg*
*1 pkg (10 oz) frozen cut*            *1 teaspoon salt*
*  asparagus*                         *2¼ cups coarsely grated natural*
*1½ cups heavy cream*                 *  Swiss cheese*
*2 eggs*

1. Preheat oven to 450F.

2. Prepare piecrust as the label directs. On floured pastry cloth, with a stockinette-covered rolling pin, roll pastry to form 13-inch circle. Use to line an 11-inch pie plate. Flute edge.

2. Prick bottom and side of pastry all over with fork. Bake 10 minutes; prick again if necessary. Let cool. Reduce oven temperature to 375F.

3. Pour ½ cup boiling water over asparagus in medium saucepan; return to boiling. Boil, covered, 5 minutes, or until tender. Drain. Dry on paper towels to remove excess moisture.

4. Place in blender with cream, eggs, nutmeg, and salt; blend at high speed 1 minute, or until smooth. Stir in 1½ cups grated cheese to mix well.

5. Turn into pastry shell. Bake 20 minutes. Remove from oven. Sprinkle remaining ¼ cup grated cheese over top, forming a lattice pattern. Return to oven about 3 minutes, or until cheese melts slightly. Serve warm.

Makes 6 servings.

## LIME SHERBET

| | |
|---|---|
| *1 envelope unflavored gelatine* | *2 cups light cream* |
| *2 cups milk* | *½ cup lime juice* |
| *1½ cups sugar* | *¼ cup lemon juice* |
| *½ teaspoon salt* | *2 tablespoons grated lemon peel* |

1. In small heavy saucepan, sprinkle gelatine over ½ cup milk to soften.

2. In medium bowl combine remaining milk, sugar, salt, and cream. Stir until sugar is dissolved. Stir in lime juice, lemon juice, and peel.

3. Heat gelatine mixture over low heat, stirring constantly until gelatine is dissolved. Remove from heat; slowly stir into mixture in bowl.

4. Turn into ice-cube tray; freeze until frozen 1 inch in from edge.

5. Turn into chilled bowl; with electric mixer or rotary beater beat mixture quickly until smooth but not melted. Return to ice-cube tray.

6. Freeze several hours or until firm.

7. To serve: Spoon into sherbet glasses.

Makes 6 servings.

# Menu IV

Shrimp Salad Orientale *
French Bread
Lemon Chiffon Pie *

## SHRIMP SALAD ORIENTALE

*1 honeydew melon*
*1 cup cantaloupe balls*
*¾ cup seedless green grapes*
*½ cup celery, cut into ½-inch*
*    cubes*
*Boiled Shrimp, below*

*1 cup mayonnaise or cooked*
*    salad dressing*
*¼ cup chutney, chopped*
*1½ tablespoons lemon juice*
*1½ teaspoons soy sauce*
*½ teaspoon salt*
*Dash pepper*

1. Using a sharp knife, cut lengthwise through honeydew melon, two thirds of the way up, making a zigzag edge. Scoop out flesh from larger half to make 1 cup of melon balls (save rest for later use). Refrigerate shell, to use as serving dish for salad.

2. In large bowl, combine honeydew and cantaloupe balls, grapes, celery and the shrimp, split in half (reserve 3 whole shrimp for garnish); refrigerate.

3. In small bowl, combine mayonnaise, chutney, lemon juice, soy sauce, salt and pepper; mix well. Refrigerate, covered, until chilled— 1 hour.

4. To serve: Add dressing to shrimp-fruit mixture; toss gently. Spoon into honeydew-melon shell, mounding. Garnish top with whole shrimp.

Makes 4 servings.

**Boiled Shrimp**
*½ lb unshelled raw shrimp*
*½ small onion, peeled and thinly*
*    sliced*

*1 sprig parsley*
*½ tablespoon salt*
*½ bay leaf*
*1 slice lemon*

1. Rinse shrimp; remove shells and devein: Using a small sharp knife, slit each shrimp down back; lift out sand vein.

2. In medium skillet, combine 2 cups water, the onion, parsley, salt, bay leaf, lemon. Bring to boiling, covered, over medium heat; simmer 10 minutes.

3. Add shrimp; return to boiling. Reduce heat and simmer, covered, 3 to 5 minutes, or just until tender.

4. Drain; let cool. Refrigerate, covered, until ready to use.

## LEMON CHIFFON PIE

9-inch baked pie shell or
    *unbaked graham-cracker crust*
*4 egg whites*
*1 envelope unflavored gelatine*
*4 egg yolks*
*½ cup lemon juice*

*1 cup granulated sugar*
*¼ teaspoon salt*
*1 tablespoon grated lemon peel*
*Yellow food color (optional)*
*1 cup heavy cream*
*Confectioners' sugar*

1. Prepare and bake pie shell; let cool completely before filling. In large bowl, let egg whites warm to room temperature—about 1 hour.

2. Sprinkle gelatine over ¼ cup cold water, to soften; set aside. With wooden spoon, beat yolks slightly. Stir in lemon juice, ½ cup sugar, and the salt.

3. Cook, stirring, over hot, not boiling, water (water should not touch bottom of double-boiler top) until mixture thickens and forms coating on metal spoon—8 to 10 minutes.

4. Add gelatine; stir to dissolve. Add lemon peel, 2 drops color, if desired. Remove from water.

5. Turn into medium bowl; set in a larger bowl of ice cubes to chill, stirring occasionally, until as thick as unbeaten egg white—10 minutes.

6. Meanwhile, beat whites at high speed until soft peaks form when beater is slowly raised (peaks bend slightly).

7. Beat in ½ cup sugar, 2 tablespoons at a time, beating after each addition. Beat until stiff peaks form when beater is raised.

8. With rotary beater, beat ½ cup cream until stiff. With wire whisk, gently fold gelatine mixture into whites just until combined. Gently fold in whipped cream. Mound high in pie shell. Refrigerate until firm—3 hours.

9. Beat ½ cup cream with 2 tablespoons confectioners' sugar until stiff. Turn into pastry bag with number-5 tip; make lattice on top, rosettes around edge.

Serves 8.

# Tea and Coffee Parties

## Tea Sandwiches, Petits Fours, Tartlets and Confections

### LOBSTER-SALAD-AND-CUCUMBER SANDWICHES

3 (8-oz size) frozen lobster tails
Salt
1 tablespoon chopped chives
½ cup mayonnaise

1 loaf (1 lb) unsliced white bread
3 tablespoons soft butter or
   margarine
24 thin slices unpared cucumber

1. In large saucepan, bring 1 quart water to boiling. Add lobster tails and ½ teaspoon salt; return to boiling; boil 7 to 10 minutes. Drain. cool; refrigerate.

2. Several hours before serving: Remove lobster meat from shells; chop medium fine. Add chives, ¼ teaspoon salt, and the mayonnaise; mix well. Refrigerate while preparing bread rounds.

3. With sharp knife, trim crusts from bread. Slice lengthwise into ¼-inch-thick slices. With 2-inch cutter, cut out 24 rounds.

4. Spread bread rounds lightly with butter. Top each with a cucumber slice, then with a mound of lobster salad.

5. To store: Arrange in shallow pan. Cover with damp paper towels, then with plastic film. Refrigerate until serving.

Makes 24.

## ROLLED WATERCRESS SANDWICHES

1 large bunch watercress
¾ cup soft butter or margarine
¼ teaspoon salt

1 tablespoon lemon juice
1½ loaves (1-lb size) thinly sliced
   white bread

1. Wash and drain watercress. Reserve small center sprigs for garnish—about 50.
2. Remove stems from remaining watercress. Finely chop enough watercress to measure ½ cup.
3. Beat butter and salt with electric mixer until smooth. Gradually beat in lemon juice. Then beat in chopped watercress.
4. With sharp knife, trim crusts from bread. Roll each slice lightly with rolling pin.
5. Spread bread slices evenly with watercress butter, using about 1½ teaspoons for each. Roll up, jellyroll fashion. Trim ends. Insert a reserved watercress sprig in each end.
6. Refrigerate, between damp paper towels, until serving. (Sandwiches may be made several hours ahead and stored this way.)
Makes about 25.

## TOMATO-CURRY ROUNDS

2 loaves (1-lb size) unsliced
   white bread
3 tablespoons soft butter or
   margarine
½ teaspoon lemon juice

¼ teaspoon curry powder
Dash salt
3 large tomatoes, washed and
   very thinly sliced

1. With sharp knife, trim crusts from bread. Slice lengthwise into ¼-inch-thick slices. Using a 2-inch scalloped cookie cutter, cut into 48 rounds.
2. With truffle cutter or sharp knife, remove and discard a small scalloped round, about ¾ inch in diameter, from center of 24 bread rounds. Cover all rounds with damp paper towels.
3. In small bowl, combine butter, lemon juice, curry powder, and salt; mix well. Spread over the 24 uncut bread rounds.
4. Using same 2-inch scalloped cutter, cut 24 tomato rounds. Place tomato rounds on bread. Top with cutout bread rounds; press together lightly.

5. To store: Arrange in shallow pan. Cover with damp paper towels, then with plastic film. Refrigerate until serving.
Makes 24.

―――――

## CREAM-CHEESE-AND-OLIVE RIBBON SANDWICHES

*1 pkg (8 oz) soft cream cheese*
*2 tablespoons mayonnaise*
*⅓ cup chopped pimiento-stuffed*
  *olives*

*½ cup soft butter or margarine*
*12 thin slices white bread*
*12 thin slices whole-wheat bread*

1. In medium bowl, combine cream cheese, mayonnaise, and chopped olives. Blend well with wooden spoon.
2. Lightly butter 8 slices of white bread and 4 slices of whole-wheat bread. Spread 4 of the buttered white-bread slices and the buttered whole-wheat-bread slices with cream-cheese mixture, using about 2 teaspoons for each slice.
3. To make ribbon sandwiches: Place whole-wheat slices, cheese side up, on white slices, cheese side up. Top with 4 buttered white slices, buttered side down. With sharp knife, trim crusts from each stack. Cut each stack into 6 strips, or ribbons. Keep sandwiches covered with damp paper towels, to prevent drying out.
4. Repeat with rest of bread, butter, and cheese-olive mixture. Place whole-wheat slices on top and bottom this time.
5. To store: Arrange close together in shallow pan. Cover with damp paper towels, then with plastic film. Refrigerate until serving.
Makes 48.

―――――

## PETITS FOURS

*2 pkg (1-lb, 1-oz size) poundcake*
  *mix*
*4 eggs*
*Apricot Glaze, below*

*Fondant Frosting, below*
*Pink and green cake-decorating*
  *tubes*

1. Preheat oven to 350F. Lightly grease and flour a 15½-by-10½-by-1-inch jelly-roll pan.
2. Prepare both packages of pound-cake mix as package label directs, using 4 eggs and liquid called for.
3. Turn into prepared pan. Bake 30 to 35 minutes, or until top springs back when pressed with fingertip.

4. Cool 10 minutes in pan. Turn out on wire rack; let cool completely.

5. Meanwhile, make Apricot Glaze and Fondant Frosting.

6. Using a 2-inch cookie cutter, cut out diamond, heart and round shapes from cooled cake. (You'll have 32 or 33.)

7. To glaze cakes: Place on fork, one at a time. Hold over bowl of glaze, and spoon glaze over cake, completely covering top and sides.

8. Place cakes, uncoated side down and 2 inches apart, on wire racks placed on cookie sheets. Let stand until glaze is set—at least 1 hour.

9. To frost: Place glazed cakes on fork, one at a time. Spoon frosting over cake, to run over top and down side evenly. Frost half of cakes white and half pink.

10. Let cakes dry completely on wire racks—about one hour. Repeat frosting, if necessary. Let dry.

11. To decorate: Make little posies and leaves with decorating tubes, or drizzle any remaining frosting over tops. Refrigerate several hours. Let stand at room temperature 1 hour.

Makes 32 or 33.

**Apricot Glaze** ½ cup sugar
1½ cups apricot preserves

1. In medium saucepan, combine preserves, sugar and ½ cup water; bring to boiling over medium heat. Boil, stirring, 5 minutes.

2. Remove from heat. Press through sieve into a bowl.

Makes 1½ cups.

**Fondant Frosting** About 2¼ cups sifted (see Note)
2¾ cups granulated sugar confectioners' sugar
Dash salt ½ teaspoon almond extract
¼ teaspoon cream of tartar Food color (optional)

1. In medium saucepan, combine granulated sugar, salt and cream of tartar with 1½ cups water. Over low heat, cook, stirring, until sugar is dissolved.

2. Over medium heat, cook, without stirring, to 226F on candy thermometer.

3. Transfer to top of double boiler; let cool to lukewarm (110F on candy thermometer).

4. With wooden spoon, gradually beat in just enough confectioners' sugar to make frosting thick enough to coat spoon but thin enough to

pour. Add almond extract. Remove half of frosting (about 1½ cups) to small bowl. Add a few drops food color, to tint a delicate color.

5. Keep white frosting over hot, not boiling, water, to keep thin enough to pour. If frosting is too thin, add a little more confectioners' sugar; if too thick, thin with a little warm water. After using white frosting, heat tinted frosting, and use in same way.

Makes 3 cups.

*Note:* Sift sugar before measuring.

---

## STRAWBERRY CREAM PUFFS

**Cream-Puff Dough**
¼ cup butter or margarine
⅛ teaspoon salt
½ cup sifted * all-purpose flour
2 large eggs

\* Sift before measuring.

**Filling**
½ cup heavy cream
2 tablespoons confectioners'
   sugar
¼ teaspoon vanilla extract
36 medium strawberries, washed
   and hulled
Confectioners' sugar

1. Preheat oven to 400F. Make cream-puff dough: In small saucepan, slowly bring ½ cup water with the butter and salt to boiling.

2. Remove from heat. With wooden spoon, beat in flour all at once.

3. Return to low heat; continue beating until mixture forms ball and leaves side of pan.

4. Remove from heat. Beat in eggs, one at a time, beating hard after each addition until smooth.

5. Continue beating until dough is shiny and breaks into strands.

6. For cream puffs, drop dough by slightly rounded teaspoonfuls, 2 inches apart, onto ungreased cookie sheet.

7. Bake until puffed and golden-brown—20 to 25 minutes.

8. Let cool completely on wire rack, away from drafts.

9. Meanwhile, beat cream with 2 tablespoons confectioners' sugar until stiff. Stir in vanilla extract. Refrigerate, covered.

10. With sharp knife, cut a slice from top of each puff. Fill each with a scant teaspoonful of whipped cream; press a strawberry into each; replace top. Refrigerate if not serving at once.

11. To serve: Sprinkle with confectioners sugar.

Makes 36 cream puffs.

————

# COFFEE ÉCLAIRS

*Cream-Puff Dough (see recipe for Strawberry Cream Puffs, above)*

**Filling**

*½ cup heavy cream*
*2 tablespoons confectioners' sugar*
*½ teaspoon powdered instant coffee*

*¼ teaspoon vanilla extract*

*Coffee Frosting, below*
*Chocolate Frosting, below*

1. Preheat oven to 400F. Make cream-puff dough.

2. For éclairs, put cream-puff dough into small pastry bag with round decorating tip, ½ inch in diameter. On an ungreased cookie sheet, 2 inches apart, press mixture in 2-inch strips.

3. Bake 20 to 25 minutes, or until golden-brown.

4. Let cool completely on wire rack, away from drafts.

5. Make filling: Beat cream with sugar, coffee and vanilla just until stiff. Refrigerate, covered, until ready to use.

6. With sharp knife, cut a slice from top of each éclair. Fill each with a scant teaspoon of filling; replace tops.

7. To decorate: Frost tops with Coffee Frosting. To make a spiral effect, put Chocolate Frosting through a small pastry bag with a plain decorating tip for writing; decorate.

8. Refrigerate until serving.

Makes 32 éclairs.

**Coffee Frosting**

*2½ cups sifted * confectioners' sugar*

*2 tablespoons light corn syrup*
*1 teaspoon vanilla extract*
*1 teaspoon powdered instant coffee*

* *Sift before measuring.*

1. In top of double boiler, combine all ingredients with 2 tablespoons water.

2. Stir over hot, not boiling, water just until frosting becomes smooth and shiny and coats a wooden spoon. Remove from hot water.

3. If frosting thickens on standing, thin it with a little water.

Makes about 1 cup.

**Chocolate Frosting**
*1 tablespoon butter or margarine*
*2½ tablespoons sugar*

*1 square unsweetened chocolate*
*½ teaspoon vanilla extract*

1. In small saucepan, combine butter, sugar, chocolate and 2 tablespoons water.

2. Stir over medium heat, until chocolate melts and mixture is smooth and just starts to boil. Remove from heat.

3. Add vanilla; let stand 2 minutes before using. Makes ⅓ cup.

## MADELONS

Cream-Puff Dough, *page 194*
*½ cup heavy cream*
*2 tablespoons confectioners'*
  *sugar*

*½ teaspoon vanilla extract*
*¾ cup cherry preserves*
*Confectioners' sugar*

1. Preheat oven to 400F. Make cream-puff dough.

2. Place dough in pastry bag with number-6 star tip. Pipe the dough, 2 inches apart, onto ungreased cookie sheet, to make 12 S shapes 3 inches long.

3. Bake 25 to 30 minutes, or until they are puffed and deep golden-brown. Remove to wire rack; cool completely.

4. Meanwhile, beat cream with 2 tablespoons sugar and the vanilla until stiff. Refrigerate, covered.

5. To assemble madelons: With sharp knife, cut each S-shape puff in half crosswise. Scoop out any filaments of soft dough.

6. Spoon 1 tablespoon cherry preserves into each bottom half, then a rounded tablespoon of whipped cream. Replace top. Sprinkle with confectioners' sugar. Refrigerate if not serving at once.

Makes 12.

## JEWEL COOKIES

½ cup butter or margarine,
   softened
¼ cup light-brown sugar, firmly
   packed
1 egg yolk
1 teaspoon vanilla extract
1 cup sifted * all-purpose flour
1 egg white, slightly beaten

½ cup finely chopped walnuts or
   pecans

4 tablespoons confectioners'
   sugar
2 teaspoons milk
3 tablespoons apricot preserves

* Sift before measuring.

1. In medium bowl, with wooden spoon, beat butter, brown sugar, egg yolk and vanilla until smooth.

2. Stir in flour just until combined. Refrigerate 30 minutes.

3. Meanwhile, preheat oven to 375F. Using hands, roll dough into balls ½ inch in diameter. Dip in egg white; then roll in chopped nuts.

4. Place, 1 inch apart, on ungreased cookie sheets. With thimble or thumb, press center of each cookie.

5. Bake 8 minutes, or just until a delicate golden-brown. Remove to wire rack; cool.

6. Meanwhile, in small bowl, combine confectioners' sugar and milk, mixing well.

7. Place ⅛ teaspoon icing in center of each cookie; top with a little of the apricot preserves.

Makes 4 dozen.

## ALMOND TILE COOKIES

⅓ cup egg whites
½ cup sugar
¼ teaspoon vanilla extract
3 tablespoons butter or
   margarine, melted

3 tablespoons flour
½ cup sliced blanched almonds

1. Preheat oven to 375F. Grease a large cookie sheet with salad oil; then dust with flour ( omit if using a pan with nonstick coating).

2. In medium bowl, combine egg whites, sugar and vanilla; beat with wire whisk about 2 minutes, or until sugar is dissolved and mixture is syrupy.

3. Add melted butter and flour; beat until smooth. Stir in almonds.

4. Drop by one-half teaspoonfuls, about 4 inches apart, onto prepared cookie sheet. With small spatula, spread each to a 1½-inch round. Make no more than eight at a time.

5. Bake 5 minutes, or until cookies are golden-brown around edge and very lightly browned in center.

6. With small spatula, carefully remove cookies at once, and place over rolling pin, to curve them. (If cookies get too cool, return to oven just until hot and soft again.)

7. Repeat with remaining batter, oiling and flouring cookie sheet each time.

Makes about 5 dozen.

## FONDANT-DIPPED STRAWBERRIES

2 pint boxes large strawberries
2½ cups confectioners' sugar
3 tablespoons lemon juice

2 tablespoons light corn syrup
4 drops red food color

1. Wash strawberries gently; drain well on paper towels. Leave hulls and stems on.

2. In top of double boiler, combine sugar, lemon juice, and corn syrup. Cook, stirring, over hot water until mixture is smooth and shiny and thin enough to coat strawberries. Tint a delicate pink with food color. Remove from heat; keep warm over hot water.

3. Holding each strawberry by the stem, dip into fondant, covering berry. Place dipped berries, hull end down, 2 inches apart, on wire racks placed on cookie sheets.

4. Let strawberries dry on racks at least 1 hour before serving. (Strawberries can be dipped in the morning for serving later in the day; but do not hold overnight.)

Makes about 30.

## PECAN TARTLETS

1 pkg (9½ or 11 oz) piecrust mix

**Filling**
2 eggs
½ cup sugar
⅓ cup light corn syrup
2 tablespoons golden rum

1 teaspoon flour
½ teaspoon salt
½ teaspoon vanilla extract
2 tablespoons butter or regular
  margarine, melted
1 cup pecan halves

1. Prepare piecrust mix as package label directs. Divide in half. Using palms of hands, roll each half into a 15-inch-long roll. Cut roll into 15 pieces. Press each piece evenly into a shallow 2-inch tart pan, to line pan. Refrigerate while making filling.

2. Preheat oven to 350F.

3. Make Filling: In medium bowl, with rotary beater, beat eggs.

4. Add sugar, syrup, rum, flour, salt, and vanilla; beat until well combined. Stir in butter and pecans, mixing well.

5. Spoon about 1 tablespoon filling into each pastry-lined pan.

6. Bake 20 to 25 minutes, or until filling is firm and golden.

7. Let tarts cool in pans on wire rack at least 10 minutes, or until completely cool.

Makes 30 tarts.

―――――

## FRUIT TARTLETS

**Tart Shells**
*1 pkg (11 oz) piecrust mix*

**Pastry Cream**
*1 pkg (3½ oz) vanilla-pudding-*
*  and-pie-filling mix*
*1½ cups milk*
*½ teaspoon vanilla extract*

*½ cup heavy cream*
*Fruits: Sliced strawberries, red*
*  raspberries, sliced bananas,*
*  canned apricot halves, pine-*
*  apple tidbits, Mirabelle plums,*
*  mandarin-orange sections*
*Apricot Glaze, below*
*Red-Currant Glaze, below*

1. Make Tart Shells: Prepare piecrust mix as package label directs. Shape into a ball.

2. For each tart, use 2 teaspoons dough. Press evenly into assorted 2½- to 3-inch tart pans. Set pans on cookie sheet. Refrigerate 30 minutes.

3. Make Pastry Cream: Prepare pudding mix as package label directs, using 1½ cups milk instead of the 2 cups called for. Bring to boiling; remove from heat. Stir in vanilla. Turn into bowl; cover surface with waxed paper. Refrigerate until well chilled.

4. Preheat oven to 375F. Bake tart shells 12 to 15 minutes, or until light golden. Cool in pans on wire rack a few minutes. Loosen around edges with small knife, and turn out. Cool completely before filling.

5. Beat heavy cream until stiff. Fold into chilled vanilla pudding.

6. Half fill each tart shell with pastry cream. Refrigerate while making glazes.

7. Top with fruit. (Drain fruits very well before using.) Brush yellow or light fruit with warm Apricot Glaze, red fruit with warm Red-Currant Glaze.

8. Refrigerate until ready to serve.

Makes 24 tarts.

*Note:* If desired, make tart shells and cook pudding day before. Several hours before serving, fold cream into pudding and assemble tarts.

**Apricot Glaze**
*½ cup apricot preserves*

1. In small saucepan, over medium heat, stir preserves until melted. If preserves seem too thick, thin with ½ to 1 tablespoon hot water.

2. Strain. Use warm.

Makes about ½ cup, enough to glaze 12 tarts.

**Red-Currant Glaze**                  *1 tablespoon kirsch or sherry*
*½ cup red-currant jelly*

1. In small saucepan, over medium heat, stir jelly until melted. Remove from heat.

2. Stir in kirsch. Use warm. If glaze becomes too thick, reheat gently, and add a little hot water.

Makes about ½ cup, enough to glaze 12 tarts.

## LEMON SANDBAKELS

*½ cup butter or regular
   margarine, softened*
*1 cup unsifted all-purpose flour*
*¼ cup sugar*
*1 egg yolk*
*2 tablespoons ground blanched
   almonds*
*½ teaspoon almond extract*

**Lemon Filling**
*1 egg*
*1 egg yolk*
*½ cup sugar*
*¼ cup butter or regular
   margarine*
*1 tablespoon grated lemon peel*
*¼ cup lemon juice*

*Flaked coconut*

1. Preheat oven to 400F.

2. In medium bowl, with pastry blender, cut ½ cup soft butter into the flour and ¼ cup sugar until mixture resembles coarse crumbs.

3. Add 1 egg yolk, the almonds and almond extract; stir with fork until well blended. Press one teaspoon of mixture into each (1¾-inch) fluted tart pan. Arrange on cookie sheet.

4. Bake 8 to 10 minutes, or until golden. Remove to wire rack. Let

cool about 5 minutes. Loosen around side with small spatula and turn out of pans. Let cool on wire rack.

5. Meanwhile, make lemon filling: In top of double boiler, combine 1 whole egg and the egg yolk; beat with spoon just until blended. Add sugar, butter, lemon peel and lemon juice.

6. Cook over hot, not boiling, water, stirring constantly, until consistency of mayonnaise—about 10 minutes. Turn into small bowl; place waxed paper directly on surface. Refrigerate until well chilled.

7. Just before serving, fill each tart shell with 1 teaspoonful of lemon filling. Sprinkle with coconut.

Makes 3½ dozen.

## MAIDS-OF-HONOR TARTLETS

½ pkg (11-oz size) piecrust mix

**Almond Topping**
1 egg white
Dash salt
½ cup confectioners' sugar
½ cup ground blanched almonds

¼ teaspoon almond or vanilla
   extract

⅓ cup raspberry or cherry jam
Sliced unblanched almonds

1. Make pastry as label directs.
2. Press 1 teaspoon of dough into each (2-inch) fluted tart pan. Chill.
3. Preheat oven to 375F.
4. Make almond topping: In small bowl of electric mixer, beat egg white with salt until soft peaks form when beater is slowly raised. Gradually beat in confectioners' sugar, 2 tablespoons at a time, beating well after each addition; continue beating until well blended and thick. Stir in almonds and extract.
5. Spoon ½ teaspoon jam into each pastry-lined tart pan. Spoon 1 teaspoon almond topping over jam; decorate each with a sliced almond.
6. Bake 25 to 30 minutes, or until topping is puffy and golden. Carefully remove from pans to wire rack; cool completely.

Makes 26.

## ROSETTES OR BUTTERFLIES

Salad oil or shortening for
   deep-frying
1 egg
1 cup milk

½ teaspoon salt
1 cup unsifted all-purpose flour
2 tablespoons granulated sugar
Confectioners' sugar

1. In large saucepan or Dutch oven, slowly heat at least 2 inches oil to 375F on deep-frying thermometer.

2. In medium bowl, beat egg with milk and salt until well blended. Gradually beat in flour, then granulated sugar, beating until batter is smooth.

3. Preheat rosette or butterfly timbale iron in hot oil 30 seconds. Shake off excess oil.

4. Dip hot iron in batter just until batter comes to top of iron, not over top; hold 15 seconds.

5. Immeditely immerse batter-coated iron in hot fat. As soon as rosette begins to brown, lift iron, and let rosette drop into hot oil. Let brown ½ minute; turn, and brown other side.

6. Drain well on paper towels. Repeat until all batter is used.

7. To serve: Sprinkle liberally with confectioners' sugar.
Makes about 30.

## DUNDEE CAKE

2 cups sifted * all-purpose flour
1 teaspoon baking powder
½ teaspoon salt
⅛ teaspoon nutmeg
1 cup dried currants
¾ cup diced mixed candied fruits
   and peels
¾ cup seeded dark raisins

½ cup light raisins
¼ cup candied cherries, halved
¾ cup butter or regular
   margarine, softened
⅔ cup sugar
3 eggs
3 tablespoons sliced blanched
   almonds

* Sift before measuring.

1. Preheat oven to 325F. Grease well a 9-inch tube pan.

2. Reserve 2 tablespoons flour. Sift remaining flour with baking powder, salt, and nutmeg. Set aside.

3. In medium bowl, combine currants, candied fruits and peels, raisins, cherries, and reserved flour; mix well. Set aside.

4. In large bowl, with electric mixer at medium speed, beat butter with sugar until light and fluffy. Add eggs, one at a time, beating well after each addition.

5. At low speed, gradually add flour mixture, beating until well combined.

6. Stir fruit mixture into batter until combined. Turn into prepared pan; smooth top with spatula. Sprinkle with almonds; gently press into top.

7. Bake 60 to 65 minutes, or until cake tester inserted in center comes out clean. Let cool in pan on wire rack 15 minutes. Remove from pan; let cool completely.

Makes a 9-inch tube cake.

## WALNUT POUNDCAKE LOAF

| | |
|---|---|
| *5 eggs* | *1 cup butter or regular* |
| *1½ cups sifted * all-purpose flour* | *margarine* |
| *½ teaspoon baking powder* | *½ teaspoon vanilla extract* |
| | *1 cup sugar* |
| *\* Sift before measuring.* | *¾ cup finely chopped walnuts* |

1. Preheat oven to 325F. Grease well and flour 9-by-5-by-3-inch loaf pan.

2. Separate eggs, putting whites in large bowl.

3. Sift flour with baking powder; set aside.

4. In large bowl of electric mixer, at medium speed, cream butter and vanilla until light. Gradually add ½ cup sugar, beating until very light and fluffy.

5. Then add egg yolks, one at a time, beating well after each addition.

6. At low speed, beat in flour mixture only until combined. Stir in walnuts.

7. Beat egg whites, with rotary beater or portable electric mixer, just until soft peaks form when beater is slowly raised.

8. Add remaining sugar, 2 tablespoons at a time, beating until stiff peaks form when beater is slowly raised.

9. With wire whisk or rubber scraper, using an under-and-over motion, gently fold egg whites into batter just until combined.

10. Pour batter into prepared pan; bake 1 hour and 10 minutes, or until cake tester inserted in center comes out clean.

11. Cool in pan, on wire rack, 15 minutes. Then turn out on rack, cool completely. To serve, slice thinly.

Makes one loaf.

# To Serve
# with Coffee

Rolls and Coffee Cake
for Morning Coffee
Hearty Sandwiches and
Cakes for Evening

### BASIC SWEET-ROLL DOUGH

¾ cup milk
½ cup sugar
2 teaspoons salt
¾ cup sweet butter or
   regular margarine
½ cup warm water (105 to 115F)

2 pkg active dry yeast
2 eggs
4¾ cups unsifted all-purpose
   flour
Sweet butter or regular
   margarine, softened

1. In small saucepan, heat milk just until bubbles form around edge of pan; remove from heat. Add sugar, salt and ¾ cup butter, stirring until butter is melted. Let cool to lukewarm (a drop sprinkled on wrist will not feel warm).

2. If possible, check temperature of warm water with thermometer. Pour into large, warm bowl. Sprinkle the yeast over the water, and stir to dissolve.

3. Add milk mixture, eggs and 3 cups flour; beat with electric mixer until smooth—about 2 minutes. Add rest of flour; using wooden spoon, beat until dough is smooth and leaves side of bowl. Brush with soft butter.

4. Cover the bowl tightly with foil; refrigerate 2 hours, or until double in bulk. (This dough may be refrigerated up to three days.)

5. To use: Cut off amount needed; refrigerate the remainder. Shape and bake as directed.

Makes 2 dozen rolls.

## CHEESE SWIRLS

**Cheese Filling**
½ cup creamed small-curd
    cottage cheese
2 tablespoons sugar
1 tablespoon flour
1 egg yolk

½ teaspoon grated lemon peel
Dash cinnamon

⅓ recipe Sweet-Roll Dough,
    above
1 egg yolk

1. Lightly grease a large cookie sheet.

2. Make cheese filling: In small bowl, with rubber scraper, cream cottage cheese, sugar and flour. Add egg yolk, lemon peel, cinnamon; mix well.

3. On lightly floured pastry cloth, roll dough into a rectangle 15 by 4 inches.

4. With pastry wheel or sharp knife, cut dough lengthwise into eight ½-inch-wide strips. Twist ends of each strip in opposite directions.

5. On prepared cookie sheet, coil each twisted strip of dough, not too tightly, beginning with one end of strip, to form a round, 2½ to 3 inches in diameter. Seal end firmly underneath.

6. Press with finger to make an indentation in center of each. Fill each with heaping tablespoon of cheese filling.

7. Let rise, uncovered, in a warm place (85F), free from drafts, until double in bulk—about 1 hour. Meanwhile, preheat oven to 350F.

8. With fork, beat egg yolk slightly with 1 tablespoon water. Use to brush tops of rolls.

9. Bake 15 minutes, or until golden-brown. Let cool on wire rack. Makes 8.

## APRICOT SHEATH TARTS

⅓ recipe Sweet-Roll Dough,
  page 204
3 tablespoons sweet butter or
  margarine, melted
¾ cup apricot preserves or orange
  marmalade

Sugar Glaze
½ cup unsifted confectioners'
  sugar
2 teaspoons milk

1. Lightly grease a large cookie sheet.
2. On lightly floured pastry cloth, shape dough into a round.
3. Roll dough into a 16-by-8-inch rectangle. Brush with half of melted butter. With sharp knife or pastry wheel, cut into eight 4-inch squares.
4. Arrange squares, 1½ inches apart, on prepared cookie sheet. In center of each, place a rounded tablespoon of apricot preserves.
5. Bring two diagonally opposite corners to center over filling; pinch together, to seal. Cover loosely with a sheet of waxed paper.
6. Let rise in warm place (85F), free from drafts, until double in bulk—about 45 minutes. Meanwhile, preheat oven to 350F.
7. Brush the tops of tarts with the rest of melted butter.
8. Bake 15 to 20 minutes, or until golden-brown. Let cool slightly on wire rack.
9. Meanwhile, make sugar glaze: In small bowl, combine sugar and milk, mixing until smooth. Using teaspoon, drizzle glaze on top of rolls, going back and forth.
Makes 8.

## WALNUT CRESCENTS

⅓ cup light-brown sugar, packed
⅓ cup finely chopped walnuts
¾ teaspoon cinnamon
⅓ recipe Sweet-Roll Dough,
  page 204

2 tablespoons sweet butter or
  margarine, softened
1 egg yolk
¼ teaspoon cinnamon mixed with
  1 tablespoon granulated sugar

1. Lightly grease a large cookie sheet.
2. In small bowl, toss the brown sugar, chopped walnuts and ¾ teaspoon cinnamon, mixing well.
3. On lightly floured pastry cloth, flatten dough into a round.
4. Roll out dough to a 12-inch circle; brush with butter. Sprinkle

with brown-sugar mixture to within ½ inch of edge. Cut into 8 equal pie-shape wedges.

5. Starting from wide end, roll up each wedge toward point. Place, with center point down, 2 inches apart, on prepared cookie sheet. Curve ends to form crescents.

6. Cover loosely with sheet of waxed paper. Set in warm place (85F), free from drafts, until double in bulk—about 45 minutes. Meanwhile, preheat oven to 350F.

7. With fork, beat egg yolk with 1 tablespoon water. Use to brush tops of rolls. Sprinkle lightly with cinnamon-sugar mixture.

8. Bake 15 minutes, or until golden-brown.

9. Let cool slightly on wire rack.

Makes 8.

## ALMOND HORNS

⅓ recipe Sweet-Roll Dough,
   page 204
2 tablespoons sweet butter or
   margarine, melted
3 tablespoons raspberry or
   strawberry preserves

1 egg yolk
¼ cup toasted sliced almonds or
   chopped peanuts

1. Lightly grease a large cookie sheet.

2. On lightly floured pastry cloth or surface, shape dough into a round.

3. Roll out dough to a 12-inch circle. Brush with melted butter; then spread with the preserves to within ½ inch of the edge.

4. With sharp knife, cut into 8 equal pie-shape wedges. Beginning at narrow end, roll up each wedge to within 1½ inches from edge.

5. Make three or four 1-inch cuts at wide end of each one. Bring up strips over filling. Pinch edges, to seal.

6. Place horns on cookie sheet; cover loosely with sheet of waxed paper.

7. Let rise in warm place (85F), free from drafts, until double in bulk—about 45 minutes. Meanwhile, preheat oven to 350F.

8. With fork, beat egg yolk slightly with 1 tablespoon water. Use to brush tops of rolls. Sprinkle with almonds or peanuts.

9. Bake 15 minutes, or until golden-brown. Let cool on wire rack.

Makes 8.

## CINNAMON BEAR CLAWS

⅓ recipe Sweet-Roll Dough,
    page 204
3 tablespoons sweet butter or
    margarine, melted
½ teaspoon cinnamon mixed with
    2 tablespoons granulated
    sugar
½ cup chopped walnuts or pecans

¼ cup chopped raisins
1 teaspoon grated lemon peel

**Sugar Glaze**
½ cup unsifted confectioners'
    sugar
¼ teaspoon vanilla extract
2 teaspoons milk

1. Lightly grease a large cookie sheet.
2. On lightly floured pastry cloth, shape dough into a round.
3. Roll dough to an 18-by-9-inch rectangle. Brush with half of butter; then sprinkle generously with cinnamon-sugar mixture, leaving a ¼-inch edge all around.
4. Combine walnuts, raisins and lemon peel. Sprinkle evenly over sugared surface.
5. From longer side, fold ⅓ of the dough over. Then bring opposite side over this, to make a 3-layer strip, 18 by 3 inches. Pinch together, to seal.
6. With sharp knife, cut strip crosswise into six sections. On folded side of each, make three 1-inch cuts, evenly spaced.
7. Arrange on prepared cookie sheet. Separate "claws" slightly. Brush tops with rest of butter. Cover loosely with a sheet of waxed paper.
8. Let rise in warm place (85F), free from drafts, until double in bulk—about 45 minutes. Meanwhile, preheat oven to 350F.
9. Bake 15 to 20 minutes, or until golden-brown. Let cool slightly on wire rack.
10. Meanwhile, make sugar glaze: In small bowl, combine confectioners' sugar, vanilla extract and milk; mix well. Drizzle over warm rolls to glaze thinly.
    Makes 6.

## CHERRY PINWHEELS

⅓ recipe Sweet-Roll Dough,
    page 204
Cherry or apricot preserves or
    prune butter

1 egg yolk

1. Lightly grease a large cookie sheet.

2. On lightly floured pastry cloth, shape dough into a round.

3. Pinch off a small piece of dough and reserve for centers. Roll rest of dough into a rectangle, 12 by 8 inches. With sharp knife or pastry wheel, cut into six (4-inch) squares.

4. Arrange squares, 1½ inches apart, on prepared cookie sheet. From each corner of each square, make cut at 45-degree angle, 1½ inches long.

5. In center of each square, place 1 tablespoon preserves.

6. To make pinwheels: Bring every other point of dough to center of square; then press in center, to fasten.

7. Roll out the small piece of reserved dough ⅛ inch thick. Using a 1¼-inch round cutter, cut 6 rounds. Moisten bottom of rounds slightly with water; place in center of each pinwheel, to cover points. Cover loosely with a sheet of waxed paper.

8. Let rise in warm place (85F) free from drafts, until double in bulk—about 45 minutes. Meanwhile, preheat oven to 350F.

9. With fork, beat egg yolk slightly with 1 tablespoon water. Use to brush tops of rolls.

10. Bake 15 minutes, or until golden-brown. Let cool on wire rack. Makes 6.

### KUGELHOF

| | |
|---|---|
| 1 cup seedless raisins | 14 to 16 whole blanched almonds |
| 3 tablespoons brandy or kirsch | 1 cup butter or regular |
| 2 tablespoons grated lemon peel | margarine, softened |
| 1 cup milk | 1 teaspoon salt |
| 1 cup granulated sugar | 6 eggs |
| ½ cup warm water (105 to 115F) | ¼ cup butter or regular |
| 1 pkg active dry yeast | margarine, melted |
| 5 cups unsifted all-purpose flour | Confectioners' sugar |
| ½ cup slivered blanched almonds | |

1. In medium bowl, combine raisins, brandy and lemon peel; toss lightly to mix well. Set aside.

2. In small saucepan, heat milk until bubbles form around edge of pan; remove from heat. Stir in ¼ cup granulated sugar; let cool to lukewarm.

3. If possible, check temperature of warm water with thermometer. Sprinkle yeast over water in large bowl; stir until dissolved. Stir in lukewarm milk mixture and 2½ cups flour; with wooden spoon, beat until smooth—about 2 minutes.

4. Cover bowl with towel; let rise in warm place (85F), free from drafts, until double in bulk—about 1 hour. Batter will be light and spongy.

5. Meanwhile, butter generously a 4-quart Turk's-head tube mold, 10½ inches in diameter. Sprinkle inside of mold with slivered almonds. Place a whole almond in each indentation in bottom of mold.

6. In large bowl, with electric mixer at medium speed, beat softened butter with remaining granulated sugar and the salt until light and fluffy. Beat in eggs, one at a time, beating until smooth.

7. At low speed, beat in 1 cup flour and the risen batter until smooth and well blended.

8. With wooden spoon, stir in the remaining flour and the raisin mixture, beating until well combined.

9. Pour batter into prepared mold. Cover with towel; let rise in warm place (85F), free from drafts, 1 hour and 20 minutes, or until batter rises almost to top of pan.

10. Meanwhile, preheat oven to 350F.

11. Bake kugelhof 50 to 60 minutes, or until a cake tester inserted near the center comes out clean. Let cool in pan on wire rack about 20 minutes.

12. Run spatula around sides of pan to loosen; turn out on wire rack. Brush with melted butter. Let cool completely.

13. To store: Wrap in waxed paper, then in foil. Store in a cool, dry place or in the refrigerator if storing for a week or two. Store in freezer if keeping longer.

14. To serve: Let warm to room temperature. Sprinkle lightly with confectioners' sugar. Slice thinly; serve, lightly buttered, with coffee.

Makes 1 large kugelhof.

---

## SOUR-CREAM CRUMB CAKE

2 cups sifted (see Note)
  all-purpose flour
1 teaspoon baking powder
½ teaspoon baking soda
¼ teaspoon salt
½ cup butter or regular
  margarine, softened
1 cup granulated sugar
3 eggs
1 teaspoon vanilla extract
¾ cup sour cream

**Crumb Topping**
½ cup granulated sugar
¼ cup sifted (see Note)
  all-purpose flour
2 tablespoons soft butter or
  margarine
1 teaspoon cinnamon

Confectioners' sugar

1. Preheat oven to 350F. Grease well and flour a 9-inch tube pan.

2. Sift 2 cups flour with the baking powder, soda and salt.

3. In large bowl of electric mixer, at high speed, beat ½ cup butter, 1 cup granulated sugar, the eggs and vanilla until light and fluffy—about 5 minutes—occasionally scraping bowl with rubber scraper.

4. At low speed, beat in flour mixture (in fourths) alternately with sour cream (in thirds), beginning and ending with flour mixture. Beat just until smooth—about 1 minute.

5. Turn batter into prepared tube pan. Bake 50 minutes, or until cake tester inserted in center comes out clean.

6. Meanwhile, make crumb topping: In small bowl, combine all topping ingredients; toss lightly with fork until mixture is crumbly.

7. Remove cake from oven; sprinkle crumb topping evenly over top. Return to oven 10 minutes.

8. Let cool in pan on wire rack 10 minutes. Remove from pan; sprinkle crumb-topped surface with confectioners' sugar. Serve warm.

Makes 10 servings.

*Note:* Sift before measuring.

# Hearty Open Face Sandwiches

### SLICED EGG AND ANCHOVY

*4 slices white or rye bread*
*2 tablespoons butter or*
*margarine*
*2 large tomatoes, cut into 8 slices*
*4 hard-cooked eggs, sliced*

*Salt and pepper*
*1 can (2 oz) rolled anchovy fillets*
*(8), drained*
*Parsley sprigs*

1. Spread bread with butter. For each sandwich, cut one tomato slice in half; arrange on each side of bread.

2. Arrange three egg slices on each piece of tomato. In center of each sandwich, place a whole tomato slice; sprinkle egg and tomato slices lightly with salt and pepper. Top with an egg slice and two rolled anchovies. Decorate with parsley sprigs.

Makes 4 sandwiches.

## HAM AND ASPARAGUS

3 slices rye or white bread
2 tablespoons butter or
   margarine
2 tablespoons mayonnaise,
   combined with 2 teaspoons
   brown mustard

3 slices baked or boiled ham
9 cooked asparagus spears
   (fresh, frozen or canned)

Spread bread with butter, then with mayonnaise-mustard mixture. Fold ham on each bread slice so that asparagus can be placed between folds. Arrange 3 asparagus spears on each.

Makes 3 sandwiches.

## SMOKED FISH AND EGG SALAD

2 canned smoked whitefish
   (about 4 oz), bones removed,
   chopped
3 hard-cooked eggs, chopped
2 tablespoons mayonnaise

4 slices pumpernickel
2 tablespoons butter or
   margarine
4 radishes, thinly sliced
Dill or parsley sprigs

1. In small bowl, combine fish, eggs and mayonnaise; mix well. Refrigerate to chill well.

2. To serve: Spread bread with butter. Top each bread slice with fish mixture. Decorate with radish slices and dill.

Makes 4 sandwiches.

## TOMATO AND CAVIAR

4 slices rye bread
2 tablespoons butter or
   margarine
4 leaves Boston or iceberg lettuce
3 medium tomatoes, thinly sliced

½ cup chopped onion
4 teaspoons black caviar
   (lumpfish)
1 lemon, quartered

1. Spread bread with butter. Arrange a lettuce leaf on each slice. Arrange thin tomato slices to cover bread.

2. Combine onion and caviar; place on top of tomatoes. Serve with lemon quarters.

Makes 4 sandwiches.

## HERBED SMOKED SALMON

*¼ cup butter or margarine*
*1 tablespoon snipped dill*
*1 tablespoon chopped parsley*
*1 tablespoon chopped chives*
*Dash dried oregano leaves*

*4 slices white, rye or*
*    pumpernickel bread*
*8 slices smoked salmon*
*4 thin slices lemon*
*Fresh dill or parsley sprigs*

1. In small bowl, mix butter with snipped dill, parsley, chives and oregano. Use to spread on bread slices.

2. Fold salmon slices; place 2 on each slice of bread. Decorate with lemon slices and dill sprigs.

Makes 4 sandwiches.

## SLICED EGG AND SARDINE

*4 slices white or rye bread*
*2 tablespoons butter or*
*    margarine*
*½ small cucumber, thinly sliced*
*4 hard-cooked eggs, sliced*

*Salt and pepper*
*1 can (3¼ oz) sardines in tomato*
*    sauce, drained*
*Watercress or parsley*
*Mayonnaise*

1. Spread bread with butter. Arrange cucumber slices and egg slices, alternately, to cover bread. Sprinkle with salt and pepper.

2. Arrange three sardines in center of each. Decorate with watercress or parsley. Serve with mayonnaise.

Makes 4 sandwiches.

## LIVER PÂTÉ ON RYE

*2 slices white or rye bread*
*2 tablespoons butter or*
*    margarine*
*1 can (4½ oz) liver pâté, chilled*
*    and cut into 10 thin slices*

*¼ red pepper*
*Capers, drained (about 10)*
*Parsley sprigs*

1. Spread bread with butter. Arrange 5 slices pâté on each bread slice.

2. Chop red pepper rather coarsely. Make a "flower" on each pâté slice, with a caper in center, surrounded by pieces of red pepper.

3. Place parsley sprigs in corners.
Makes 2 sandwiches.

---

## CRABMEAT SALAD

*4 slices white or rye bread*
*2 tablespoons butter or*
   *margarine*
*4 leaves Boston or iceberg lettuce*
*1 can (7½ oz) crabmeat, drained*

*¼ cup mayonnaise*
*¼ cup chopped celery*
*1 lemon*
*Watercress or parsley sprigs*

1. Spread bread with butter. Arrange a lettuce leaf on each.
2. Remove any cartilage from crabmeat. Combine crabmeat with mayonnaise and celery; mix well. Chill well.
3. To serve: Mound crabmeat mixture on lettuce. Decorate each with 3 lemon slices, halved, and watercress.
Makes 4 sandwiches.

---

## DEVILED HAM

*5 tablespoons butter or*
   *margarine, softened*
*2½ tablespoons brown mustard*
*8 slices boiled ham, coarsely*
   *chopped*

*4 thin slices rye bread*
*1 tablespoon chopped parsley*
*Finely chopped egg white from*
   *2 hard-cooked eggs*

Combine butter and mustard; add chopped ham and mix well. Spread liberally on bread. Sprinkle top of each with a little chopped parsley, then chopped egg white.
Makes 4 sandwiches.

---

## SALAMI WITH COTTAGE CHEESE

*4 slices rye bread*
*2 tablespoons butter or*
   *margarine*
*Sliced salami, rind removed*

*½ green pepper, cut into*
   *4 thick rings*
*1 container (8 oz) cottage cheese*
*Chives*

1. Spread bread with butter. On each slice, arrange 2 or 3 salami slices. Place a green-pepper ring on one side.

2. Fill rings with cottage cheese; sprinkle with snipped chives.
Makes 4 sandwiches.

————

## SEAFOOD DELUXE

*4 slices white bread*
*2 tablespoons lemon butter or*
   *margarine (see Note)*
*4 leaves Boston or iceberg lettuce*
*¼ cup heavy cream, whipped*
*2 teaspoons prepared horse-*
   *radish, drained*

*12 cooked shrimp, halved*
   *lengthwise*
*4 slices smoked salmon*
*Black caviar (lumpfish)*
*Dill sprigs*

1. Spread bread with lemon butter. Arrange a lettuce leaf on each slice.
2. Combine whipped cream and horseradish; mix well.
3. Arrange shrimp on each bread slice in a row. Roll up each salmon slice; place one at end of each row of shrimp.
4. Decorate with horseradish-cream, caviar and dill.
Makes 4 sandwiches.
*Note:* Melt butter or margarine slightly; stir in 1 tablespoon lemon juice; mix well.

————

## SLICED TONGUE WITH HORSERADISH

*4 slices rye bread*
*2 tablespoons butter or*
   *margarine*
*4 leaves Boston or iceberg lettuce*

*2 tablespoons prepared*
   *horseradish*
*¾ cup heavy cream, whipped*
*12 slices tongue*
*Chopped parsley*

1. Spread bread with butter. Place a lettuce leaf on each slice.
2. Mix horseradish with whipped cream. Use to spread on 12 tongue slices—about 1 rounded tablespoon for each.
3. Roll up tongue (3 slices for each sandwich). Arrange on lettuce. Sprinkle with chopped parsley.
Makes 4 sandwiches.

## HAZELNUT TORTE

**Torte Layers**
7 eggs
¼ teaspoon salt
1 cup granulated sugar
1 teaspoon vanilla extract
1¼ cups ground hazelnuts
1¼ cups ground pecans
¼ cup packaged dry bread
　crumbs
1 teaspoon baking powder
½ teaspoon salt

**Filling**
1 cup heavy cream, chilled
½ cup confectioners' sugar
1 teaspoon vanilla extract

**Chocolate Frosting**
4 squares unsweetened chocolate
¼ cup butter or regular margarine
3 cups sifted (see Note)
　confectioners' sugar
½ cup hot water
1 teaspoon vanilla extract

1 cup raspberry preserves
½ cup whole hazelnuts

**Coffee Frosting**
2 teaspoons instant coffee
2 tablespoons hot water
¼ cup butter or regular
　margarine, softened
1¾ cups sifted (see Note)
　confectioners' sugar

1. Separate eggs, putting whites into large bowl of electric mixer, yolks in smaller one. Let whites warm to room temperature—about 1 hour.

2. Preheat oven to 375F. Line bottom of three (8-inch) round layer-cake pans with circles of waxed paper.

3. With mixer at high speed, beat whites with ¼ teaspoon salt until soft peaks form when beater is slowly raised. Gradually beat in ½ cup granulated sugar, 2 tablespoons at a time, beating until stiff peaks form.

4. With same beater, beat yolks until thick and light. Gradually beat in rest of granulated sugar, beating until thick—3 minutes; beat in 1 teaspoon vanilla.

5. Combine ground nuts, crumbs, baking powder and ½ teaspoon salt; turn into yolk mixture; mix well. With an under-and-over motion, fold into the egg whites just to combine.

6. Pour into prepared pans, dividing evenly; smooth surfaces. Bake 25 minutes, or until surface springs back when gently pressed with fingertip. To cool, hang each pan upside down between two other pans—1 hour.

7. Make filling: In medium bowl, combine cream, ½ cup confectioners' sugar and 1 teaspoon vanilla. Beat until stiff; refrigerate.

8. Make chocolate frosting: In top of double boiler, over hot water,

melt chocolate and ¼ cup butter. Remove from water; add 3 cups confectioners' sugar, the hot water and vanilla; mix until smooth. Set in larger bowl of ice cubes to chill. Stir until thickened.

9. Loosen sides of layers from pans with spatula. Turn out of pans; peel off paper. On plate, assemble layers, spreading each layer with half raspberry preserves, then with half of filling.

10. Frost torte with chocolate frosting; refrigerate 1 hour.

11. Slice hazelnuts, reserving 6 whole ones for top. Make coffee frosting: In medium bowl, dissolve coffee in hot water. Add butter and confectioners' sugar; mix until smooth.

12. Place coffee frosting in pastry bag with number-4 star tip. Decorate, making ruching around bottom of cake and three even triangles on top. Arrange sliced hazelnuts inside the three triangles. Place whole hazelnuts in center.

13. For easier cutting, refrigerate 2 hours before serving.

Makes 12 servings.

*Note:* Sift sugar before measuring.

---

## BLACK FOREST CHERRY CAKE

*6 eggs, at room temperature*
*1 cup granulated sugar*
*1 teaspoon vanilla extract*
*½ cup sifted (see Note) flour*
*½ cup unsweetened cocoa*
*⅔ cup sweet butter or regular*
  *margarine, melted*

**Syrup**
*⅓ cup granulated sugar*
*3 tablespoons kirsch or Cointreau*

*Glazed Cherries, below*

**Filling**
*3 cups heavy cream*
*½ cup confectioners' sugar*

*Maraschino cherries with stems,*
  *well drained, or whole candied*
  *cherries*
*1 (8 oz) milk-chocolate bar*

1. Preheat oven to 350F. Grease well and flour three (8-by-1½-inch) layer-cake pans.

2. In large bowl of electric mixer, at high speed, beat eggs until light and fluffy. Beat in 1 cup granulated sugar gradually; continue beating until very thick—about 10 minutes. Add vanilla.

3. Sift flour with cocoa. Then fold into egg mixture in fourths, using a wire whisk or rubber scraper. Also fold in butter, in fourths, just until combined. Gently turn into prepared pans. Bake 15 minutes, or until surface springs back when gently pressed with finger.

4. Let layers cool in pans on wire rack 5 minutes. Then loosen edges with metal spatula; turn out on wire rack to cool completely.

5. Meanwhile, make syrup: In small saucepan, combine ⅓ cup granulated sugar with ½ cup water. Stir over medium heat, to dissolve sugar. Then bring to boiling; boil, uncovered, 5 minutes. Set aside to cool; add kirsch.

6. Also, make Glazed Cherries.

7. To assemble: Place layers on cookie sheets. Make several holes with toothpicks; spoon syrup over cake layers.

8. Make filling: Beat cream with confectioners' sugar until stiff. Invert one cake layer on cake plate for bottom. Spread glazed cherries over bottom layer. Then spread with 1 cup whipped cream.

9. Place second layer on top; spread with 1 cup whipped cream. Place third layer on top. Spread top and side with remaining whipped cream, making 12 whipped-cream rosettes around top edge. You may use a spoon or put some of whipped cream through a pastry tube with a number-5 tip. Refrigerate.

10. Make chocolate curls: Let chocolate bar soften slightly. Using vegetable parer, scrape across chocolate to make curls; refrigerate.

11. To serve: Place chocolate curls around side of cake, covering completely. Place cherry on each rosette.

Makes 12 servings.

*Note:* Sift flour before measuring.

**Glazed Cherries**
*1 cup canned pitted Bing
    cherries, drained*
*2 tablespoons kirsch or Cointreau*
*1 tablespoon cornstarch*
*⅔ cup cherry juice*

1. In small bowl, combine cherries and kirsch; let stand about 1 hour.

2. Meanwhile, in small saucepan, combine cornstarch and ⅓ cup cherry juice; stir to dissolve cornstarch. Stir in remaining juice.

3. Bring to boiling, stirring; reduce heat and simmer 5 minutes, or until thickened and translucent. Let cool completely.

4. Add cherries in kirsch to cooled cornstarch mixture; mix well. Use to fill Black Forest Cherry Cake.

===

## CHOCOLATE-MOUSSE DESSERT CAKE

*Chocolate Chiffon Cake, below*

**Chocolate Mousse**
*3 cups heavy cream*
*1½ cups sifted * confectioners'*
 *sugar*

*¾ cup unsweetened cocoa*
*2 teaspoons vanilla extract*
*¼ teaspoon salt*
*1 teaspoon unflavored gelatine*

*\* Sift before measuring.*

1. Make and cool cake as directed.
2. Make chocolate mousse: Pour cream into large bowl; refrigerate until very cold—about 30 minutes.
3. Add sugar, cocoa, vanilla and salt; beat until stiff enough to hold its shape. Refrigerate.
4. Sprinkle gelatine over 2 tablespoons cold water to soften. Heat over hot water, stirring until dissolved. Cool.
5. Prepare cake for filling: Cut 1-inch slice crosswise from top of cake; set aside. With sharp knife, outline a cavity in cake, being careful to leave 1-inch-thick walls around center hole and side. With spoon, carefully remove cake from this area, being sure to leave 1-inch-thick base. Reserve 1¼ cups crumbled cake.
6. Measure 2⅔ cups chocolate cream into small bowl; fold in cooled gelatine. Use to fill cavity in cake. Replace top.
7. Mix ½ cup chocolate cream with reserved crumbled cake. Use to fill center hole of cake.
8. Frost top and side of cake with remaining chocolate cream. Refrigerate until well chilled.
 Makes 12 servings.

**Chocolate Chiffon Cake**
*1 cup egg whites (7 or 8)*
*½ cup sifted * unsweetened cocoa*
*¾ cup boiling water*
*1¾ cups sifted * cake flour*
*1¾ cups sugar*

*1½ teaspoons baking soda*
*1 teaspoon salt*
*½ cup salad oil*
*7 egg yolks*
*2 teaspoons vanilla extract*
*½ teaspoon cream of tartar*

*\* Sift before measuring.*

1. In large bowl of electric mixer, let egg whites warm to room temperature—about 1 hour.
2. Preheat oven to 325F.
3. Place cocoa in small bowl; add boiling water, stirring until smooth. Let mixture cool about 20 minutes.

4. Into a second large bowl, sift flour with sugar, soda and salt. Make a well in center; pour in salad oil, egg yolks, vanilla and cooled cocoa. With spoon or electric mixer, beat just until smooth.

5. Sprinkle cream of tartar over egg whites. With mixer at high speed, beat until very stiff peaks form when beater is slowly raised. Do not underbeat.

6. Pour batter over egg whites; with rubber scraper or wire whisk, gently fold into egg whites just until blended. Turn batter into ungreased 10-inch tube pan.

7. Bake 65 to 70 minutes, or until cake tester inserted in center comes out clean.

8. Invert pan over neck of bottle; let cake cool completely—about 1½ hours. With spatula, carefully loosen cake from pan; remove.

Makes 10-inch tube cake.

---

## MEXICAN CHOCOLATE CAKE

½ cup regular margarine
½ cup salad oil
2 squares unsweetened chocolate
2 cups unsifted all-purpose flour
1 teaspoon baking soda
2 cups granulated sugar
½ cup sour milk (place 1½ teaspoons vinegar in a 1-cup measure; fill with milk to measure ½ cup)

2 eggs, beaten
1 teaspoon cinnamon
1 teaspoon vanilla extract

Mexican Chocolate Frosting, below

1. Preheat oven to 350F. Lightly grease a 15½-by-10½-inch jelly-roll pan.

2. Combine margarine, oil, chocolate and 1 cup water in a sauce pan and heat until chocolate is melted.

3. Combine flour, baking soda, sugar, milk, eggs, cinnamon and vanilla in large bowl; then combine with chocolate mixture. Pour batter into prepared pan; bake 20 to 25 minutes, or until surface springs back when gently pressed with fingertip.

4. Five minutes before cake is done, make Frosting. Frost cake while still warm. Cut into squares.

Makes 10 to 12 servings.

**Mexican Chocolate Frosting**
½ cup regular margarine
2 squares unsweetened chocolate
6 tablespoons milk

1 pkg (1 lb) confectioners' sugar
1 teaspoon vanilla extract
½ cup chopped pecans

1. Combine margarine, chocolate and milk in a saucepan and heat until bubbles form around the edge. Remove from heat.

2. Add confectioners' sugar, vanilla and pecans; beat. Ice cake while still warm. (Frosting is not stiff.)

## WARM CREAM-CHEESE STRUDEL

1 pkg (4 leaves) Hungarian-style
  strudel leaves

½ cup light raisins
2 teaspoons grated lemon peel

**Filling**
4 pkg (3-oz size) cream cheese,
  softened
½ cup granulated sugar
3 egg yolks

⅓ cup melted butter or margarine
⅓ cup packaged dry bread
  crumbs
Confectioners' sugar

1. Let strudel leaves stand at room temperature overnight.

2. Next day, preheat oven to 375F. Grease a cookie sheet.

3. Prepare Filling: In small bowl of electric mixer, combine cream cheese, sugar, and egg yolks; beat at medium speed until well blended and smooth. Stir in raisins and lemon peel. Refrigerate.

4. Place a damp cloth (larger than 23-by-17-inch strudel leaves) on work surface. Remove one package of two leaves from box of strudel leaves. Unfold leaves on damp cloth. Quickly brush one leaf with melted butter; then sprinkle with about 1 tablespoon bread crumbs. Top with second leaf; quickly brush with butter, and sprinkle with crumbs.

5. Remove remaining two leaves; brush each with butter, and sprinkle with crumbs. Place on first two leaves, to make 4 layers. Spread filling over half of top leaf, starting from one short end. Then, from same end, roll up pastry loosely, jelly-roll fashion, using cloth to roll and guide it.

6. Roll strudel onto prepared cookie sheet, placing seam side down. Brush with butter.

7. Bake 50 to 55 minutes, or until deep golden-brown. Brush with any remaining butter.

8. Remove to wire rack. Let cool 30 minutes; then sprinkle with confectioners' sugar. Serve warm, cut into thick slices.

Makes 6 servings.

## SCOTCH CHOCOLATE CAKE SQUARES

2 cups sifted * all-purpose flour
2 cups granulated sugar
½ teaspoon salt
½ cup regular margarine
½ cup shortening
¼ cup unsweetened cocoa
2 eggs, slightly beaten
½ cup buttermilk
1 teaspoon baking soda

* Sift before measuring.

1 teaspoon cinnamon
1 teaspoon vanilla extract

**Icing:**
½ cup regular margarine
¼ cup unsweetened cocoa
6 tablespoons milk
1 pkg (1 lb) confectioners' sugar
1 teaspoon vanilla extract
2 cups flaked coconut
1 cup chopped pecans

1. Preheat oven to 350F. Into large bowl, sift flour with granulated sugar and salt; set aside. Grease a 13-by-9-by-2-inch baking pan.

2. In small saucepan, combine ½ cup margarine, the shortening, ¼ cup cocoa, and 1 cup water; bring to boiling. Pour over flour mixture.

3. Add eggs, buttermilk, soda, cinnamon, and 1 teaspoon vanilla; with portable electric mixer, beat just until smooth. Immediately pour into prepared pan.

4. Bake 40 to 45 minutes, or until surface springs back when gently pressed with fingertip.

5. Meanwhile, make Icing: In medium saucepan, combine margarine, cocoa, and milk; bring just to boiling. Remove from heat.

6. Add sugar and vanilla; with spoon, beat until smooth. Stir in coconut and nuts. Spread over hot cake as soon as it is removed from oven. Cool in pan on wire rack. Cut into squares.

Makes 15 servings.

## DATE-WALNUT BARS

1 cup sifted (see Note)
   all-purpose flour
½ teaspoon baking powder
¼ teaspoon salt
⅓ cup butter or regular
   margarine, softened
1 cup sugar

2 eggs
1 teaspoon vanilla extract
1 teaspoon grated orange peel
1 pkg (8 oz) pitted dates,
   quartered
½ cup coarsely chopped walnuts
Granulated sugar

1. Preheat oven to 375F. Grease a 9-inch-square baking pan.

2. Sift together flour, baking powder and salt.

3. In medium bowl, with portable electric mixer at medium speed, beat butter with sugar until light and fluffy. Add eggs and vanilla; beat until well blended.

4. At low speed, beat in flour mixture; add orange peel, dates and nuts.

5. Turn batter into pan. Bake 25 to 30 minutes, or until golden-brown.

6. Remove pan to wire rack, cut into bars while hot. Sprinkle top with sugar. Cool completely in pan.

Makes 18 bars.

*Note:* Sift before measuring.

## TOFFEE BARS

**Cookie Crust**
*½ cup butter or regular*
  *margarine, softened*
*½ cup light-brown sugar, packed*
*1 egg yolk*
*1 teaspoon vanilla extract*
*½ cup sifted (see Note)*
  *all-purpose flour*
*½ cup raw quick-cooking oats*
  *(not instant)*

**Topping**
*3 squares semisweet chocolate*
*1 tablespoon butter or margarine*

**Frosting**
*2 squares semisweet chocolate*
*2 tablespoons butter or regular*
  *margarine*
*1½ cups sifted confectioners'*
  *sugar (See note)*
*¼ cup hot water*

1. Preheat oven to 375F. Lightly grease a 13-by-9-by-2-inch pan. Line bottom with foil.

2. Make cookie crust: In large bowl, with wooden spoon or portable electric mixer at medium speed, beat ½ cup butter, the brown sugar, egg yolk and vanilla until smooth.

3. Add flour and oats; stir until well combined.

4. Press mixture evenly in bottom of prepared pan.

5. Bake 15 minutes, or until golden. Cool slightly.

6. Meanwhile, make topping: Melt 3 squares chocolate and 1 table-spoon butter over hot, not boiling, water.

7. Spread over warm cookie crust.

8. With sharp knife, cut into bars while still warm. Let cool completely in pan before removing.

9. Meanwhile, make frosting: In top of double boiler, over hot water, melt chocolate and butter. Remove from water; stir in con-

fectioners' sugar and hot water, mixing until smooth. Refrigerate, covered, about 10 minutes. Put frosting into pastry bag with number-27 tip. Decorate.

Makes 32.

*Note:* Sift flour before measuring.

# Barbecues
# and
# Picnics

## Menu I

Barbecued Beef Round
on French Bread *
Garbanzo-Bean Salad *
Marinated Sliced Tomatoes *
Apple Kuchen *
Coffee     Cold Beer     or     Red Wine

### BARBECUED BEEF ROUND ON FRENCH BREAD

6-lb eye-of-beef-round roast
½ cup salad oil
½ cup catsup
¼ cup lemon juice
1 bay leaf, crumbled
1½ teaspoons salt

1½ teaspoons dried rosemary
  leaves
¼ teaspoon pepper

1 loaf French bread

1. Day before: Wipe beef with damp paper towels. Place in shallow baking dish.
2. In small bowl, combine oil, catsup, lemon juice, bay leaf, salt,

rosemary, and pepper. Pour over beef. Refrigerate, covered, overnight; turn meat at least twice.

3. Next day: Remove beef from refrigerator 1 hour before roasting. Leave in marinade, and turn occasionally.

4. Secure roast on spit, balancing evenly. Insert barbecue meat thermometer into thickest part; be sure it doesn't touch spit.

5. Adjust spit 5 to 6 inches from prepared coals. Place foil drip pan under roast, to catch drippings.

6. Roast, basting occasionally with marinade, 1¾ hours, or until meat thermometer registers 150F, for medium rare.

7. To serve: Remove meat from spit to carving board. Let stand 10 minutes before carving. Slice thinly. Serve on slices of buttered French bread, with meat juices.

Makes 12 servings.

=====

## GARBANZO-BEAN SALAD

3 cups diced potato
1½ cups thinly sliced carrot
1 large red onion, thinly sliced
⅓ cup salad or olive oil
3 cans (1-lb size) garbanzo beans

¾ cup bottled Italian-style
    dressing
2 cloves garlic, crushed
3 teaspoons salt
1½ teaspoons sugar
Chopped parsley

1. In large saucepan, in 1 inch salted boiling water, cook potato and carrot until tender—about 10 minutes. Drain; turn into large bowl.

2. In medium, heavy skillet, sauté onion in oil until soft but not brown. Add to potato and carrot.

3. Drain garbanzos. Add to potato mixture.

4. In small bowl, combine dressing, garlic, salt, and sugar; mix well. Pour over vegetable mixture.

5. Toss gently until well mixed. Serve warm. Or refrigerate 2 hours, or until well chilled. Sprinkle with chopped parsley.

Makes 12 servings.

=====

## MARINATED SLICED TOMATOES

8 large tomatoes (1½ lb)
½ cup salad oil
2 tablespoons lemon juice

1 teaspoon minced garlic
1 teaspoon salt
1 teaspoon dried oregano leaves

1. Peel and slice tomatoes. Arrange in shallow dish.

2. Combine oil, lemon juice, garlic, salt, and oregano; mix well.

3. Pour over tomatoes. Refrigerate, covered, several hours, until well chilled.

Makes 12 servings.

## APPLE KUCHEN

1¼ cups sifted * all-purpose flour
¼ cup sugar
1½ teaspoons baking powder
½ teaspoon salt
¼ cup butter or margarine
1 egg, beaten
¼ cup milk
1 teaspoon vanilla extract
5 cups thinly sliced, pared tart apple

Topping:
¼ cup sugar
1 teaspoon cinnamon
¼ cup butter or margarine, melted
⅓ cup apricot preserves

Cinnamon-Ice-Cream Sauce, below.

* Sift before measuring.

1. Preheat oven to 400F. Lightly grease a 13-by-9-by-2-inch baking pan.

2. Into medium bowl, sift flour with ¼ cup sugar, the baking powder, and salt. With pastry blender, cut in ¼ cup butter until mixture resembles coarse crumbs.

3. Add beaten egg, milk, and vanilla extract, stirring with a fork until the mixture is smooth—will take about 1 minute.

4. Spread batter evenly in bottom of prepared pan. Arrange apple slices, thin sides down and slightly overlapping, in parallel rows over the batter.

5. Make Topping: Combine sugar, cinnamon, and melted butter. Sprinkle sugar mixture over the apple slices.

6. Bake 35 minutes, or until apple slices are tender. Remove to wire rack.

7. Mix apricot preserves with 1 tablespoon hot water. Brush over apple. Cut apple kuchen into rectangles, and serve it warm, with Cinnamon-Ice-Cream Sauce.

Makes 12 servings.

## CINNAMON-ICE-CREAM SAUCE

1 teaspoon cinnamon                    1½ pints soft vanilla ice cream
1 tablespoon sugar

Combine cinnamon and sugar. Stir into ice cream until well blended and smooth. Serve immediately.
Makes 2 cups.

# Menu II

Glazed Loin of Pork
on a Spit *
Chilled Curried Fruit *
Baked Sweet Potatoes
Hot Cornbread
Chicory and Endive Salad
Raspberry-Cream Torte *

## GLAZED LOIN OF PORK ON A SPIT

**Marinade**                           ½ teaspoon ground ginger
1 can (6 oz) frozen lime or lemon      ¼ teaspoon pepper
   juice concentrate, thawed
1 tablespoon prepared mustard          5-lb loin-of-pork roast (12 ribs)
1 teaspoon salt

1. Day before: Make Marinade: In small bowl, combine undiluted lime-juice concentrate, mustard, salt, ginger, and pepper.

2. Wipe pork with damp paper towels; trim fat to ¼-inch thickness. Place in shallow baking dish; pour marinade over pork. Refrigerate, covered, several hours or overnight; turn pork occasionally.

3. One hour before roasting, remove pork from refrigerator. Leave in marinade, and turn occasionally.

4. Secure roast on spit, balancing evenly. Insert barbecue meat thermometer into thickest part; be sure it does not touch spit.

5. Adjust spit 5 to 6 inches from prepared coals. Place foil drip pan under roast, to catch drippings.

6. Roast, basting frequently with marinade, 1½ to 1¾ hours, or until meat thermometer registers 185F.

7. To serve: Remove meat from spit to carving board or large platter. Let stand 10 minutes before carving. Serve with Chilled Curried Fruit.

Makes 8 servings.

**Chilled Curried Fruit**
1 can (1 lb, 1 oz) salad fruits
¼ cup butter or margarine

1 tablespoon curry powder
¼ cup chutney
2 cups cantaloupe balls

1. Drain salad fruits, reserving syrup.

2. In small saucepan, combine butter, curry powder, chutney, and ¾ cup of the reserved syrup. Bring to boiling, stirring; boil, uncovered, stirring occasionally, 10 minutes, or until mixture is thickened.

3. Stir in salad fruits, cantaloupe. Refrigerate, covered, until chilled. Makes 2 cups.

## RASPBERRY-CREAM TORTE

4 egg whites
1¼ cups sifted (see Note)
    all-purpose flour
¼ teaspoon salt
1 cup granulated sugar
4 egg yolks
2 tablespoons fresh lemon juice

2 teaspoons grated lemon peel
2 cups heavy cream
¼ cup confectioners' sugar
1 jar (12 oz) raspberry or
    strawberry preserves
½ cup coarsely chopped pistachio
    nuts

1. In large bowl of electric mixer, let egg whites warm to room temperature—about 1 hour.

2. Meanwhile, preheat oven to 350F.

3. Sift flour with salt.

4. With electric mixer at high speed, beat egg whites until foamy. Gradually beat in ½ cup granulated sugar, beating after each addition. Continue beating until soft peaks form when beater is slowly raised.

5. In small bowl of electric mixer, at high speed and with the same beater, beat egg yolks until thick and lemon-colored. Gradually beat in the remaining ½ cup granulated sugar; continue beating until mixture is fluffy.

6. At low speed, blend in flour mixture, guiding it into beater with rubber scraper.

7. Add 2 tablespoons lemon juice, 2 tablespoons water and the lemon peel, beating just until combined—about 1 minute.

8. With wire whisk or rubber scraper and using an under-and-over motion, gently fold yolk mixture into egg-white mixture just until blended.

9. Pour the batter into two ungreased, round, 8-by-1½-inch layer-cake pans; bake 25 minutes, or until the surface springs back when it is gently pressed with fingertip.

10. Invert cake layers by hanging pan between two other pans. Cool completely—about 1 hour. With spatula, carefully loosen cake from pan; remove.

11. Beat cream with confectioners' sugar until stiff; refrigerate. Slice layers in half horizontally, to make four layers.

12. To assemble: Place a layer, cut side up, on cake plate. Spread with ⅓ cup raspberry preserves and ½ cup whipped cream. Repeat with remaining layers, ending with top layer cut side down.

13. Frost top and side of torte with whipped cream, reserving about ½ cup for decoration. With remaining whipped cream in pastry bag with number-6 decorating tip, make ruching around top edge of cake. Sprinkle with nuts. For easier cutting, refrigerate 1 hour. Makes 8 to 10 servings.

*Note:* Sift before measuring.

# Menu III

Grilled Lamb with Mint *
Mushroom Ratatouille *
Crusty Rolls
Green Salad
Deep-dish Peach Pie *

## GRILLED LAMB WITH MINT

4-lb boned lamb shoulder or
   4½- to 5-lb boned leg of lamb
2 cloves garlic, slivered

1 teaspoon black pepper
1 teaspoon salt
2 tablespoons olive or salad oil

**Marinade**
½ bunch fresh mint, chopped
   (1 cup)
1 teaspoon sugar
2 cups dry white wine
½ cup wine vinegar

**Sauce**
1½ cups marinade
½ cup canned condensed beef
   broth, undiluted
1 tablespoon chopped fresh mint

1. Have butcher flatten lamb to 1½-inch thickness. Wipe lamb with damp paper towels. Make a number of deep cuts, and insert garlic slivers.

2. Make marinade: In deep bowl, combine mint with rest of marinade ingredients; mix well. Place lamb in marinade, turning to coat well. Refrigerate, covered, several hours or overnight, turning lamb several times.

3. To cook indoors: Preheat broiler. Remove lamb from marinade, reserving 2½ cups of marinade. Wipe lamb with paper towels. Place on rack in roasting pan. Broil, 4 inches from heat, 20 minutes on each side, basting several times with 1 cup marinade. To serve, slice crosswise into ½-inch-thick slices.

4. One half hour before lamb is done, make sauce: Strain 1½ cups reserved marinade; in medium saucepan, bring to boiling. Boil, uncovered, about 15 minutes, to reduce marinade to about 1 cup; skim surface. Add beef broth; boil 5 minutes more. Add 1 tablespoon mint; serve with lamb.

5. To cook outdoors: Adjust grill 5 inches from prepared coals. Remove lamb from marinade, reserving 2½ cups. Lay lamb flat on grill, fat side up.

6. Grill lamb 17 to 20 minutes on each side, basting several times with 1 cup marinade. (Test for doneness with sharp knife.) Make sauce as in Step 4.

Makes 8 to 10 servings.

## MUSHROOM RATATOUILLE

2 medium green peppers (1 lb)
3 medium zucchini (1 lb)
1 lb small mushrooms
½ cup salad or olive oil
1 cup thinly sliced onion
2 cloves garlic, crushed

4 medium tomatoes (1½ lb),
    peeled and cut into wedges
2 teaspoons salt
¼ teaspoon pepper
2 tablespoons chopped parsley

1. Wash peppers; halve. Remove ribs and seeds. Cut lengthwise into ¼-inch-thick slices.

2. Scrub zucchini. Cut crosswise into ½-inch-thick slices. Wash mushrooms; cut in halves.

3. In ¼ cup hot oil in large skillet, sauté green pepper, onion, and garlic about 5 minutes, or until onion is transparent. With slotted spoon, remove to medium bowl.

4. Add 2 tablespoons oil to skillet. In hot oil, sauté zucchini, turning

frequently, until tender—about 10 minutes. With slotted utensil, remove from skillet to same bowl.

5. Add remaining oil to skillet. In hot oil, sauté mushrooms until golden—about 5 minutes.

6. Return vegetables to same skillet. Layer half of tomato wedges on top. Sprinkle with salt, pepper, and 1 tablespoon parsley. Stir gently just to combine.

7. Layer remaining tomato on top. Sprinkle with remaining parsley.

8. Simmer mixture, covered and over low heat, 10 minutes.

9. Remove cover; cook 5 minutes longer, or until liquid has evaporated.

10. Turn into large, shallow serving dish. Serve hot. Or refrigerate, covered, until very well chilled.

Makes 8 to 10 servings.

## DEEP-DISH PEACH PIE

| | |
|---|---|
| 1 pkg (11 oz) piecrust mix | ⅛ teaspoon cloves |
| 4 to 4½ lb fresh peaches | ⅛ teaspoon cinnamon |
| ¼ cup lemon juice | ½ cup heavy cream |
| 1½ cups light-brown sugar | ¼ cup butter or margarine |
| ¼ cup unsifted all-purpose flour | 1 egg yolk |

1. Prepare piecrust mix as package label directs. Shape into a ball; refrigerate while preparing peaches.

2. Peel and slice enough peaches to make 9 cups. Turn into large bowl. Add lemon juice; toss gently.

3. In small bowl, mix well sugar, flour, cloves, and cinnamon. Sprinkle over peaches; stir until combined. Stir in cream. Turn into a 12-by-8-by-2-inch shallow baking dish. Dot with butter.

4. Preheat oven to 425F.

5. On lightly floured pastry cloth or board, roll out pastry to a 12-inch square. Cut into 1-inch-wide strips.

6. Arrange 4 strips lengthwise over peaches; arrange remaining strips across them, slightly on diagonal. Trim strips, pressing ends to edge of dish. If you wish, arrange leftover pastry strips, end to end, around edge of dish, to make a border.

7. Mix egg yolk with 1 tablespoon cold water; brush over pastry.

8. Bake 35 to 40 minutes, or until pastry is golden-brown and juice bubbles.

9. Let pie cool on wire rack about 30 minutes.

Makes 8 to 10 servings.

*Note:* To make pie with canned peaches, use 3 cans (1-pound, 14-ounce size) sliced peaches. Drain peaches, reserving syrup. Reduce sugar to 1 cup and use ½ cup reserved syrup in place of cream.

# Menu IV

Salmon Steaks Tarragon *
New Potatoes with Parsley
Tomato and Avocado Salad
Buttered Whole Wheat Bread Slices
Raspberries Sabayon *

## SALMON STEAKS TARRAGON

4 salmon steaks, 1 inch thick
½ teaspoon hickory salt
Fresh tarragon sprigs
12 slices bacon, slightly cooked
1 teaspoon dried tarragon leaves

**Sauce**
2 tablespoons butter or
  margarine

1 tablespoon chopped shallot
1 tablespoon chopped fresh
  tarragon
1 tablespoon chopped parsley
1 cup dry white wine
½ teaspoon salt
¼ teaspoon sugar

1. Rinse salmon steaks under cold running water. Drain; pat dry with paper towels. Sprinkle both sides with hickory salt. On each, place several sprigs of fresh tarragon; completely wrap each in bacon slices. Sprinkle with dried tarragon.

2. To cook indoors: Preheat broiler. Arrange salmon steaks on rack in broiler pan. Broil, 4 inches from heat, 10 minutes. Turn; broil about 8 minutes longer, or until fish flakes easily.

3. Make sauce: In hot butter in small saucepan, sauté shallot until tender—about 5 minutes. Add tarragon and parsley; cook 1 minute. Add wine, salt, and sugar; cook, stirring, until hot.

4. To cook outdoors: Adjust grill 4 inches from prepared coals. Grease grill well. Grill fish 10 minutes on one side, or until bacon is browned. Turn; grill 5 minutes longer. Fish should flake easily when tested with fork. Serve with sauce.

Makes 4 servings.

## RASPBERRIES SABAYON

**Sabayon Sauce:**
*4 egg yolks*
*2 tablespoons sugar*
*¼ cup Grand Marnier*
*⅓ cup heavy cream, whipped*

*2 pint boxes red raspberries,*
*washed and drained; or 3 pkg*
*(10-oz size) frozen raspberries,*
*thawed and drained*

1. Make Sabayon Sauce: In top of double boiler, with electric mixer at medium speed, beat egg yolks until thick. Gradually beat in sugar; beat until mixture is light and soft peaks form when beater is slowly raised.

2. Place double-boiler top over simmering water (water in bottom should not touch base of top). Slowly beat in Grand Marnier; continue beating until mixture is fluffy and mounds—takes about 5 minutes.

3. Remove double-boiler top from hot water; set in ice water. Beat the custard mixture until cool. Gently fold in whipped cream.

4. Refrigerate sauce, covered, until serving.

5. Place berries in serving bowl or dessert dishes. Stir sauce; pour over fruit.

Makes 6 servings.

# Picnics

## Menu I

White Wine Spritzer *
Pâté Stuffed Chicken Breasts en Gelée *
Romaine Salad Bowl
Assorted Rolls and Crackers
Platter of Assorted Cheeses
Poached Fresh Peaches *
Sugar Cookies

### WHITE-WINE SPRITZER

*1 bottle (4/5 qt) dry white wine,
   chilled*

*1 bottle (12 oz) club soda, chilled
Ice cubes*

1. Pour wine and soda into large pitcher; stir just to combine. Add ice cubes.
2. Serve in chilled wineglasses.
Makes 8 (6-oz) servings
*Note:* To carry to a picnic, pack wine and soda in cooler, along with wineglasses. Combine at picnic spot.

## PÂTÉ-STUFFED CHICKEN BREASTS EN GELÉE

1 large onion, sliced
2 celery stalks, sliced
2 carrots, sliced
2 parsley sprigs
1½ teaspoons salt
½ teaspoon dried thyme leaves
2 small bay leaves
2 cans (10¾-oz size) condensed
    chicken broth, undiluted
5 (1-lb size) whole chicken
    breasts, split in half
Wine Aspic, below

2 cans (4¾-oz size) liver pâté

**Glaze**
1 env unflavored gelatine
1 cup heavy cream

Chives, cucumber, radishes,
    carrots, black olives and
    capers, to make flowers
Clear Glaze, below
Watercress sprigs

1. In 6-quart kettle, combine onion, celery, carrot, parsley, salt, thyme, bay leaves, undiluted chicken broth, 1 cup water and the split chicken breasts; bring to boiling.

2. Reduce heat and simmer, covered, 30 minutes, or just until chicken is fork-tender.

3. Remove kettle from heat; let the chicken cool in broth. Meanwhile, make Wine Aspic.

4. Remove chicken from broth; reserve broth. Remove and discard skin and bone from chicken breasts; trim edges evenly.

5. On underside of each chicken breast, spread about 1 tablespoon liver pâté, mounding it slightly. Refrigerate chicken breasts, covered, 1 hour.

6. Meanwhile, strain broth; skim off fat. Reserve 2 cups broth.

7. Make glaze: In medium saucepan, bring reserved broth to boiling. Reduce heat; simmer, uncovered, 30 minutes, or until reduced to 1 cup.

8. In ¼ cup cold water in medium bowl, let gelatine stand 5 minutes, to soften. Add hot broth, stirring to dissolve gelatine.

9. Add heavy cream, mixing until well combined with gelatine mixture.

10. Set bowl with gelatine mixture in ice water; let stand about 20 minutes, or until well chilled but not thickened. Stir occasionally. Remove from ice water.

11. Place chicken breasts, pâté side down, on a wire rack; set rack on a tray. Spoon glaze over chicken breasts.

12. Refrigerate on tray for 30 minutes, or until glaze is set.

13. Scrape glaze from tray; reheat and set in saucepan in ice water

again to chill. Spoon glaze over chicken breasts, coating completely.

14. To make decoration: Use chives for stems. Cut skin from cucumber with sharp knife to make leaves. Use radish skin, thin slices of partially cooked carrot and thin slices of black olive, cut with small aspic cutter or sharp knife, for flowers. Use capers for flower centers. Press flowers into glaze, to decorate. Refrigerate until glaze is set—about 1 hour. Meanwhile, make Clear Glaze. Spoon Clear Glaze on top to cover completely. Refrigerate 1 hour longer.

15. To serve: Arrange chicken breasts, in a single layer, on chilled serving platter. Decorate platter with Wine Aspic and watercress.

Makes 8 to 10 servings.

**Wine Aspic**
*3 env unflavored gelatine*
*2 cans (13¾-oz size) chicken broth*

*3 tablespoons lemon juice*
*½ cup dry white wine*
*¼ teaspoon Kitchen Bouquet*

1. Sprinkle gelatine over 1 cup chicken broth in small saucepan; let stand 5 minutes to soften.

2. Stir over medium heat to dissolve gelatine. Add remaining chicken broth, lemon juice, wine and Kitchen Bouquet.

3. Strain into a 13-by-9-by-2-inch pan. Refrigerate until firm—3 hours or overnight.

4. Cut firm gelatine into eight crosswise strips; cut two strips to make ten triangles. Cut remaining gelatine into cubes.

5. Use triangles to decorate outside of platter; mound cubes in center.

**Clear Glaze**
*1 env unflavored gelatine*

*1 can (13¾ oz) chicken broth*

1. In ¼ cup cold water in medium bowl, let gelatine stand 5 minutes, to soften. Heat broth; add to gelatine mixture, stirring to dissolve gelatine.

2. Set bowl with gelatine mixture in ice water; let stand about 20 minutes, or until well chilled but not thickened, stirring occasionally. Remove from ice water. Use to glaze decorated chicken breasts.

## POACHED FRESH PEACHES

*½ cup apricot preserves*
*2 teaspoons grated orange peel*
*6 tablespoons sugar*

*8 ripe, fresh peaches (about 1½ lb), peeled, halved and pitted*
*½ cup sherry*

1. In large saucepan, combine preserves, orange peel and sugar with cup water.

2. Cook, stirring, over low heat until mixture is syrupy and falls in heavy drops from side of spoon—about 8 minutes.

3. Add peach halves to syrup. Simmer, uncovered, about 10 minutes, or until peaches are tender.

4. Add ½ cup sherry. Refrigerate, covered, several hours, or until well chilled.

5. Serve peaches with syrup spooned over them.
Makes 8 servings.

# Menu II

Cold Roast Meat Loaf *
Macaroni Salad *
Relishes—Carrot Sticks,
Celery, Radishes, Black and Green Olives
Fruit-glazed Cream-Cheesecake *
Carafe of Red Wine      Coffee

## COLD ROAST MEAT LOAF

2 eggs
½ cup packaged dry bread
    crumbs
2 tablespoons prepared mustard
1 teaspoon dried basil leaves
1½ teaspoons salt
½ teaspoon pepper
Dash Tabasco

½ cup finely chopped onion
½ cup finely chopped green
    pepper
1 cup chopped parsley
1½ lb ground veal
½ lb lean ground pork
1 lemon, thinly sliced
6 slices bacon

1. Preheat oven to 350F.

2. In large bowl, combine eggs, bread crumbs, mustard, basil, salt, pepper, Tabasco, onion, green pepper and parsley; beat with fork until well combined. Let stand 5 minutes.

3. Add veal and pork; mix well with fork.

4. Line a 13-by-9-by-1¾-inch pan with foil (use piece long enough to hang over ends of pan). Turn meatloaf mixture into pan; shape with hands to form a loaf 8 inches long and 4 inches wide. Overlap lemon slices on top; place bacon slices lengthwise on top.

5. Bake, uncovered, 1 hour and 15 minutes.

6. Let cool in pan on wire rack 30 minutes. Lifting with foil, remove meat loaf to serving platter; refrigerate several hours, covered, to chill well.

7. Serve with mustard if desired.

Makes 8 servings.

## MACARONI SALAD

1 pkg (1 lb) elbow macaroni
1 jar (9½ oz) sweet-pepper relish
1 can (4 oz) pimientos, drained
   and chopped
½ cup diced green pepper
1 tablespoon chopped parsley
2 teaspoons grated onion

1½ teaspoons salt
1½ cups mayonnaise or cooked
   salad dressing
½ cup dairy sour cream
½ cup milk
Crisp salad greens

1. Cook macaroni as the label directs. Drain, and rinse with cold water.

2. In large bowl, combine relish, pimiento, green pepper, parsley, onion, salt, 1 cup mayonnaise, the sour cream, and ¼ cup milk; blend well. Add macaroni; toss lightly until well combined.

3. Refrigerate, covered, until well chilled—several hours or overnight.

4. To serve: Combine remaining mayonnaise and milk; stir into salad. Turn into salad bowl; garnish with salad greens.

Makes 12 servings.

## FRUIT-GLAZED CREAM-CHEESECAKE

**Crust:**
2½ cups packaged graham-
   cracker crumbs
¼ cup sugar
½ cup butter or regular
   margarine, softened

**Filling:**
3 pkg (8-oz size) cream cheese,
   softened

3 tablespoons grated lemon peel
1½ cups sugar
3 tablespoons flour
4 eggs
½ cup lemon juice

Fruit Glazes, below
Sour cream

1. Make Crust: In medium bowl, with hands or back of metal spoon, mix graham-cracker crumbs with ¼ cup sugar and the butter until well combined.

2. With back of spoon, press crumb mixture to the bottom and sides of a greased 12-by-8-by-2-inch baking dish or 3-quart shallow baking dish.

3. Preheat oven to 350F.

4. Make Filling: In large bowl of electric mixer, at medium speed, beat cream cheese, lemon peel, sugar, and flour until they are smooth and well combined.

5. Beat in eggs, one at a time. Beat in lemon juice.

6 Pour filling into crust-lined dish. Bake 35 to 40 minutes, or until center of filling seems firm when dish is shaken.

7. Cool completely on wire rack. Refrigerate 4 hours or overnight, or until very well chilled.

8. Meanwhile, make Fruit Glazes.

9. Divide surface of cheesecake into thirds. Spoon glazes, each in one third, over cheesecake. Refrigerate 1 hour.

10. To serve, cut into squares. Pass sour cream.

Makes 12 servings.

**Strawberry Glaze**
1 pkg (10 oz) frozen strawberries, thawed
1 tablespoon sugar
2 teaspoons cornstarch

1. Drain the strawberries, reserving ½ cup of the liquid.

2. In a small saucepan, combine sugar and cornstarch. Stir in reserved liquid.

3. Over medium heat, bring to boiling, stirring; boil 1 minute.

4. Remove from heat; cool slightly. Stir in strawberries; cool completely.

**Pineapple Glaze**
1 tablespoon sugar
2 teaspoons cornstarch
1 can (8¼ oz) crushed pineapple,
 undrained

1. In small saucepan, combine sugar and cornstarch. Stir in pineapple.

2. Over medium heat, bring to boiling, stirring; boil 1 minute. Cool completely.

**Blueberry Glaze**
1 pkg (10 oz) frozen blueberries,
 thawed
1 tablespoon sugar
2 teaspoons cornstarch

1. Drain blueberries, reserving liquid. Measure liquid; add water, if necessary, to make ½ cup.

2. In small saucepan, combine sugar and cornstarch. Stir in reserved liquid.

3. Over medium heat, bring to boiling, stirring; boil 1 minute.

4. Remove from heat; cool slightly. Stir in blueberries. Cool completely.

# Menu III

Salade Niçoise *
French Potato Salad *
French Bread
Bowl of Strawberries and Green Grapes
McCall's Best Chocolate Loaf Cake *
Carafe of White Wine     Iced Coffee

## SALADE NIÇOISE

**Dressing:**
½ cup olive oil
¼ cup salad oil
¼ cup red-wine vinegar
1 teaspoon sugar
¾ teaspoon salt
¼ teaspoon cracked pepper

**Salad:**
1 lb fresh green beans, trimmed
    and washed; or 2 pkg
    (9-oz size) frozen whole green
    beans

1 medium red onion, thinly sliced
2 medium tomatoes, cut in
    wedges
½ cup pitted ripe olives
1 can (2 oz) anchovy fillets
2 cans (7-oz size) solid-pack tuna,
    drained and broken into
    chunks
2 hard-cooked eggs, sliced

1. Make Dressing: In jar with tight-fitting lid, combine oil, vinegar, sugar, salt, and pepper; shake vigorously until well combined.

2. Cook whole fresh beans in small amount of boiling salted water, covered, 17 to 20 minutes, or until tender. Cook frozen beans, as package label directs, 5 minutes, or just until tender. Drain well; turn into shallow dish. Add ½ cup dressing; toss until beans are well coated.

3. Refrigerate beans, covered. Also refrigerate remaining dressing

and the salad ingredients until well chilled—at least 2 hours.

4. To serve: Turn green beans into salad bowl. Add all but a few onion slices, tomato wedges, olives, and anchovy fillets; toss gently. Then add tuna chunks, egg slices; toss again.

5. Garnish with reserved onion, tomato, olives, and anchovy. Drizzle remaining dressing over all.

Makes 6 servings.

## FRENCH POTATO SALAD

3 lbs waxy or new potatoes
¼ cup wine vinegar
1½ teaspoons salt
1 teaspoon freshly ground pepper
3 tablespoons canned condensed
    consommé, undiluted
⅓ cup dry white wine

1 tablespoon chopped fresh
    tarragon or 1 teaspoon dried
    tarragon leaves
2 teaspoons chopped fresh
    chervil or ½ teaspoon dried
    chervil leaves
1½ tablespoons chopped parsley
1 tablespoon chopped chives
¾ cup salad or olive oil

1. Cook potatoes, covered, in enough boiling, salted water to cover, 30 minutes, or just until fork-tender.

2. Drain, peel; slice while still warm into ¼-inch-thick slices into salad bowl.

3. In bowl or jar with tight-fitting lid, combine vinegar and rest of ingredients; mix very well.

4. Pour over warm potatoes; toss gently to coat with liquid. Serve warm, or let cool and refrigerate. Before serving, toss gently again.

Makes 8 servings.

## McCALL'S BEST CHOCOLATE LOAF CAKE

1 cup boiling water
2 squares unsweetened
    chocolate, cut-up
2 cups sifted * all-purpose flour
¼ teaspoon salt
1 teaspoon baking soda

* Sift before measuring.

½ cup butter or regular
    margarine, softened
1 teaspoon vanilla extract
1¾ cups light-brown sugar, firmly
    packed
2 eggs
½ cup sour cream
Confectioners' sugar

1. In small bowl, pour boiling water over chocolate; let cool.

2. Meanwhile, preheat oven to 325F. Grease well and flour a 9-by-5-by-3-inch loaf pan.

3. Sift flour with salt and soda; set aside.

4. In large bowl of electric mixer, at high speed, beat butter, vanilla, sugar, and eggs until light and fluffy—about 5 minutes—occasionally scraping side of bowl with rubber scraper.

5. At low speed, beat in flour mixture (in fourths), alternately with sour cream (in thirds), beginning and ending with flour mixture.

6. Beat in chocolate mixture just until combined.

7. Pour batter into prepared pan. Bake 60 to 70 minutes, or until cake tester inserted in center comes out clean.

8. Cool in pan 15 minutes. Remove from pan; cool on wire rack. Serve sprinkled with confectioners' sugar, or frost as desired.

# Menu IV

Herring in Sour Cream *
Glazed Veal-and-Ham Loaf *
Bean Salad Vinaigrette *
Party Rye and Pumpernickel Bread
Fresh Peach and Blueberry Pie *
Iced Tea or Coffee

### HERRING IN SOUR CREAM

| | |
|---|---|
| 2 cans (6-oz size) matjes-herring fillets, or 3 matjes-herring fillets | 24 whole black peppercorns 2 bay leaves ¾ cup sour cream |
| 1 medium onion | ¼ cup dry white wine |

1. Rinse fillets in cold water; drain; dry on paper towels. Cut crosswise into 1-inch pieces. Then slice onion into thin rings.

2. In medium bowl, layer onion rings, black peppercorns, bay leaves, herring pieces.

3. Combine sour cream, wine. Pour over herring mixture, mixing gently to combine.

4. Refrigerate, covered, 8 hours, or overnight.

Makes 2 cups.

Pass as an hors d'oeuvre with wooden picks.

*Note:* Herring in Sour Cream may be stored, covered, in refrigerator 3 days.

―――――

### GLAZED VEAL-AND-HAM LOAF

5 slices bacon
2 lbs veal for scaloppini, pounded
  thin
2 lb thinly sliced ham
1 tablespoon salt
½ teaspoon black pepper

½ cup chopped parsley
⅓ cup finely chopped shallot
1 teaspoon dried thyme leaves
1 bay leaf
⅔ cup dry white wine
Parsley Glaze, below

1. Line a 9-by-5-by-3-inch loaf pan with bacon. Preheat oven to 325F.

2. Then, in loaf pan, layer veal and ham alternately, beginning and ending with veal and sprinkling each layer with a little salt, pepper, parsley, shallot and thyme. Place bay leaf on top; pour white wine over all.

3. Cover top with foil. Bake 2 hours. Cool on wire rack several hours (while loaf cools, place a heavy casserole on top to weight it down).

4. Unmold loaf on serving platter. Remove and discard bacon slices. Refrigerate loaf.

5. Several hours before serving, make Parsley Glaze. Brush slightly thickened glaze over top of loaf several times, to coat well. (If glaze becomes too thick, reheat slightly.) Refrigerate at least 1 hour before serving.

6. To serve: Garnish platter with parsley sprigs and tiny sweet gherkins, if desired. Cut loaf crosswise into thin slices.

Makes 8 to 10 servings.

**Parsley Glaze**
1 env unflavored gelatine
¼ cup white wine

¼ cup lemon juice
½ cup chopped parsley

1. Sprinkle gelatine over ½ cup water in small saucepan; let stand 5 minutes to soften. Heat gently, stirring, to dissolve gelatine.

2. Stir in ½ cup cold water, the wine, lemon juice and parsley. Place in a large bowl of ice; stir occasionally until slightly thickened —about 15 minutes.

## BEAN SALAD VINAIGRETTE

**Vinaigrette Dressing**
*1 cup olive or salad oil*
*⅓ cup red-wine-vinegar*
*1 teaspoon salt*
*⅛ teaspoon pepper*
*2 tablespoons chopped capers*
*2 tablespoons chopped green
onion*

*1 can (1 lb, 4 oz) chick peas,
drained*

*1 can (1 lb) whole baby carrots,
drained and sliced*
*1 can (1 lb) red kidney beans,
drained*
*1 can (1 lb, 4 oz) white kidney
beans, drained*
*Romaine-lettuce leaves, washed
and crisped*
*¼ cup chopped green onion*

1. Make vinaigrette dressing: Combine all ingredients in jar with tight-fitting lid. Shake vigorously.
2. Refrigerate dressing until ready to use. Shake it again just before using.
3. In large bowl, combine vinaigrette dressing with chick peas, carrots and red and white kidney beans; toss lightly to combine; refrigerate.
4. Just before serving, line salad bowl with romaine leaves. Turn bean mixture into bowl. Sprinkle with ¼ cup chopped green onion.
Makes 8 to 10 servings.

## FRESH PEACH AND BLUEBERRY PIE

*2 tablespoons lemon juice*
*3 cups sliced, pitted, peeled
peaches (2¼ lb)*
*1 cup blueberries*
*1 cup sugar*

*2 tablespoons quick-cooking
tapioca*
*½ teaspoon salt*
*Pastry for 2-crust pie*
*2 tablespoons butter or
margarine*

1. Sprinkle lemon juice over fruit in large bowl.
2. Combine sugar with tapioca and salt. Add to fruit, tossing lightly to combine. Let stand 15 minutes.
3. Meanwhile, preheat oven to 425F.
4. On lightly floured surface, roll out half of pastry into an 11-inch circle. Use to line 9-inch pie plate; trim.
5. Turn fruit mixture into pastry-lined pie plate, mounding in center; dot with butter.

6. Roll out remaining pastry into an 11-inch circle. Make several slits near center, for steam vents; adjust over filling; trim.

7. Fold edge of top crust under bottom crust; press together with fingertips. Crimp edge decoratively.

8. Bake 45 to 50 minutes, or until fruit is tender and crust is golden-brown.

9. Cool partially on wire rack; serve slightly warm.

Makes 8 servings.

# Parties for the Young

## Menu I

Egg Salad Sandwiches
Stuffed Dates
Crudités
Pink Party Cake *

### PINK PARTY CAKE

1 pkg (10 oz) frozen sliced
  strawberries, thawed
1 pkg (14½ oz) angel food cake
  mix

Strawberry Frosting:
2 egg whites
½ cup sugar
¼ teaspoon salt

Small pink and yellow gumdrops

1. Preheat oven to 375F. Drain strawberries, reserving juice.
2. Prepare cake mix as package label directs, using ⅓ cup juice from strawberries and 1 cup water.
3. Bake in 10-inch tube pan. Let cool completely.
4. Make Frosting: In top of double boiler, combine strawberries and remaining juice with egg whites, sugar and salt.
5. Place over boiling water (water in lower part of double boiler should not touch upper section); cook, beating constantly with portable electric mixer, until stiff peaks form when beater is slowly raised —5 to 7 minutes.

6. Remove from boiling water; cool slightly.

7. Spread frosting over top and side of cake. Decorate with gum-drops cut into flowers.

Makes 12 servings.

# Menu II

Pizza With Meatball and Mozzarella Filling *
Creamy Coleslaw *
Banana Split

## BEST OF ALL PIZZAS

| | |
|---|---|
| *1⅓ cups warm water* | *Salad oil* |
| *(105 to 115F)* | *2 teaspoons salt* |
| *1 pkg active dry yeast* | *4⅓ cups sifted * all-purpose flour* |

*\* Sift before measuring.*

1. Prepare Crust: If possible, check temperature of warm water with thermometer. Sprinkle yeast over water in large bowl, stirring until dissolved.

2. Add 2 tablespoons salad oil, the salt, and 4 cups flour; stir, with wooden spoon, until all flour is moistened.

3. Turn out on lightly floured surface. Knead in remaining flour until smooth—this will take about 10 minutes.

4. Place in medium bowl; brush very lightly with salad oil. Cover with towel; let rise in warm place (85F), free from drafts, until double in bulk—about 2 hours. (Or, if desired, refrigerate dough, covered, to rise overnight. Next day, remove from refrigerator; let stand at room temperature 30 minutes.)

5. Punch down dough; divide in half. Pat and stretch each half to fit a 14-inch pizza pan.

6. Move oven rack to lowest position; place cookie sheet on rack to heat. (This ensures a crisp crust.) Preheat oven to 500F.

7. Arrange filling over dough, as directed. Let set 10 minutes.

8. Bake pizza, placing pan on cookie sheet, about 20 minutes, or until crust is golden-brown and filling is bubbly.

Makes 2 pizzas.

## MEATBALL AND MOZZARELLA FILLING

2 lbs ground chuck
2 eggs
½ cup packaged dry bread
  crumbs
2 teaspoons salt

½ teaspoon pepper
4 tablespoons salad oil
3 cups Pizza Sauce, below
2 pkgs (8 oz) mozzarella cheese,
  coarsely grated (3 cups)

1. In medium bowl, combine beef, egg, bread crumbs, salt, and pepper; with fork, mix gently until well blended. Shape into 1-inch meatballs—about 60.

2. Heat salad oil in large skillet. Add meatballs, and sauté until browned on all sides—about 5 minutes. Drain on paper towels.

3. Spread sauce over unbaked crusts; cover with meatballs. Sprinkle mozzarella over all.

4. Bake as directed.

Makes enough filling for 2 (14-inch) pizzas.

**Pizza Sauce**
3 tablespoons olive or salad oil
1 cup sliced onion
1 clove garlic, crushed
2 cans (15-oz size) Italian plum
  tomatoes, undrained

1 tablespoon chopped parsley
1½ teaspoons salt
1 teaspoon dried oregano leaves
½ teaspoon sugar
¼ teaspoon dried basil leaves
¼ teaspoon pepper

1. In hot oil in medium saucepan, sauté onion and garlic until onion is golden—5 minutes.

2. Add rest of ingredients; bring to boiling. Reduce heat; simmer, uncovered, 25 minutes; stir occasionally.

Makes 3 cups; enough for 2 (14-inch) pizzas.

## CREAMY COLESLAW

**Dressing:**
2 cups mayonnaise or cooked
  salad dressing
¼ cup prepared horseradish
1 tablespoon sugar
1 tablespoon lemon juice
1 tablespoon grated onion
2 teaspoons salt
½ teaspoon paprika

3 quarts finely shredded green
  cabbage (3 lb)
1½ cups shredded carrots (½ lb)
½ cup shredded radishes

Green-pepper strips
Shredded radishes

1. In large bowl, combine mayonnaise, horseradish, sugar, lemon juice, onion, salt, and paprika; mix well.

2. Add cabbage, carrots, and ½ cup radishes; toss until vegetables are well coated with dressing.

3. Refrigerate, covered, until well chilled—several hours, or overnight.

3. To serve: Garnish with green-pepper strips and shredded radishes.

Makes 12 servings.

# Menu III

Spaghetti With White Clam Sauce *
Sliced Fresh Tomatoes
Italian Bread
Ice Cream Sundaes

## SPAGHETTI WITH WHITE CLAM SAUCE

*2 cans (7½-oz size) minced clams*
*¼ cup olive or salad oil*
*¼ cup butter or margarine*
*2 or 3 cloves garlic, crushed*

*2 tablespoons chopped parsley*
*1½ teaspoons salt*
*1 pkg (8 oz) cooked spaghetti*
*Grated Parmesan cheese*

1. Drain clams, reserving ¾ cup liquid. Set aside.

2. In skillet, slowly heat oil and butter. Add garlic, and sauté until golden. Remove from heat.

3. Stir in clam liquid, parsley, salt; bring to boiling. Reduce heat; simmer, uncovered, 10 minutes.

4. Add clams; simmer 3 minutes.

5. Serve hot over spaghetti, with Parmesan cheese.

Makes 4 to 6 servings.

# Menu IV

Tamale Casserole *
Breadsticks
Tossed Green Salad
Deep-Dish Apple Pie *

## TAMALE CASSEROLE

2 tablespoons salad or olive oil
1 cup chopped onion
2 cloves garlic, crushed
1½ lb ground chuck
3 to 5 teaspoons chili powder
2 teaspoons salt
1 can (8 oz) tomato sauce

1 can (12 oz) Mexican-style corn,
    undrained
1 can (15¼ oz) red kidney beans,
    undrained
½ cup pitted ripe olives,
    quartered
½ pkg (6¼-oz size) tortilla chips
1 cup grated Cheddar cheese

1. In hot oil in Dutch oven, sauté onion and garlic until golden —about 3 minutes. Add ground chuck, breaking up with fork.

2. Cook, stirring occasionally, over medium heat until browned— about 10 minutes. Drain off excess fat.

3. Add chili powder, salt, tomato sauce, corn, and kidney beans. Bring to boiling, stirring; reduce heat; simmer, uncovered and stirring occasionally, 20 minutes.

4. Preheat oven to 375F.

5. Turn meat mixture into 10-inch round, shallow casserole. Sprinkle with olives. Arrange tortilla chips around edge; sprinkle chips with cheese. Bake 10 minutes, or until cheese is melted.

Makes 6 servings.

## DEEP-DISH APPLE PIE

Pastry for 1-crust pie
2 lbs tart cooking apples
1 tablespoon lemon juice
1 cup sugar
3 tablespoons flour

½ teaspoon nutmeg
¼ teaspoon cloves
1 egg yolk
½ cup heavy cream

1. Prepare pastry. Refrigerate, wrapped in waxed paper, until ready to use.

2. Preheat oven to 400F. Lightly grease 1½-quart casserole.

3. Wash apples; core; slice thinly into large bowl. Sprinkle with lemon juice.

4. Combine sugar, flour and spices; gently toss with apples, mixing well. Turn into prepared casserole.

5. On lightly floured surface, roll out pastry into a 9½-inch circle. Fit over top of casserole; flute edge.

6. Make several cuts, 1 inch long, in center, for vents.

7. Brush lightly with egg yolk beaten with 1 tablespoon water; bake 50 to 60 minutes. Top should be golden-brown and apples tender. Remove from oven to rack. Pour cream into vents. Serve warm.

Makes 8 servings.

# Home Weddings

## An Afternoon Wedding Reception Planned for 50

### NOTES ON PREPARATION

For 50 people, we have planned seven kinds of canapés, approximately 50 of each kind. In addition, there are about 60 Cream-Cheese-and-Watercress Sandwiches and 100 small servings of hot Chicken-and-Seafood Newburg.

Everything is finger food except for the cake. You may need to rent champagne glasses, plates and forks for the cake, a punch bowl and punch cups and several serving trays.

All of our canapés and the Cream-Cheese-and-Watercress Sandwiches and Bread Basket can be made a day ahead and stored as directed. Several hours before serving the canapés may be sliced and arranged on serving trays. These can then be refrigerated, covered with a damp towel, until serving. Arrange Cream-Cheese Sandwiches in Bread Basket just before serving.

The Chicken-and-Seafood Newburg and Toast Cups may be made a day ahead and stored as directed. Reheat seafood mixture just before turning into heated chafing dish for serving. (If mixture seems too thick, add a little more sherry.)

The cake may be made and frosted the day before and stored in the refrigerator. Decorate with fresh flowers some time before serving.

The champagne must be chilled in ice several hours ahead.

The Ice Ring may be made and frozen the day before. When it's frozen, it may also be unmolded and stored in freezer. The white wine and cassis for the punch bowl should be well chilled. Just before serving combine wine and cassis in chilled punch bowl (to chill bowl, fill with ice until chilled, then empty out); float Ice Ring on top.

Champagne
Assorted Canapés *
Cream-Cheese-and-
Watercress Sandwiches en Croûte *
Seafood-and-Chicken Newburg *
in Chafing Dish
Wedding Cake*
White-Wine-Cassis Punch Bowl *
Salted Almonds     Pastel Mints

---

### SWISS-CHEESE-AND-OLIVE ROLLS

1 lb loaf unsliced white bread
1 cup softened butter or
    margarine
24 to 32 large stuffed olives

8 slices Swiss cheese (about 8 oz)
2 tablespoons strong mustard
2 cups chopped parsley

1. With long serrated knife, trim all crusts from bread. Slice into eight lengthwise slices. Using a rolling pin, gently roll bread to make thin.

2. Spread each slice with butter, using about ½ cup in all.

3. Place 3 or 4 olives at one end of each slice of bread.

4. Arrange cheese slices over rest of bread; spread lightly with mustard.

5. Roll up each slice of bread, starting from olive end.

6. Spread outside of rolls with remaining butter. Sprinkle ¼ cup parsley on waxed paper, and roll sandwich rolls in it to cover completely with parsley.

7. To store, wrap in damp paper towels, and refrigerate. To serve, slice each roll crosswise into seven sandwiches.

Makes 56.

## EGG-SALAD RIBBONS

*1 lb loaf thin-sliced white bread*
*1 lb loaf thin-sliced whole-wheat*
*  bread*
*6 hard-cooked eggs, finely*
*  chopped*
*⅓ cup mayonnaise or cooked*
*  salad dressing*
*2 tablespoons sour cream*

*¼ teaspoon salt*
*1 tablespoon finely chopped*
*  onion*
*1 tablespoon chopped fresh dill*
*  or ½ teaspoon dried dillweed*
*Dash black pepper*
*Fresh dill sprigs (optional)*

1. With sharp knife, trim crusts from bread.

2. Combine eggs, mayonnaise, sour cream, salt, onion, dill and pepper; mix well.

3. Make three-decker sandwiches, with 1 rounded tablespoon egg salad on two slices: five sandwiches with white, whole-wheat, then white bread; and five sandwiches with whole-wheat, white, then whole-wheat bread. Press each down with a plate for 30 minutes.

4. To store: Wrap in damp paper towels. Refrigerate. To serve, slice each into six ribbons; cut each ribbon crosswise in half; then cut in half again. Decorate each with sprig of dill.

Makes 120 ribbons of each design.

## PINEAPPLE-CREAM-CHEESE-AND-WALNUT ROLLS

*1 lb loaf unsliced white bread*
*2 cans (8-oz size) crushed*
*  pineapple*
*2 pkg (8-oz size) cream cheese,*
*  softened*

*4 slices bacon, cooked and*
*  crumbled*
*2 tablespoons chopped walnuts*
*2 tablespoons chopped raisins*
*1 cup finely chopped walnuts*

1. With long serrated knife, trim all crusts from bread. Slice into eight lengthwise slices. Using a rolling pin, gently roll bread to make thin.

2. Drain pineapple, reserving liquid. Mix 1 package cream cheese with the bacon, 2 tablespoons chopped walnuts, the raisins, pineapple and 1 tablespoon reserved pineapple juice.

3. Spread 3 tablespoons cream-cheese mixture on each bread slice; roll up from short end. Mix remaining package of cream cheese with 2 tablespoons reserved pineapple juice. Use to spread on outside of

each sandwich roll. Then roll in finely chopped nuts placed on sheet of waxed paper.

4. To store: Wrap in damp paper towels; refrigerate. To serve, slice each roll crosswise into seven sandwiches.

Makes 56.

## HAM ROLLS

2 pkg (8-oz size) sliced ham
(12 slices in all)
1½ cups whipped cream cheese

1 jar (8 oz) midget gherkins,
drained

1. Spread 1 slice ham with 1 tablespoon cream cheese. Top with slice of ham; spread with 2 tablespoons cream cheese.

2. Arrange several gherkins in a row along short edge. Roll up from gherkin side. There will be six rolls.

3. To store: Arrange on tray; cover with damp towel. Refrigerate.

4. To serve: Slice each roll into eight crosswise slices.

Makes 48.

## CUCUMBER SPIRALS

1 lb loaf unsliced white bread
⅔ cup softened butter or
    margarine
3 tablespoons chopped parsley
½ teaspoon grated lemon peel

2 teaspoons lemon juice
1 long cucumber, washed
½ cup softened butter or
    margarine
2 cups chopped parsley

1. With long serrated knife, trim all crusts from bread. Slice into eight lengthwise slices. Using rolling pin, gently roll slices, to make them thin.

2. Combine ⅔ cup butter, 3 tablespoons parsley, the lemon peel and lemon juice; mix well.

3. Spread bread with butter mixture.

4. Slice unpared cucumber into 8 lengthwise strips. Trim ends from each. Place 1 strip on each of 4 bread slices. (Refrigerate leftover cucumber to use another time.) Roll up from long side. Place each cucumber roll on a remaining slice of buttered bread, cut edge down; roll up again.

5. Spread outside of each roll with butter. Sprinkle 2 cups chopped

parsley on waxed paper, and roll sandwich rolls in it, to cover completely with parsley.

6. To store, wrap each in damp paper towels. To serve, slice each roll crosswise into 15 spirals.

Makes 60.

## HAM-AND-SWISS-CHEESE ROLLS

1½ cups whipped cream cheese
2 teaspoons chopped parsley
2 pkg (8-oz size) sliced ham
    (12 slices in all)

6 slices Swiss cheese (about 8 oz)
2 tablespoons strong mustard

1. Combine cream cheese and parsley; mix well. Spread 1 slice ham with 2 tablespoons cream-cheese mixture; top with 1 slice Swiss cheese. Spread with 1 teaspoon mustard.

2. Top with 1 slice ham; spread with 2 tablespoons cream-cheese mixture. Repeat to make six in all.

3. Roll up each from short side. To store: Arrange on tray; cover with damp towel. Refrigerate.

4. To serve: Slice each roll into eight crosswise slices.

Makes 48.

## PÂTÉ SPIRALS

16 slices thin-sliced white bread
8 slices thin-sliced whole-wheat
    bread
1 can (4¾ oz) liver pâté

2 tablespoons mayonnaise or
    cooked salad dressing
2 tablespoons finely chopped
    scallion
1 tablespoon chopped parsley

1. Trim crusts from bread. Roll gently with rolling pin.

2. Combine pâté, mayonnaise, scallion and parsley; mix well.

3. Spread one slice white bread with 1 rounded teaspoon filling; top with whole-wheat slice; spread with 1 rounded teaspoon filling; then top with white slice, and spread with 1 rounded teaspoon filling. Continue with rest of bread and filling, to make eight stacks of three slices each.

4. Roll up each from long side. To store: Refrigerate, wrapped with damp paper towels. To serve, cut crosswise into six spirals.

Makes 48 spirals.

## CREAM-CHEESE-AND-WATERCRESS SANDWICHES EN CROÛTE

*2 large bunches watercress*
*1½ cups soft butter or margarine*
*½ teaspoon salt*
*4 pkg (3-oz size) cream cheese*
  *with chives, softened*

*2 tablespoons lemon juice*
*4 loaves (1-lb size) thinly sliced*
  *white bread*
*Bread Basket, below*

1. Wash and drain the watercress. Reserve small center sprigs for garnish—about 64.
2. Remove stems from remaining watercress. Finely chop enough watercress to measure ½ cup.
3. Beat the butter and the salt with electric mixer until smooth. Beat in the cream cheese. Gradually beat in lemon juice. Then beat in the chopped watercress.
4. With sharp knife, trim crusts from each slice of bread, to make a 3-inch square. Roll each slice with rolling pin.
5. Spread bread slices evenly with watercress butter, using about 2½ teaspoons for each. Roll up, jelly-roll fashion. Insert a reserved watercress sprig in one end.
6. To store: Arrange rolls in single layer on tray; cover with damp paper towels. Refrigerate. To serve, arrange in Bread Basket.
Makes 64.

### BREAD BASKET

*1 loaf (2 lb, 3 oz) sandwich bread*
  *(about 16 inches long)*

*¼ cup butter or margarine,*
  *melted*

1. With a long serrated knife, slice off the top from bread lengthwise. Carefully cut all around the inside edge of the loaf to make a shell about ¼ inch thick.
2. Carefully remove bread. (Save bread for bread crumbs.)
3. Cut scallops along sides of bread. Cut four arcs on each long side and one on each end.
4. Preheat oven to 350F. Brush outside of basket with melted butter. Place on cookie sheet. Toast in oven just until light golden —about 8 to 10 minutes. Let cool.
5. Store at room temperature until ready to use.
Makes 1 basket.

## SEAFOOD-AND-CHICKEN NEWBURG

2 cans (5-oz size) crabmeat
½ cup butter or margarine
6 tablespoons flour
1 teaspoon salt
Dash pepper
Dash cayenne
1 can (13¾ oz) chicken broth
   (see Note 1)
1 cup heavy cream
3 tablespoons dry sherry
2 hard-cooked eggs, finely
   chopped
2 cooked whole chicken breasts,
   chopped (see Note 2)

2 tablespoons finely chopped
   onion
1 cup coarsely chopped fresh
   mushrooms
2 tablespoons finely chopped
   parsley
2 tablespoons finely chopped
   chives
3 jars (4.4-oz size) baby shrimp,
   drained
Chopped parsley
Toast Cups, page 260

1. Drain crabmeat, and remove any cartilage.

2. Melt 3 tablespoons butter in medium saucepan. Remove from heat; stir in flour, salt, pepper and cayenne until smooth. Gradually stir in chicken broth and cream.

3. Bring mixture to boiling, stirring; sauce will be thickened and smooth.

4. Stir in sherry, chopped egg, crabmeat and chicken.

5. Heat rest of butter in small skillet; sauté onion, mushrooms, parsley and chives until mushrooms are tender—about 5 minutes. Stir into crab-chicken mixture. Turn into chafing dish to keep warm. Decorate edge with shrimp. Sprinkle with parsley.

6. To serve, fill Toast Cups with Newburg mixture (about 1 rounded teaspoon for each); decorate each with shrimp and parsley.

Makes about 100 servings.

*Note 1:* Or use chicken broth reserved from cooking chicken breasts.

*Note 2:* Cook chicken breasts as directed in Pâté-Stuffed Chicken Breasts en Gelée, page 236.

## TOAST CUPS

*50 slices thin-sliced white bread*       *⅔ cup butter or margarine,*
   *(3½ [1-lb size] loaves)*           *melted*

1. Preheat oven to 350F.
2. With 2-inch round cookie cutter, cut out 100 rounds of white bread. Brush both sides with melted butter. Press into 1¾-inch muffin-pan cups.
3. Bake 10 to 15 minutes, or until golden around edge. Gently lift out of pans; cool on wire racks.
4. Store, lightly covered, at room temperature. To serve, fill each cup with 1 rounded teaspoon filling.

Makes 100 toast cups.

## WEDDING CAKE

**Cake**
*4 pkg (1-lb, 2.5-oz or 18½-oz size)*
   *yellow or devil's-food-cake mix*
*8 eggs*

**Decoration**
*1½ dozen fresh pink or white*
   *roses in various sizes*
*Other small pink or white flowers*

*White Frosting, below*

1. Day before serving, make cake: Preheat oven to 350F. Grease well and flour a 12-by-2-inch tier-cake pan, a 9-by-2-inch tier-cake pan and a 6-by-2-inch tier-cake pan.
2. Prepare 2 packages cake mix together, as package label directs, using 4 eggs. Measure 3 cups batter; pour into prepared 9-inch pan. Pour 6¼ cups batter into prepared 12-inch pan. Pour 1½ cups batter into prepared 6-inch pan.
3. Bake large layer 40 to 45 minutes, medium-size layer 35 to 40 minutes, small layer 30 to 35 minutes, or until surface springs back when gently pressed with fingertip.
4. Cool in pans on wire rack 15 minutes. Remove from pans; cool thoroughly on wire racks.
5. Prepare remaining 2 packages of cake mix together, using 4 eggs. Bake in 9-, 6-, and 12-inch tier-cake pans, as directed above.
6. When the six layers are completely cool, make White Frosting. Cut an 8-inch and a 5-inch circle from thin cardboard. Cover each with foil or plastic film.

7. To assemble and frost cake: If necessary, trim the tops of layers so they will stack evenly. Spread a teaspoonful of frosting in middle of a large round tray—at least 14 inches in diameter. Place one 12-inch layer, top side down, in center of tray; spread 1½ cups frosting on layer. Top with second 12-inch layer, bottom side down; spread with 1 cup frosting.

8. Place prepared 8-inch cardboard circle in center, then one 9-inch cake layer, top side down; spread with ¾ cup frosting. Add second 9-inch layer, bottom side down, and spread with ¾ cup frosting.

9. Top with prepared 5-inch cardboard circle, then one 6-inch cake layer, top side down; spread with ½ cup frosting. Then top with remaining 6-inch layer, bottom side down.

10. Reserve 3 cups frosting. Spread remaining frosting on cake: First, frost side of each layer; then, starting at top layer, frost remaining surfaces, making all frosting smooth with a spatula dipped in warm water.

11. Using reserved frosting in pastry bag with number-30 star tip, make a border on rim of each layer and around base of cake. To make border: Make slight curve on slant from left to right around edge of each layer.

12. Cover with a tent of foil, and store in a cool place, or, if possible, refrigerate overnight.

13. Early next day, decorate cake: Trim stems of roses; remove leaves and set aside.

14. Arrange roses on cake. Arrange rose leaves around base of cake.

15. Keep cake in a cool place, or, if possible, refrigerate until shortly before serving.

16. To serve cake: Cut top layer into eight wedges; remove cardboard. Cut next layer into 16 wedges; remove cardboard. Cut a circle in 12-inch-layer, 2½ inches from edge, to make a ring. Cut the ring into 20 pieces; cut remaining cake into eight wedges.

Makes 52 servings.

**White Frosting** ° °
¾ cup shortening
¼ cup butter or regular
   margarine, softened

2 pkg (1-lb size) confectioners'
   sugar
½ cup water
2 teaspoons vanilla extract
½ teaspoon almond extract

1. In large bowl of electric mixer, at low speed, beat shortening and butter until light and fluffy.

2. Beat in sugar, 1 cup at a time, alternately with water, beating until smooth after each addition.

3. Add vanilla and almond extracts; continue beating until smooth and of spreading consistency.

4. Keep frosting covered with damp cloth to prevent drying out. Beat again just before using.

** You will need to make this recipe twice. Make it in separate batches.

## WHITE-WINE–CASSIS PUNCH BOWL

*3 gallons dry white wine*  
*6 cups crème de cassis*  
*Ice Ring, below*

*1 pint box strawberries, washed*  
*and hulled*

1. Several hours ahead, chill white wine and cassis. Also, fill punch bowl with ice to chill well.

2. Just before serving, empty punch bowl of ice. Combine 1 gallon white wine and 2 cups cassis in punch bowl; mix well. (The punch bowl may not be large enough to serve any more than this at one time. As more punch is needed, mix 1 gallon white wine with 2 cups cassis.) Float Ice Ring on top. Add strawberries.

**Ice Ring**  
*2 large navel oranges, washed*

*Distilled water*

1. Slice unpeeled oranges crosswise into slices about ⅛ inch thick. Arrange in single layer in bottom of a 5-cup ring mold, overlapping on sides.

2. Gradually pour in enough distilled water to measure 1 inch deep, without disturbing orange slices.

3. Freeze until firm. Then fill the rest of the mold with distilled water. Freeze until ice ring is firm—overnight.

4. When ice ring is firm, place in warm water a few seconds to loosen ice. Turn out on waxed paper. Return to freezer at once until ready to use.

# A Wedding Luncheon for 25

Warm Quiche Lorraine * or
Hot Cheese-Ball Appetizer *
Breast of Chicken in White Wine *
Marinated Asparagus Salad *
Assorted Hot Buttered Rolls
Raspberry Sherbet Mold
Wedding Cake
Champagne     Coffee

## WARM QUICHE LORRAINE

| | |
|---|---|
| 1½ pkg (11-oz size) piecrust mix | 4 cups light cream |
| 1 lb sliced bacon | 1½ teaspoons salt |
| 2 cups finely chopped onion | 1 teaspoon sugar |
| 3 cups grated natural Swiss | ¼ teaspoon nutmeg |
| cheese (¾ lb) | ¼ teaspoon pepper |
| 6 eggs | Dash cayenne |

1. Prepare piecrust mix as package label directs.

2. On lightly floured surface, roll out pastry to an 18-by-15-inch rectangle. Use to line a 15½-by-10½-by-1-inch jelly-roll pan; flute edge. Refrigerate until needed.

3. Preheat oven to 375F.

4. Fry bacon until crisp. Drain on paper towels; crumble. Sauté onion in 2 tablespoons bacon drippings until golden.

5. Sprinkle cheese over bottom of pastry shell; sprinkle bacon and onion over cheese.

6. In large bowl, with rotary beater, beat eggs with cream, salt, sugar, nutmeg, pepper and cayenne until well combined. Pour into prepared shell.

7. Bake 35 to 40 minutes, or until golden and center is firm when gently pressed with fingertip.

8. Let cool on wire rack 10 minutes. To serve, cut quiche into squares—about 1½ inches.

Makes about 25 appetizer-size servings; 60 to 70 cocktail servings.

## HOT CHEESE-BALL APPETIZER

1 lb grated Parmesan cheese
1 lb cream cheese, softened
4 eggs
1 teaspoon salt

Dash cayenne
2 cups fresh white-bread crumbs
Peanut or salad oil for deep
    frying

1. In large bowl, combine both kinds of cheese, the eggs, salt and cayenne. Beat with wooden spoon until smooth. Refrigerate, covered, 1 hour.

2. Form into 1-inch balls. Roll each ball lightly in bread crumbs on waxed paper. Refrigerate.

3. In a deep skillet or deep-fat fryer, slowly heat oil (about 2 inches) to 350F on deep-frying thermometer. Fry cheese balls, turning once, 1 minute, or until golden-brown. Drain on paper towels. Serve hot.

Makes 60.

*Note:* If desired, make day ahead and refrigerate, covered. Fry as in Step 3.

## BREAST OF CHICKEN IN WHITE WINE

25 halves (about 5 lbs in all)
    chicken breasts, skinned and
    boned
1 cup butter or margarine
½ cup salad oil
3 cups sliced onion
2 lbs small fresh mushrooms,
    washed and stems removed
1½ teaspoons salt
1 teaspoon pepper

1 tablespoon dried thyme leaves
2 bay leaves, crushed
2 cups dry white wine
2 cans (13¾-oz size) chicken
    broth

**Sauce**
¼ cup dry white wine
2 tablespoons flour

1. Wipe chicken breasts well with damp paper towels.

2. In a large skillet, heat ¼ cup butter and ¼ cup oil. Add chicken breasts, several pieces at a time; sauté until golden—about 10 minutes in all. Remove to large roasting pan. Continue to brown rest of chicken, adding more butter and oil as needed.

3. Overlap browned chicken breasts in bottom of 17-by-12½-by-2¼-inch roasting pan. Preheat oven to 350F.

4. Heat remaining butter and oil in skillet. Add onion and mush-

rooms; sauté stirring, until onion is golden—about 5 minutes. Spread onion-mushroom mixture over chicken breasts.

5. Combine drippings left in skillet with salt, pepper, thyme and bay leaves. Add wine and chicken broth; bring to boiling, stirring. Pour over chicken. Cover pan tightly with foil.

6. Bake, basting twice, 1 hour, or until chicken breasts are tender.

7. Remove cooked chicken breasts and mushrooms; keep warm. Strain mixture remaining in roasting pan into large saucepan. Bring to boiling; boil, uncovered, to reduce to 2 cups—for sauce.

8. Make sauce: Combine wine with flour; add to mixture in skillet. Bring to boiling; reduce heat; simmer 2 minutes.

9. Just before serving, spoon sauce over chicken breasts; garnish with whole mushrooms and watercress.

Makes 25 servings.

*Note:* If desired, bake in two 13-by-9-by-2-inch roasting pans. Chicken breasts may be cooked ahead; bake 1 hour, as in Step 6; cool completely; refrigerate, covered. Before serving, heat chicken breasts until hot; proceed with Step 7.

## MARINATED ASPARAGUS SALAD

*4 cans (15-oz size) green asparagus spears*
*4 cans (15-oz size) white asparagus spears*

**Lemon Vinaigrette**
*1 bottle (8 oz) herb-and-garlic salad dressing*

*½ cup lemon juice*
*2 tablespoons snipped chives*
*¼ teaspoon white pepper*

*2 heads Boston lettuce*
*1 bunch watercress*

1. Drain asparagus spears.

2. Make lemon vinaigrette: In a small bowl, combine all of the vinaigrette ingredients.

3. In large, shallow, glass baking dish arrange asparagus spears. Pour dressing over asparagus.

4. Refrigerate, covered, several hours to chill well.

5. Cut core from lettuce; discard. Wash leaves; dry on paper towels. Refrigerate in crisper several hours or overnight. Wash watercress; drain. Refrigerate in crisper.

6. To serve: Arrange lettuce leaves on chilled large serving platter. Remove asparagus from vinaigrette; arrange around the outside of platter in groups, alternating green and white asparagus. Place watercress in center. Spoon vinaigrette over top.

Makes 25 servings.

## RASPBERRY-SHERBET MOLD

*6 pints raspberry sherbet*          *Creme de cassis*
*½ pint heavy cream, whipped*
  *stiff*

1. Day ahead: Line 3-quart heart-shape mold with plastic film.

2. Remove sherbet from freezer; let stand at room temperature to soften—about 20 minutes. Pack into mold. Smooth surface with spatula.

3. Place in freezer until firm—overnight.

4. To unmold: Grasp plastic film and pull out sherbet mold; invert on chilled serving tray. Discard plastic film.

5. Decorate outside edge and around bottom with whipped-cream ruching, using a pastry bag and number-6 rosette tube. Return to freezer until serving. (If stored more than one day, freezer-wrap in foil.)

6. Pass creme de cassis to serve over each portion of sherbet—about 1 tablespoon per serving.

Makes 25 servings.

# Holiday
# Entertaining

## Menu I

An Informal Christmas Gathering
For the adults:
Vodka Wassail Bowl *
Cream Cheese with Red Caviar
on Pumpernickel *
Platter of Smoked-Salmon Rolls
with Capers
Cucumber Sandwiches
Coffee

For the children:
Hot Mulled Cider *
Peanut-Butter-and-Bacon Sandwiches
Warm Sugared Doughnuts
Gingerbread Men
Peppermint-Stick-Ice-Cream
Sundaes

## VODKA WASSAIL BOWL

*Whole cloves*
*3 large oranges*
*1 gallon apple juice*
*½ cup lemon juice*

*10 (2-inch) cinnamon sticks*
*2 cups vodka*
*¼ cup brandy*

1. Preheat oven to 350F.
2. Insert cloves, ½ inch apart, in unpeeled oranges. Place in shallow pan; bake, uncovered, 30 minutes.
3. Meanwhile, heat apple juice in large kettle until bubbles form around edge of kettle.
4. Add lemon juice, cinnamon sticks, and baked oranges. Heat, covered, over low heat, 30 minutes. Remove from heat.
5. Add vodka, brandy; mix well. Pour into punch bowl. Serve warm. Makes about 36 (4-oz) servings.

## CREAM CHEESE WITH RED CAVIAR

*2 pkg (8-oz size) cream cheese*
*1 jar (4 oz) red caviar, slightly*
  *drained*

*Pumpernickel slices*

1. Let cream cheese stand at room temperature, to soften—about 1 hour. Then, on serving tray, shape into a mound about 5 inches in diameter; flatten top. Refrigerate, covered.
2. To serve: Spoon caviar over top of cream cheese, letting a little drizzle over side. Surround with pumpernickel. If desired, decorate with holly.
Makes 30 servings.

## HOT MULLED CIDER

*1 quart cider*
*¼ cup sugar*
*Dash salt*

*12 whole cloves*
*2 (4-inch) cinnamon sticks*
*8 whole allspice*

1. Combine all ingredients in 2-quart saucepan; bring to boil, stirring until sugar is dissolved.

2. Cool. Refrigerate, covered, several hours.

3. Just before serving, reheat slowly. Strain to remove spices. Serve hot, in mugs or punch cups.

Makes 8 (4-oz) servings.

# Menu II
# New-Year's-Day Open House

Old English Eggnog *
Champagne Punch Bowl *
Molded Chicken-Liver Pâté *
on White-Toast Squares
Hot Biscuits Filled
with Deviled Ham
Tray of Assorted Cheeses and Crackers
Smoked-Turkey Sandwiches
Tiny Shrimp-Salad Sandwiches
Christmas Cake      Poundcake
Winter Fruit Bowl
Coffee

## OLD ENGLISH EGGNOG

6 egg yolks
1 cup granulated sugar
2 quarts light cream
1 pint cognac

1 cup light rum
6 egg whites
½ cup confectioners' sugar

1. In large bowl, beat egg yolks until thick. Gradually add granulated sugar, beating until light.

2. Add cream; beat until very well combined. Slowly stir in cognac and rum. Refrigerate, covered, until well chilled.

3. About 1 hour before serving, beat the egg whites until they are foamy. Gradually add the confectioners' sugar, beating well after each addition. Continue beating until soft peaks form when the beater is slowly raised.

4. Gently fold into egg-yolk mixture.

5. Refrigerate, covered, until serving time.

Makes about 28 (4-oz) servings.

## CHAMPAGNE PUNCH BOWL

*1 large bunch seedless green
grapes (about 1½ lb)*
*2 cups dry white wine*
*1 cup cognac*
*2 tablespoons sugar*

*2 bottles (7-oz size) club soda,
chilled*
*6 strawberries, hulls on, washed
(optional)*
*1 bottle (4/5 quart) champagne,
chilled*

1. Day ahead: Wash grapes; place on small tray. Place in freezer.
2. Several hours before serving: In pitcher or bowl, combine sauterne, cognac, and sugar; stir until sugar is dissolved. Refrigerate.
3. To serve: Pour sauterne mixture into punch bowl. Stir in soda. Add frozen grapes and the strawberries.
4. Pour champagne into punch just before serving.
Makes about 16 (4-oz) servings.

## MOLDED CHICKEN-LIVER PÂTÉ

*2 cups butter or margarine*
*1 small onion, chopped*
*1 lb chicken livers*
*1 can (10½ oz) condensed
chicken broth, undiluted*
*¼ cup Marsala or sherry*
*1 clove garlic, crushed*
*½ teaspoon paprika*
*½ teaspoon salt*

*⅛ teaspoon allspice*
*⅛ teaspoon Tabasco*
*1 env unflavored gelatine*
*⅓ cup bourbon*
*1 cup coarsely chopped walnuts*
*3 pitted ripe olives, sliced*

*White-toast squares; or
pumpernickel, thinly sliced*

1. In 1 cup hot butter in skillet, sauté onion until tender—about 5 minutes.
2. Add chicken livers; cook, stirring occasionally, 10 minutes.
3. Add 1 cup chicken broth, the wine, garlic, salt, paprika, allspice, and Tabasco; cook, stirring occasionally, 5 minutes longer.
4. Meanwhile, sprinkle gelatine over remaining chicken broth in can, to soften. Add to chicken-liver mixture; stir until gelatine is dissolved. Remove from heat.
5. Add remaining butter and the bourbon; stir until butter is melted.
6. In electric blender, blend 1 cup of mixture at a time until smooth. Turn into large bowl. Stir in nuts.

7. Refrigerate, covered, just until pâté is chilled—about 1 hour. Also, refrigerate 2½-quart bowl. Line chilled bowl with plastic film; fill with pâté.

8. Refrigerate, covered, until firm—8 hours or overnight.

9. To serve: Invert bowl of pâté on serving platter. Peel off plastic film. Decorate top with olive slices, and surround with toast squares. Makes about 60 hors-d'oeuvre servings.

# Menu III
# A Christmas Dinner

Hot Clam Bisque
Roast Goose*
Potato Stuffing *    Giblet Gravy *
Cranberry-Apple Sauce
Buttered Green Beans
Crisp Relishes    Hot Rolls
New England Plum Pudding *
With Pudding Sauce *
Fresh-Fruit Bowl    Nuts in Shell
Cider    White Wine    Coffee

### ROAST STUFFED GOOSE

Potato Stuffing, below
12-lb ready-to-cook goose
Giblet Gravy, below
1 tablespoon lemon juice
1 teaspoon salt

⅛ teaspoon pepper

Cranberries-on-a-String With
Link Sausages, below

1. Make Potato Stuffing.

2. Preheat oven to 325F. Remove giblets and neck from goose; reserve for Giblet Gravy. Wash goose inside and out; dry well with paper towels. Remove all fat from inside, and discard. Rub cavity with lemon juice, salt and pepper.

3. Spoon stuffing lightly into neck cavity; bring skin of neck over back and fasten with poultry pins. Spoon stuffing lightly into body cavity; close with poultry pins and lace with twine. Bend wing tips under body; tie ends of legs together.

4. Prick skin only (not meat) over thighs, back and breast very well. Place, breast side up, on rack in large roasting pan.

5. Roast, uncovered, 2 hours. Remove goose from oven.

6. Pour fat from pan and discard. Roast goose, uncovered, 1 hour longer. Remove goose to platter; keep warm. Make Giblet Gravy.

7. To serve, garnish with whole cranberries on a string and cooked link sausages. Serve with Giblet Gravy.

### To String Cranberries
Thread washed cranberries on a string, using a large darning needle and heavy-duty thread.

### Link Sausages
Place 1 pound pork-sausage links in a heavy skillet with water 1 inch deep. Cook over medium heat until water is evaporated. Then sauté gently 15 to 20 minutes, turning until sausages are nicely browned all over and cooked through.

### Potato Stuffing

| | |
|---|---|
| 10 medium potatoes (3 lbs) | 4 cups toasted bread crumbs (see Note) |
| Boiling water | 2 teaspoons salt |
| 1 tablespoon salt | 1 teaspoon dried sage leaves |
| ½ cup butter or margarine | 1 teaspoon dried thyme leaves |
| 1 cup chopped onion | 3 eggs, beaten |
| ½ cup chopped celery | |

1. Pare potatoes; quarter. In boiling water 2 inches deep in large saucepan, cook potatoes with salt, covered, until tender—20 minutes. Drain well; return to saucepan.

2. Beat with portable electric mixer (or mash with potato masher) until smooth. Heat slowly over low heat, stirring, to dry out—takes about 5 minutes.

3. In hot butter in medium skillet, sauté onion and celery 5 minutes, or until tender.

4. Add mashed potato to onion-and-celery mixture, along with bread crumbs, salt, sage and thyme. Beat with wooden spoon to mix well. Beat in eggs. Use potato mixture to stuff goose.

Makes 10 cups stuffing, enough for a 10-to-12-pound bird.

*Note:* Toast white bread; grate on fine grater.

**Giblet Gravy**
*Goose giblets and neck*
*2 cans (13¾-oz size) chicken*
  *broth*
*1 celery stalk, cut up*
*1 medium onion, peeled and*
  *quartered*

*1 medium carrot, pared and*
  *cut up*
*Salt*
*4 whole black peppercorns*
*⅓ cup flour*

1. While goose is roasting, wash giblets and neck well. Refrigerate liver until ready to use. Place rest of giblets and neck in 2-quart saucepan; add chicken broth, celery, onion, carrot, 1 teaspoon salt and the peppercorns.

2. Bring to boiling. Reduce heat; simmer, covered, 2¼ hours, or until giblets are tender; add liver; simmer 15 minutes. Discard neck. Chop giblets coarsely.

3. Strain cooking broth, pressing vegetables through sieve with broth. Measure broth (there should be about 3½ cups).

4. Remove goose to platter; pour drippings into 1-cup measure. Skim fat from surface, and discard. Return ¼ cup of the drippings to the roasting pan.

5. Stir in flour until smooth. Stir over very low heat, to brown flour slightly. Remove from heat; gradually stir in broth.

6. Bring to boiling, stirring. Reduce heat; simmer, stirring, 5 minutes, or until thick and smooth. Add chopped giblets and salt to taste; simmer 5 minutes.

## NEW ENGLAND PLUM PUDDING

*1 jar (8 oz) mixed candied fruit*
*¼ lb suet*
*½ cup blanched almonds*
*1 cup chopped, pared tart apple*
*1 cup raisins, 1 cup currants*
*½ teaspoon ground cinnamon*
*½ teaspoon ground nutmeg*
*½ teaspoon ground ginger*
*½ teaspoon ground cloves*
*¼ teaspoon salt*

*1 cup light-brown sugar, packed*
*1 cup packaged unflavored dry*
  *bread crumbs*
*½ cup all-purpose flour*
*3 eggs*
*¼ cup light molasses*
*½ cup milk*

*Vanilla Hard Sauce or Pudding*
  *Sauce, recipes below*

1. Chop candied fruit, suet and almonds very fine.

2. In large bowl, combine fruit, suet, almonds, raisins, currants, spices, salt, sugar, bread crumbs and flour.

3. In medium bowl, using portable electric mixer, beat eggs until very thick. Beat in molasses and milk, beating until well blended.

4. Add beaten-egg mixture to fruit mixture. With large spoon, mix well.

5. Turn batter into a well-greased 1½-quart pudding mold with tight fitting cover or a greased 1½-quart Pyrex bowl. Cover, or wrap bowl in several thicknesses of cheesecloth; tie around top with string. Place on trivet in large kettle. Pour in boiling water to come halfway up side of mold. Cover kettle.

6. Steam pudding 4 hours. (Water in kettle should boil gently; add more water as needed.)

7. Remove mold to wire rack; uncover; let cool completely in mold. If using metal mold, invert on wire rack; lift off mold.

8. To store: Wrap pudding in plastic film, then in foil. Or, if using bowl, store right in bowl in cheesecloth. Store in refrigerator several weeks.

9. To serve: Steam pudding in mold, covered, as directed above, 50 minutes, or until thoroughly hot. Decorate with candied cherries and angelica. Serve at once with Vanilla Hard Sauce or Pudding Sauce.

Makes 10 to 12 servings.

*To flame pudding:* Pour several tablespoons brandy over hot pudding. Heat ¼ cup brandy gently in a medium saucepan. When vapor begins to rise, ignite; pour flaming over pudding.

**Pudding Sauce**
*1 pkg (3 oz) cream cheese,*
*   softened*
*1 egg*
*1 cup confectioners' sugar*
*2 tablespoons butter or*
*   margarine, softened*
*1 teaspoon lemon juice*
*Pinch salt*
*1 cup heavy cream, whipped*
*About 2 tablespoons golden rum,*
*   or ½ to 1 tablespoon rum*
*   extract*

1. Day before: In medium bowl, with spoon, beat cheese until light. Add egg, sugar, butter, lemon juice and salt; beat well.

2. Fold in whipped cream and rum just until combined.

3. Refrigerate, covered, overnight.

Makes 3 cups.

**Vanilla Hard Sauce**
*½ cup soft butter or margarine*
*1 teaspoon vanilla extract*
*1 cup unsifted confectioners'*
*   sugar*

1. In small bowl of electric mixer, at high speed, cream butter until light.

2. Add vanilla and sugar; beat until fluffy and smooth.

Makes about ¾ cup.

# Menu IV
# A Seder Feast

Sweet-and-Sour Jellied Fish *
Chicken Fricassee *
Potato Pancakes *
Broccoli With Lemon Sauce
Grandpa's Dessert *

## SWEET-AND-SOUR JELLIED FISH

*3-lb striped bass, head and tail
removed*
*2 medium onions, coarsely
chopped*
*1 large carrot, pared and sliced*
*1 teaspoon salt*
*⅛ teaspoon pepper*

*1½ teaspoons mixed pickling
spice*
*2 bay leaves*
*⅓ cup sugar*
*1 cup white vinegar*

1. Wipe fish with damp paper towels. Cut into 2-inch slices.
2. In 10-inch skillet, combine onion, carrot, salt, pepper, pickling spice, bay leaves and sugar with 4 cups water.
3. Bring to boiling; simmer, covered, 30 minutes. Add vinegar.
4. Arrange fish on top; simmer, covered, 1 hour, basting occasionally, until fish flakes easily with fork.
5. Remove from heat. Cool to room temperature in marinade—½ hour. Arrange fish on serving platter with sauce spooned over. Refrigerate, covered, 4 hours, until sauce has jelled.
6. Serve as an appetizer or entrée.
Makes 4 to 6 servings.

## CHICKEN FRICASSEE

5-lb roasting chicken, cut in
  serving pieces
1½ cups coarsely chopped onion
1 medium tomato, chopped
1½ teaspoons paprika
1 teaspoon salt,
  ⅛ teaspoon pepper

¼ cup grated onion
½ cup grated carrot
2 eggs
2 tablespoons matzo meal
1½ teaspoons sour salt
½ cup sugar

1. Wash chicken; pat dry with paper towels. (Use all parts of chicken except liver, heart and gizzard.)

2. Remove skin from all pieces of chicken except wings; set breast meat aside. Cut remaining pieces of chicken into smaller pieces.

3. In 5-quart Dutch oven, over medium heat, brown chicken pieces (except breast meat), turning often, along with the chopped onion, tomato, paprika, salt and pepper—about 20 minutes. Cover; cook 20 minutes.

4. Meanwhile, remove bones from chicken breasts; chop finely.

5. In medium bowl, combine chopped chicken breast, grated onion, grated carrot, eggs and matzo meal. Shape into 1-inch balls.

6. Add to chicken mixture in Dutch oven, along with sour salt and sugar. Add water (about ½ cup) if needed.

7. Bring to boiling; simmer, covered, 1 hour.

8. Serve chicken balls with chicken-sauce mixture in pan.

Makes 6 servings.

## POTATO PANCAKES

4 large potatoes (2 lbs), pared
¼ cup grated onion
2 eggs, slightly beaten
2 tablespoons flour
¾ teaspoon salt

Dash each nutmeg, pepper
Salad oil or shortening for frying

Chilled applesauce or sour cream

1. On medium grater, grate potatoes. Drain very well; pat dry with dish towel; measure 3 cups.

2. In large bowl, combine grated potato with onion, eggs, flour, salt, nutmeg and pepper.

3. In large, heavy skillet, slowly heat oil, ⅛ inch deep, until very hot but not smoking.

4. For each pancake, drop potato mixture, 2 tablespoons at a time, into hot fat. With spatula, flatten against bottom of skillet to make a pancake 4 inches in diameter. Fry 2 or 3 minutes on each side, or until golden-brown.

5. Drain well on paper towels. Serve hot with applesauce or sour cream.

Makes 12.

## GRANDPA'S DESSERT

2 pkg (11-oz size) dried mixed
   fruit

¼ lb dried apples
½ cup light raisins
½ cup sugar

1. Place all dried fruits in 5-quart Dutch oven or saucepan. Add 6 cups hot water to cover fruit. Refrigerate, covered, several hours or overnight.

2. Next day, bring to boiling; simmer, covered, ½ hour, until soft, not mushy. Add sugar the last 5 minutes.

3. Turn into serving dish; refrigerate, covered, until well chilled—several hours or overnight.

Makes 10 to 12 servings.

# Index of Menus and Recipes